HELPING
THE TROUBLED
EMPLOYEE

_____HELPING_____
THE TROUBLED
EMPLOYEE

JOSEPH F. FOLLMANN, JR.

rancis

amacom
A DIVISION OF AMERICAN MANAGEMENT ASSOCIATIONS

Library of Congress Cataloging in Publication Data

Follmann, Joseph Francis, 1908–
    Helping the troubled employee.

    Bibliography: p.
    Includes index.
    1.   Employee counseling.   2.   Mental health
services.   I.   Title.
HF5549.5.C8F64   658.38'2   78-23474
ISBN 0-8144-5488-7

First Printing

to
JUDY

For their very appreciable help and guidance,
sincere thanks are extended to:

EDWARD M. DOLINSKY
Metropolitan Life Insurance Company

DR. ALAN A. MCLEAN
International Business Machines Corp.

EVELYN MYERS
American Psychiatric Association

DR. FRED M. SANDER
Psychiatrist, Long Island Jewish—Hillside Medical Center

Work is man's strongest tie to reality.

Civilization and Its Discontents

CONTENTS

1

INTRODUCTION

THE troubled employee is someone with problems that he or she has difficulty keeping in proper perspective. These problems lie essentially within the mind of the individual, who is basically an unhappy, sad, lonely, confused, and perhaps tortured person, although outward appearances may contradict this. Nevertheless, to a considerable extent life for this individual is ungratifying, frustrating, and unfulfilled. The consequence is that troubled employees are a problem to themselves, their family, their fellow employees, and their employer.

Sigmund Freud has described mental health as the ability to work and love. Others have expanded this concept to include the abilities to mix work with play and relaxation; to advance one's welfare without exploiting others; to conquer guilt, shame, doubt, feelings of inferiority, and indecision; to enjoy friendships, affections, and love; and to confidently take initiative. These are the abilities that are to a greater or lesser extent lacking in the troubled employee.

The troubled employee may be suffering as a consequence of various deep-seated influences. Those that go back to early childhood might include the loss of a parent by death, a broken home, rejection by a parent, or failure at school; later on, the inability to measure up to the expectations of family members, friends, or neighbors, or a deep-seated, though often unfounded, feeling of guilt or fear can be important factors. He or she may be suffering under the strain of trouble at home, unhappiness in the marriage, or a feeling of sexual inadequacy. He may be concerned over an accumulation of debts. He may be suffering from a sense of inadequacy or of rejection by his peers. He may unfavorably compare his accomplishments, his income level, his worldly goods, and his comforts with those of others. He can become plagued by the need to keep up with the Joneses or by the concept of the great American dream as portrayed in newspapers and magazines, in movie houses, or on TV. Any of these influences can result in varying degrees of mental, personality, emotional, or psychological stress or disorders.

It is becoming increasingly, though by no means universally, recognized that emotionally disturbed people are under a psychological stress with which they cannot cope. In addition there is now general recognition that mental illness *is* an illness. Like most illnesses, it can strike anyone at any time in life, and in certain instances can be prevented as well as cured. Certainly mental illnesses and disorders fall within the definition of disease given in Dorland's *Illustrated Medical Dictionary,* 24th Edition: "A definite morbid process having a characteristic train of symptoms; it may affect the whole body or any of its parts, and its etiology, pathology, and prognosis may be known or unknown." It is significant that the Council on Mental Illness of the American Medical Association has identified mental illness as America's most pressing and complex health problem.

Unfortunately, we know little of the precise causes of mental disorders, how to treat or cure them, or how to prevent them. As a consequence, the incidence and the types of mental disorders are not always clearly delineated. Many aspects of the subject remain elusive, because mental illness is not always readily identifiable, its causes are frequently unknown, its onset is inevitably obscure, and opinions differ regarding definitions, diagnostic criteria, and etiology. Furthermore, its termination is uncertain. Compounding the situation are the highly subjective aspects of mental disorders, particularly those of the personality, so that both the seeking of treatment and its continuation are decisions the individual usually makes for himself.

Such concerns are recognized by many experienced, eminent professionals. Dr. William C. Menninger, for example, has pointed out that there is considerable ambiguity in the use of such terms as mental illness, emotional illness, maladjustment, and personality defects; and that none of these include such problems as tension head-aches or marital discord. Similarly Dr. Benjamin Pasamanick has said that "there is extraordinarily little agreement on the definition of neurosis [and] I must include personality trait disorders as well." Dr. George Rosen has referred to "the confusion and obscurity, not to say obscurantism, which mark numerous current endeavors to under-stand and control mental illness"; and has remarked that "no single view of causation and pathogenesis of these disorders is currently regarded as generally acceptable; rather a multiplicity of diverse view-points prevails." Indeed, Dr. Charles Menninger says "there are no natural mental disease entities"; and Thomas S. Szasz, a professor of psychiatry, maintains that psychiatrists do not practice medicine, but rather that they are moral legislators, teachers, and social engineers. He further contends that mental illness, as such, is solely a disease of the brain and does not include functional or psychological disorders.

Where, then, does this leave the troubled employee who is aware that he has a problem of real dimensions and that he is in need of help? How is he to evaluate his own behavioral, job-related, emo-tional, or marital problems? How is he to determine the necessity for care or to judge the effectiveness of a particular form of treatment in relation to his problem when even the professionals cannot agree on the efficacy of specific approaches?

Despite the considerable progress made in developing an under-standing of mental illnesses since the end of the nineteenth century, a great deal more remains to be learned. Unfortunately too many peo-ple who should be concerned with the problem take only a passive interest, if any. Because of the paucity of useful information—includ-ing where to go for help—the troubled employee himself and his employer are frequently inclined to walk away from the subject, to pay it no heed. In addition, many of the efforts in the mental health field have been somewhat ineffectual or perhaps too specific, and have focused on such sensational aspects of the subject as drug abuse, for which, face it or not, there is little public sympathy. Consequently, the public may lack confidence in efforts to come to grips with the problem and those in trouble may fail to heed the warning signals. This can be particularly true among working people, since so much of the attention of publicly established agencies and of the reports that appear in the mass media are devoted to the unemployed. The result can be significant harm to the individual.

That the subject of mental disorders and mental health will re-ceive increased attention in the immediate future was indicated in

February 1977 when President Carter created the President's Commission on Mental Health. The Commission was mandated to hold hearings and conduct studies in order to identify the mental health needs of the nation. The final report of the Commission, which was tendered in April 1978, contained a series of recommendations for action that will probably lead to the introduction of legislation and the appropriation of public funds. The result will unquestionably be a constant flow of information through all types of mass media and an aroused public interest in the subject. The last such federal intervention in the field of mental health occurred in the 1960s, when President Kennedy's interest and encouragement led to the enactment in 1963 of the Mental Retardation Facilities and Community Mental Health Centers Construction Act. Considerable public interest was aroused in the subject at that time, only to subside as other matters of national and personal concern assumed precedence.

Historically, the original cause for concern on the part of the federal government arose out of the fact that in World War II some two million men had been rejected or discharged from duty in the armed services because of mental or emotional disorders. This situation led to the enactment by Congress of the National Mental Health Act of 1946. Three years later, the National Health Assembly recommended a "national program for mental health," and that year the National Institute of Mental Health was established as "the focal point for the Federal Government's activities to gain knowledge about the causes of mental illness, to find more effective treatments, and to promote sound mental health." The report of the President's Commission on the Health Needs of the Nation in 1953 further directed attention to mental health problems, and in 1955 Congress established a Joint Commission on Mental Illness and Health "to survey the resources and to make recommendations for combatting mental illness," which tendered its report in 1961. The subject has not, therefore, been languishing because of the absence of consideration by the federal government.

This book will discuss who the troubled employee is and how to identify him, as well as the various types of mental disorders and their causes. The incidence of people with mental disorders will be examined, as will the economic costs. The types of treatment available, where to go for help, and how to finance mental health care will also be considered. Prevention of mental disorders, and the significant role that employers and labor unions can play in helping the troubled employee, will also be discussed.

Special problems often associated with the mental disorders of the troubled employee such as stress, alcoholism, drug addiction, the excessive use of tobacco, and compulsive gambling will be discussed separately, as will the problems associated with suicide.

2

A LONG HISTORY

THAT mental disorders and illnesses are not unique to our society, with its urban congestion, impersonalization, industrialization, job monotony, automation, specialization, stress, and Jet Age pace is readily substantiated by history. Mental disorders and their treatment have a long, grim, and erratic record.

Referred to through the ages as madness, mania, folly, idiocy, insanity, derangement, dementia, or melancholia, evidence of their presence over several thousands of years, in all societies and among all races and religions, is undeniably clear. And the attitudes of other members of society have always been the same: impatience, fear, lack of compassion, and a belief that the victim was possessed by devils and should be put away. This has contributed to the stigmatization that persists even to this day.

Madness Through the Ages

The Bible records that madmen were alienated, ostracized, rejected from society, and cast out beyond the gates of the city to beg and fend for themselves. However, the compassion of Jesus of Nazareth is described in Luke:

> There met him out of the city a certain man, which had devils a long time, and ware no clothes, neither abode in any house but in the tombs. When he saw Jesus, he cried out, and fell down before him, and with a loud voice said, What have I to do with thee Jesus, thou Son of God most high? I beseech thee, torment me not. (For he had commanded the unclean spirit to come out of the man. For oftentimes it had caught him: and he was kept bound with chains and in fetters; and he brake the bands, and was driven of the devil into the wilderness.) And Jesus asked him, saying, What is thy name? And he said, Legion: because many devils were entered into him. . . . and they besought him . . . Then went the devils out of the man, and entered into the swine: and the herd ran violently down a steep place into the lake and were choked. . . . Then they went out to see what was done; and came to Jesus, and found the man, out of whom the devils were departed, sitting at the feet of Jesus, clothed and in his right mind: and they were afraid. [8:27–35]

During the Middle Ages the mentally ill were considered useless, consumed with vice, nonproductive, or odd, and were publicly whipped, raped, ostracized, incarcerated, chained, and even deprived of access to the church. The fools and simpletons, including the Court Jester, furnished good subjects for merriment and hilarity. At times those who were mad were placed aboard ships of fools and exhibited for a fee at the various ports of Europe. Even after they were institutionalized, the mentally ill provided entertainment for the general public: upon payment of an admission charge, people were permitted to view the inmates. At best, the mentally ill were subjected to derision or neglect.

With the virtual disappearance of leprosy in Europe about the thirteenth century, the estimated 19,000 leprosariums were gradually emptied. The deranged, along with criminals and the poor, were incarcerated in these lazar houses. Their alternative was confinement to a workhouse, where they provided an excellent source of cheap labor. From the hindsight of modern concepts this was barbarous, inhumane treatment, even though vestiges remain today. Nevertheless, aspects of the compulsory work requirement could well have had a salutary effect similar to today's occupational therapy. Even certain forms of the cruel treatment that were commonly practiced might have been therapeutic in nature, perhaps by having an effect similar to modern-day shock treatment.

The Madhouses

By the later Middle Ages and the Renaissance, the concept of hospitalization for the deranged gradually took hold. In the thirteenth and fourteenth centuries hospitals for the mentally ill were established at Gheel, Belgium; Seville, Spain; and Padua, Italy. In 1567 the Juliusspital was built in Wurtzburg, in 1616 a hospital for the insane was opened at Lyon, and by 1620 there were similar hospitals in Germany, Holland, Italy, Spain, and England.

In 1656, the General Hospital of Paris, popularly known as the Madhouse, held 6,000 people (a third of all arrests in that city were said to be insane). The Narrenturm, a fortress-like structure that was part of the General Hospital of Vienna, was referred to as the Fool's Tower. In Barking, England, a structure built to care for insane priests, and later for others, became known as All Hollow's. St. Mary's of Bethlehem was built in 1247 at Bishopgate outside London to care for the sick, but in the fourteenth century began housing the mentally ill. As late as 1815 the inmates at Bedlam were exhibited to the curious public upon payment of a fee, a practice which produced an income of more than £400 annually for the hospital. William Gregory, Lord Mayor of London, had provided for its maintenance in his will, referring to the legatee as "a church of Our Lady that is called Bedlam"—and in so doing coined a term that has remained a part of our language.

Despite the use of the word hospital, these establishments were not built to provide treatment for the unfortunates, but rather to furnish a place for their incarceration and custodial care in order to protect the safety, welfare, and property of other citizens. There is evidence that in some instances the care provided was kindly and tolerant, and that the surroundings were clean. However, in many hospitals the inmates, along with criminals and debtors, were housed in cages, and chains, iron fetters, stocks, and hard work were used as punishment.

Speculation on Causes and Cures

Meanwhile, other forces were at work attempting to determine the causes of mental derangement and searching for cures. Theories of the causative factors varied. Some blamed yellow and black bile, bad blood, humours, or the heat of dog days. Others cited sloth, envy, jealousy, or self-abuse. Some looked to hereditary factors, others to the presence of evil spirits. Later, emotional blockage, glandular imbalance, germs, and viruses were seen as causative factors. It cannot pass unnoted that psychiatric evaluations of these causes, which took place in the Middle Ages, bear marked resemblance to certain twentieth century concepts.

The search for cures led to experimentation in many directions. Purgatives, emetics, honey and vinegar, baths, immersions, and the consumption of large amounts of water were highly favored, and their effects on certain forms of therapy can be seen today. Various herbs and drugs, including opium pills, belladonna, camphor, afetida, oriental saffron, and tincture of quinine, were also used, and again have had an influence on modern approaches. Other substances used were soluble tartar, coffee, oil of amber, burnt leather and feathers, chimney soot, wood lice, and powdered lobster claws. There were those who resorted to prescribing soap internally as well as the direct absorption of iron filings. Some physicians rubbed the head with vinegar, others used superficial abscesses, and still others innoculated the patient with scabies, an attempted cure that was still being recommended in 1785. One example is the treatment given King Henry VI of England, who lost his reason about 1460, when he was in his later years. He was given potions, waters, sirop, electuaries, clysters, and fomentations. Across the Atlantic Ocean, the Delaware Indians thought insanity resulted if the family failed to perform certain traditional ceremonies. They treated the condition with sweating and charms.

Bloodletting was practiced and by 1662 some physicians had tried blood transfusions in an attempt at cure. Many felt that severe punishment, gun shots, or burning had a therapeutic effect. Somewhat later, treatments included exhortation or reasoning, occupational therapy, exercise, sea voyages, and music.

As strange as some of these attempts at cure might seem today, and recognizing that in several instances they have survived in modified form in modern therapy, the important fact is this: gradually mental disorders came to be more generally recognized as afflictions which could be subject to treatment, and perhaps to cure.

A More Rational Approach

Throughout the ages there were also some who attempted to more rationally understand and cope with madness. In the fourth century B.C., during the Golden Age of Greece, the great physician Hippocrates regarded mental illness as a brain function disorder, and discoursed on depression and melancholia. Aristotle remarked that melancholics had more intelligence than other men. And Galen, a physician who was to influence the concept of medicine for centuries, discussed such matters as psychology, psychopathology and function, diseases of the nervous system, and sensory perception. Greek and Egyptian physicians also used occupational therapy as treatment for mental disorders.

In ancient Rome Horace, Juvenal, and Persius wrote discourses on insanity; Suetonius discussed the mental disorders of the Caesars; and in the second century A.D. Plutarch wrote about the symptoms of melancholia. In an effort to cure insanity, Roman physicians administered a form of electroshock therapy using eels, and the Byzantine physicians of the day treated disturbed paupers in a variety of ways.

By the Middle Ages some of the most qualified and respected physicians of the day were experimenting with a variety of treatments for mania and melancholia. As early as 1160 the famous Roger of Salerno advised that an incision in the form of a cross be made on the head "in order that the humours may escape to the exterior." Later Constantine Africanus bored holes in the skull, foreshadowing the modern procedure of lobotomy. In England during the late thirteenth century, Gilbertus Anglicus, who had an admirable grasp of this complex subject, attributed such ailments to disturbances in the anterior or middle cell of the brain, which caused imagination and reason to diminish.

Meanwhile, the outstanding Arabian physicians of the period were employing a form of verbal counseling combined with milieu therapy in an attempt to exercise the patient's powers of reason. While these men were most certainly rare (this is always the case), their explorations unquestionably led to further advancements.

In 1672, Richard Lower in England published *De Catarrhis,* in which he discussed his theories of the brain's function. About that same time Georg Ernst Stahl in Bavaria began advocating psychotherapy. In England, Richard Blackmore discoursed on hysteria and hypochondria in 1725, paving the way for the subsequent recognition of such symptoms as mental disorders, and by 1743 Robert James had recognized mania as a disease. In 1758, *A Treatise on Madness,* the revolutionary work of William Battie and John Monro in England, was to become a turning point in the development of psychiatry by alerting the medical profession to the problem of insanity. Three years later Leopold Auenbrugger in Germany published his *Inventum Novum ex Percussione Thoracis Humani ut Signo Abstrusos Pectoris Morbos.* It was also in the eighteenth century that Anton Mesmer experimented with the therapeutic use of hypnotism, or what later came to be known as mesmerism.

About this time, in America, Benjamin Rush, a surgeon general of the Continental Army and a signer of the Declaration of Independence, published a work which broke with prevailing traditions in many respects. He demanded that mental illness be freed from moral stigma, that the insane be treated with kindness, and that physicians supervise their care. Included in his approach to treatment was the use of medicines and occupational therapy. In 1785 he published a paper in Philadelphia, "Inquiry into the Effects of Ardent Spirits on the Human Body and Mind," in which he was the first person known to have called the intemperate use of distilled spirits a disease.

Meanwhile, hospitals with some form of treatment for the mentally ill were appearing with increasing frequency. Included among these were St. Luke's Hospital in London, founded in 1751, and the Quaker Asylum in York, which opened in 1792. The Society of Friends was founding asylums for the deranged throughout England, and by the early nineteenth century these hospitals were being built throughout Europe, including ones at Munich founded in 1801, at Sonnenstein in 1811, and at Siegburg in 1815.

In the brave new world, the Philadelphia Almshouse (now the Philadelphia General Hospital) was built in 1732 to care for the poor, the sick, the unemployed, the aged, and the insane. A few years later, the Pennsylvania Hospital was founded by Benjamin Franklin "for the relief of the sick poor and for the reception and care of lunatics." Mental cases accounted for about one-third of the total case load, and their treatment is reported to have been humane and advanced for the time. Patients were provided with latrines, bathing facilities, and an exercise area, and the cells were clean and well ventilated. By 1841, the hospital extended its efforts on behalf of the mentally ill by establishing the Pennsylvania Hospital for the Insane, now the Institute of the Pennsylvania Hospital. In the interim, the first public mental hospital had been founded in Virginia, and in 1816 the Friends Asylum in Philadelphia was opened, the first private psychiatric hospital in the United States.

Samuel Tuke spotlighted the cruel treatment given the institutionalized mentally ill in England in his *Condition of the Indigent Insane.* In that same year, 1811, Sir Charles Bell published his *Idea of a New Anatomy of the Brain,* in which he discussed the functions of the spinal nerve roots and demonstrated the motor functions of the anterior root.

John Conolly, at the Middlesex County Pauper Lunatic Asylum at Hanwell, England (now St. Bernard's Hospital), provided major contributions to the field of psychiatry. In 1830, he wrote "An Inquiry

Concerning the Indications of Insanity with Suggestions for the Better Protection and Care of the Insane"; followed in 1847 by "The Construction and Government of Lunatic Asylums and Hospitals for the Insane," in which he conceived of such institutions as a therapeutic community, and in 1856 by "The Treatment of the Insane Without Physical Restraints," which was a clear revolt against earlier approaches to the care of the mentally ill. In it he advocated the abolition of mechanical restraints on the patients, thereby elevating the afflicted to the status of sick human beings.

At that same time in America, Edward Jarvis published *Insanity and Idiocy in Massachusetts: Report to the Commission on Lunacy,* in which he made a study of the mental health services available at the time and proposed several valuable recommendations for their improvement. Charles Darwin's *The Expression of the Emotions in Man and Animals,* in which he discussed the physiological effects of fright, was published in 1872, highlighting for the first time the relationship between mental disorders and physical illnesses. Four years later, Sir David Ferrier published *Functions of the Brain,* which paved the way for modern cerebral surgery. At the end of the century, psychiatrists were observing and treating battle fatigue resulting from the Boer War.

During this period, the concept that insanity was incurable and a cause for disgrace gradually diminished as a result of the works of men such as William Tuke in England, Pinel and Esquirol in France, and Reil and Wagnitz in Germany. Attempts to develop a science of mental illness soon followed, along with efforts to prevent its occurrence. The end of the nineteenth century witnessed the development of graded tests for the mentally retarded by Binet and Simon, and the evolution of the concepts underlying modern psychiatry by Kraepelin, von Krafft-Ebing, Meyer, Freud, and Jung.

In 1908 Beatrice Hinkle, a psychiatrist, opened the first psychotherapeutic clinic in America at Cornell Medical College in New York, and in 1920 Mary Jarrett began practicing psychiatric social work. During the early twentieth century in the United States, great strides were made in the fields of psychotherapy and mental health. Austen Fox Riggs began his pioneer work on the psychotherapy of neuroses, the Austen Riggs Center for psychoanalysis was founded, the Worcester State Hospital and the Post–Hall Clark University contributed to the field of psychoanalysis, and Dorothea Dix and Clifford W. Beers confronted issues concerning mental hygiene and the abuses occasioned in mental health services. About this time hospitals for psychopathic patients and those with acute mental illness were established and public outpatient clinics began to develop.

The early twentieth century also witnessed the gradual inception of industrial health programs in places of employment in America, a development which had commenced in the late nineteenth century and then gained momentum following the enactment of workmen's compensation laws after 1911. Employers began to take an interest in the mental health of their employees, and slowly developed a willingness to help those with problems. In 1914 the Cheney Silk Mills in Manchester, Connecticut, became the first known employer to engage a psychiatrist. In 1917 H. M. Adler developed the concept of mental hygiene in industry, and in 1919 E. E. Southard was asked by the Engineering Foundation of New York to study the psychiatric problems of workers. Then, in 1924 Macy's department store in New York engaged a psychiatrist to define job qualifications and to assist in job placement in an effort to match the employee's personality and physical capabilities with each job, as well as to provide counseling and therapy for troubled employees. In that same year Western Electric also engaged a psychiatrist, and in 1927 M. A. Sherman wrote the first textbook on the subject, *A Review of Industrial Psychiatry*.

By 1932 the Metropolitan Life Insurance Company had employed a psychiatrist, followed by Du Pont in 1942. World War II gave impetus to the subject for both those in the armed forces and civilian defense workers. It was at about this time, also, that employers first began to set up alcoholism control programs. In 1948, under the aegis of the Carnegie Corporation, the first postresidency training program was established at the Cornell University School of Industrial and Labor Relations. Then, in 1956, W. D. Ross published his *Practical Psychiatry for Industrial Physicians*. These were important evolutionary steps in an endeavor to assist the troubled employee.

This long history of the attempt to deal with mental health problems, the advancements and setbacks, the humanity and cruelty, roughly parallels the pattern of the gradual development of the care and treatment of physical ailments. We are not yet free of many of the injustices that have prevailed for thousands of years, but we have come a long way, and all the evidence indicates that further understanding and progress is assured.

Madness in Creative Works
Before leaving the subject it may be instructive to take note of the considerable degree to which insanity and mental disorders have attracted the interest and caught the imagination of some of the greatest creative minds of all time. Classical mythology tells us of Ajax, the tall, strong, handsome military leader of the Trojan War who went

mad with jealousy and committed suicide; of Jason, who led the Argo-
nauts in search of the Golden Fleece and was subject to fits of depression, eventually taking his own life; of Hercules, a carouser and ad-
venturer who became vengeful, went mad, and violently murdered
his wife and children.

Bacchus, or Dionysius—the god of wine and fertility—punished
the women of Attica by making them so mad that they tore their
infants to pieces, roamed the mountains in a disheveled state, imag-
ined themselves to be cows, ate the children suckling at their breasts,
and then hanged themselves. The nymph Echo could commence no
conversation but could only repeat the words of others. Narcissus,
with whom she fell hopelessly in love, was so consumed with the love
of himself that he could not partake of the life around him. There was
Alcmeon, who led the seven against Thebes only to go mad; Oedipus,
King of Thebes, who killed his father, married his mother, and then
jabbed out his own eyes; Antiope, a woman of Thebes, who the god
Dionysius made mad. In addition, it might well be suspected that the
goddess Aphrodite suffered from nymphomania.

Literature has brought us Cervantes' incomparable Don Quixote
tilting at windmills, Goethe's Faust selling his soul to the devil, Gogol's
memorable clerk in the *Memoirs of a Madman,* Robert Louis Steven-
son's unforgettable *Dr. Jekyll and Mr. Hyde,* Mary W. Shelley's *Franken-
stein,* and Lewis Carroll's Mad Hatter in *Alice in Wonderland.* Some of
the great portrayals of madness occur in the Dostoevsky characters:
Raskolnikov in *Crime and Punishment,* Prince Myshkin in *The Idiot,*
Stavrogin in *The Possessed,* and Ivan Karamazov in *The Brothers Karamazov.* Not to be ignored are such dramatic portrayals as Herman
Melville's Captain Ahab, Hawthorne's Ethan Brand, Joseph Conrad's
Mister Kurtz, Charlotte Bronte's Heathcliff, and Edith Wharton's
Ethan Frome.

In the world of drama, Euripides in the fifth century B.C. portrayed such characters as Medea, Phaedre, and Orestes. We have
Shakespeare's great portrayals of Lady Macbeth, Hamlet, Ophelia,
Othello, King Lear, and Caliban. In the nineteenth century Ibsen
gave us Oswald, Verdi gave us Rigoletto, and Puccini gave us Madame
Butterfly. The twentieth century brought the classic character study
of Willie Loman in Arthur Miller's *Death of a Salesman.*

In the world of painting and the graphic arts, we have Bosch's
Ship of Fools, painted in 1499, and the sixteenth century drawings of
the insane by the Flemish artist Brueghel and by Dürer, a German.
Goya's *Madhouse* was painted in the eighteenth century at the same
time Hogarth in England was depicting in his engravings the insane

of his day. During the nineteenth century, Kaulbach was working in Germany and Van Gogh was painting the insane asylum where he was housed in southern France.

Mental and personality problems, then, have inspired all forms of creative work throughout the centuries, including some of the most highly regarded works ever produced. It is certainly a subject that has intrigued as well as concerned mankind throughout time. "Whom the gods would destroy, they first make mad."

Some Outstanding Cases

At the risk of being prolix it cannot pass unnoted that the pages of history abound with important, influential, and powerful people who suffered from a variety of mental or personality disorders.

According to Plutarch, the incomparable Alexander the Great had a disturbed mind and was consumed with fears. King Herod, who ruled Judea at the time of the birth of Jesus, was subject in his later years to insanity, becoming highly suspicious and bloodthirsty.

Among the Romans, according to Plutarch, mental disorders were apparently quite prevalent. Julius Caesar is described as "distempered in the head and subject to epilepsy." Marc Anthony, the renowned military leader and consul, was a notorious drunkard given to overindulgence who ended his life by suicide. In his later years, the Roman consul Caius Marius is described as being extraordinarily sick, subject to nocturnal frights and auditory hallucinations, and despondent. Cato the Younger, a senator, was frank enough to describe himself as deranged and out of his senses. The Emperor Tiberius is said to have been paranoid, and Caligula, a paranoic sadist, is described as a vicious monster who tortured and killed thousands. Nero is noted for his monstrous violence and acts of cruelty, even to the point of having his mother, Agrippina, murdered.

Subsequent centuries bear evidence of serious mental disorders in Attila the Hun, the Empress Irene of Constantinople, the Byzantine Emperor Michael III, Charles "the Simple," and King Charles VI ("the Mad") of France, Vlad Dracul, Prince of Wallachia (generally known as Dracula or Vlad the Impaler), Cesare Borgia of Italy who was used by Machiavelli as the prototype for his Prince, Henry VI of England, Ivan V ("the Terrible") of Russia, George III of England, Czar Paul I of Russia, Christian VII of Denmark, Peter III of Russia, Otto I of Bavaria, Frederick William IV of Prussia, Louis II of Bavaria, and Ludwig II of Bavaria. Abraham Lincoln, with all his greatness, was by his own admission a manic-depressive. An impressive list.

Examples abound in the present century as well. In 1920 Paul

Deschanel, newly elected President of the French Republic, jumped out of the presidential train in his pajamas, rolled unhurt into a ditch, and then sought refuge from the pressures of his office in the house of a level crossing guard. Von Hindenburg became president of Germany after a long career as a top-ranking army officer, but in his later years refused to squarely face the issues confronting him. His subsequent senility paved the way for Adolph Hitler's assumption of power. Although irrefutable proof is lacking, Hitler might well have been a paranoid. Benito Mussolini described himself as stiff with terror and reportedly turned to the hypodermic needle for solace; however, the records of his examining physicians were strictly confidential and were never released. Joseph Stalin was suspected of having serious mental disorders later in life, although again, adequate records are lacking.

Other notable people who have suffered from serious mental disorders include the German philosophers Kant and Nietzsche; such writers as Tolstoy, Poe, Gide, Wilde, Fitzgerald, Hemingway, Joyce, and Jonathan Swift (the author of *Gulliver's Travels,* who later in life became hopelessly insane and at his death left his fortune to found a hospital for the insane); the composers Moussorgsky and Schumann; the painters Gauguin and Van Gogh; and the playwrights Strindberg and Andreyev.

The point of this extensive list is that mental illness is by no means a rare occurrence; it can strike anyone at any time of life. The poor and rejected of society are not its only victims, and brilliance of mind, unlimited means, and the freedom to exert either initiative or power are in no sense an assurance against its devastations.

BIBLIOGRAPHY

The Columbia Encyclopedia.
Ennis, Bruce J. *Prisoners of Psychiatry.* New York: Harcourt Brace Jovanovich, 1973.
Follmann, J. F., Jr. *Alcoholics and Business.* New York: AMACOM, 1976.
————. *The Economics of Industrial Health.* New York: AMACOM, 1978.
————. *Insurance Coverage for Mental Illness.* New York: AMACOM, 1970.
Foucault, Michel. *Histoire de la folie.* Paris: Librairie Plon, 1961.
Garrison, Fielding H. *History of Medicine.* Philadelphia: W. B. Saunders, 1929.
Goffman, Erving. *Asylums.* New York: Doubleday, 1961.
Group for Advancement of Psychiatry. *The VIP with Psychiatric Impairment,* 1973.
Hamilton, S. W. *The History of American Mental Hospitals.* New York: Columbia University Press, 1944.
Marion, John Francis. *Philadelphia Medica.* Philadelphia: Smith-Klein Corporation, 1975.

McNally, Raymond, and Radu Florescu. *In Search of Dracula.* New York: New York
    Graphic Society, 1972.
Neaman, Judith S. *Suggestion of the Devil.* Garden City, N.Y.: Doubleday-Anchor, 1975.
Plutarch's Lives. c. 110 A.D.
Talbot, C. H. *Medicine in Medieval England.* London: Oldbourne, 1967.
Tantauidgen, Gladys. *Folk Medicine of the Delaware Indians.* The Pennsylvania Historical
    Commission, 1972.
Tripp, Edward. *Crowell's Handbook of Classical Mythology.* New York: T. Y. Crowell,
    1970.

3

WHO IS THE
TROUBLED EMPLOYEE?

THE troubled employee can be anyone: chairman of the board, clerk, lathe operator, company manager, secretary, hard hat, account executive, engineer, actuary; farmer, coal miner, sailor, airline pilot, bank teller, salesperson, stock broker; physician, lawyer, scientist, architect, accountant, teacher; taxi driver, army officer, journalist, police officer, civil servant, bookie, member of the clergy; Ph.D. or grade-school dropout, suburban commuter or city dweller; fashion designer, archaeologist, actor, novelist, dancer, painter, musician; head of state, member of Congress, judge; the butcher, the baker, the candlestick maker . . . even unto me and thee. The troubled employee can be Catholic,. Protestant, Muslim, or Jew; white, black, yellow, or red: mental illness does not discriminate.

The troubled employee might be excessively sensitive or shy or may be hostile or overly agressive. He or she might be obsessive, compulsive, or irritable. The troubled employee's behavior is often marked by immaturity: he may be unduly talkative, flighty, selfish, likely to giggle unpredictably, to overreact to daily situations, or to blame others for his misfortunes. Overly self-protective, jealous, envious, suspicious, or greedy, this worker often exhibits a lack of empathy for others. He can be unduly fearful or anxious, or can lack spontaneity or a sense of humor.

At work, troubled individuals are often overly conscientious about their tasks, and deeply devoted to rules, regulations, and routines. They can overwork themselves as a result of the inner tension and stress that plague them. Concern over promotion, demotion, impending job transfers, or new assignments often preoccupies these people. Fear about issues such as inflation, recession, job layoffs, and unemployment can become obsessive. Conversely, a persistent tendency to procrastinate, failure to learn from experience, difficulty in making decisions, confusion, or resentment of authority may characterize these people. Or they may indulge in grandiose delusions, excessive exuberance, and extravagances beyond their means.

The troubled individual may be aware of his shortcomings, which can range from apathy, lack of motivation, pessimism, and a feeling of futility, to a loss of self-esteem and a sense of worthlessness. Accordingly, he often has great difficulty adjusting to change, whether at home, on the job, or socially. He can have difficulty sleeping, relaxing, playing, or enjoying himself. He can come to suffer from absent-mindedness and memory lapses and may become consumed by strong feelings of anxiety. In his problem of facing the real world he can engage in pretentions and dreams of various sorts.

Imaginary or real physical ailments may develop, ranging from frequent hypochondriacal complaints to the development of actual conditions such as gastrointestinal disorders, which include stomach ulcers, gallbladder ailments, constipation, and colitis. The aggravation of conditions such as arthritis or diabetes and the development of high blood pressure and other illnesses of the circulatory system may also have a psychological basis. Food, cigarettes, alcohol, and drugs, used excessively, are frequent palliatives to which troubled people turn.

Because any of the characteristics discussed cannot be tolerated indefinitely, life at home and at work eventually deteriorates. Alienation, separation, or divorce are common consequences, as are demotion on the job or actual dismissal. Deeper troubles are then inevitable.

Lest what has been said cause undue concern, it should be made clear that any such characteristics may very well be quirks or foibles on the part of any of us that might be long-standing patterns of behavior, or attempts to establish individuality. They also might prove to be temporary behaviors, perhaps caused by problems or situations of the moment that will pass or be overcome. They also can be signs, albeit early signs, of trouble, and therefore are not to be totally ignored. Certainly we all become anxious at times, and concerned about what is going on in our lives. We all have our eccentricities, and some of us might even enjoy them. We all have our bad days and our good days. We all get down in the doldrums, edgy, and jumpy. But, we hope we can keep these under control, not let them become too obtrusive, and not let them impair our functioning.

Lucky, indeed, is the person who has not had some unhappiness in childhood, who has not lost a loved one, who does not have family problems or financial concerns, and who does not suffer reverses on or off the job. Only a super being would never procrastinate, make a bad decision, blow his stack, foul up a task, or feel inferior. Perhaps thanks to some unknown influences in our backgrounds we are able to keep such problems or concerns in perspective, to overcome them, or to work our way out of or around them. But for all we know, they may simply be piling up inside to make their full impact felt at some later date. The fact is that the norms of psychological function are difficult if not impossible to determine.

To fellow employees, the troubled worker often inspires laughter, snickers, or hilarious jokes. He might be considered a kook, a nut, a crank, a worrier, a chronic complainer; eccentric, zany, balmy, foolhardy, unhinged, or punch-drunk. He can be referred to as off his chump, daft, harebrained, crazy as a bedbug, mad as a hatter, having a screw loose, in orbit, spaced out, or not having it all together. If his fellows are Spanish speaking he is *loco,* if Italian he is *pazzo* or she is *pazza,* if German *verrückt,* if French *fou,* if Polish *glupi,* or if Jewish *meshuggeneh.* He will be looked upon as a loner, or as one who is opinionated, rigid, inflexible, and has a closed mind, and who is unreasonable and difficult to deal with.

But there will also be those who, to some degree, will understand the troubled employee, who will sympathize with him, make excuses for his inadequacies, straighten out the messes he creates, or even try to help by suggesting that he consider seeking guidance.

To the employer, at various levels of organization from supervisor or shop steward to upper management, the troubled employee will become a source of concern in many ways. Inefficiency, carelessness about the way work is done, indecisiveness or confusion in approaching the job, dissatisfaction with the job or the work environment, or a lack of motivation are all characteristics that will eventually attract attention. When these are accompanied by an absence of gratification in accomplishment, by unresponsiveness or resistance to changes in procedures or concepts, by faulty decision making, or by a general deterioration in the employee's work performance, the situation becomes a matter for concern. If, in addition, the employee becomes hostile and overly aggressive, or creates friction among fellow employees, customers, or the general public, the employer is forced to take some form of action.

In economic terms alone, such behaviors add to the operating costs of a place of employment. Inevitably, the troubled employee is one with a record of excessive absenteeism and lateness, is inclined to be accident-prone, waste time and materials, and make too many erroneous and costly decisions. This unavoidably results in economic costs of such proportions that they *must* be reckoned with.

One course of action is to fire the troubled employee, simply get rid of him. But this approach is not always a sound economic solution. Labor turnover and the training of new employees is costly. Furthermore, many troubled employees have been with their employers for a good many years and have gained knowledge, experience, and expertise. Others are valued employees in whom management has made a considerable investment. As rational or justifiable as it might have seemed at first, discharge is essentially a wasteful approach.

The alternative, which, as will be shown, is becoming increasingly recognized in places of employment, is to identify the person in need of help before too much deterioration has taken place, and to counsel him to seek assistance. For the fact is that with help he or she can regain a sense of mental balance, can function more adequately, and can live life more fully. Only recently have people begun to recognize this and act on it. Essential to the process, however, is the recognition by the individual that help is needed, and a willingness to seek and accept it.

This, unfortunately, is easier said than done. The troubled employee will invariably deny that he has a problem, at least until the symptoms can no longer be ignored. He will not only resist treatment, he will reject the very idea that he has troubles other than those which are brought on by others. There can be many reasons for this. He does not want his job and his security threatened. Furthermore, he probably takes a dim view of any type of psychiatric treatment; a view held and substantiated by a great many of his fellow citizens. This leads to doubt concerning where to turn for help. He may have a well-founded fear of ending up in an insane asylum. Added to this is a normal concern about the time lost from work and the costs of treatment. What of his family's security?

Perhaps above all, his concerns will be tempered by the broadly held public attitudes toward mental disorders. Beyond the refusal to believe that this can actually happen to him, there is the wide public stigma and shame attached to these conditions. What will the spouse and the children, the relatives, and, heaven knows, the in-laws think? What will those characters at the shop say about this? And what about the future? How will advancement on the job, promotion, or even the job itself be affected by a history of psychiatric treatment on his record? Certainly he is aware that not so long ago a candidate for the vice-presidency of the United States withdrew from that political race when it was disclosed that he had undergone psychiatric treatment.

Too readily, the result can be that the seeking of treatment is postponed with the hope that the situation will right itself. This delay can continue until matters become unavoidably serious, often after considerable damage has been done.

The following anonymous brief case histories describe a few situations that reached these critical proportions:

● The executive of a large corporation whose thinking and behaviors became so disturbed that his ability to lead and assume initiative became adversely affected, and he had to be removed from office.

● The automobile plant employee with a long history of persecutory feelings and violent actions, who had been advised several times to seek psychiatric help, and who one day beat his foreman to death on the groundless feelings that the foreman was about to fire him.

● The middle-aged woman, an advertising copywriter, who became consumed with fears that arose from loneliness, and developed a paralysis of both legs that had no physical basis.

● The former warehouse employee, owner of quite an arsenal of firearms, who one day appeared at his former place of employment and took the lives of five innocent employees and then his own.

● The brilliant lawyer, engaged by a prestigious law firm, who became manic-depressive, highly extravagant, and eventually so consumed with fear that his marriage ended in divorce, he became unemployed, lost all his economic resources, and finally committed himself for treatment, which was ultimately successful. Then, at the age of 50, he had to commence life afresh.

● The overworked construction supervisor who functioned under pressure, was cantankerous and aggressive, felt he had to get a job done yesterday, and was unable to relax; who one evening had a few beers and on the way home lost control of his car and severely hurt himself. Two weeks later he was back in the hospital in a state of fear and dependency, having lost his sense of taste and sense of balance; his functional level was considerably decreased. In a word, he was headed for a reactive depression. He underwent treatment and returned to work in two weeks.

● The President and Board Chairman of a large publishing company that had serious financial troubles, who functioned under tremendous stress; who one day collapsed on the street vomiting blood from ulcers he had developed as a result of dieting, excessive intake of grapefruit juice, heavy smoking, overwork, economic worries, fear of a loss of reputation, and unrelieved anger and frustration; who underwent treatment and completely readjusted his life pattern as well as his means of earning a living.

● The junior executive who was highly capable and efficient, but whose personality suddenly began to change, as did his work patterns; who became depressed and was hospitalized, and upon release went home and eventually shot himself.

● The happily married saleswoman who periodically went into a deep depression and attempted to take her own life three times; who underwent various episodes of treatment, each of which appeared to be successful until recidivism occurred.

● The highly successful advertising executive who lost his major account, was given early retirement, became an alcoholic, and finally committed suicide at the age of 56.

● The middle-management executive with a steady history of advancements who, following his most recent promotion, began to develop psychophysical symptoms that threatened to become serious. Seeking treatment, he finally followed the advice of his physician and reported to management that he would be unable to assume his new responsibilities because of health reasons. He was reassigned and his physical symptoms disappeared.

These brief case histories are sad indeed. Most certainly they indicate how devastating mental disorders can be and the fact that they can affect people working at all levels of employment.

The problem, then, is one of early identification of the troubled employee, the worker suffering from a mental disorder, and of providing him or her with guidance for appropriate treatment, which, hopefully, will help alleviate the problems. One of the best and most resourceful loci where this can be accomplished is at the place of employment. As will be shown subsequently, employers are devoting more and more efforts toward this end. Unfortunately, this humane and sensible approach is not always taken. Too often the employee is fired or euphorically given early retirement, which much too frequently can prove fatal.

4

CLASSIFICATIONS OF MENTAL DISORDERS

THERE are many types of mental disorders, the identification and classification of which have evolved, to their present status, only in relatively recent years. Some types reflect underlying physical conditions, particularly in cases of mental retardation and the various organic brain syndromes; others do not. Some individuals, furthermore, have more than one mental disorder; for example, a person with anxiety neurosis may also develop morphine or alcohol addiction. This chapter presents several classification systems, which have been developed by outstanding authorities in the field.

The *Diagnostic and Statistical Manual of Mental Disorders,* prepared by the American Psychiatric Association in 1968, has a detailed categorization of mental disorders. According to the APA, the following are the major types of disorders:

Mental Retardation
A subnormal general intellectual functioning associated with impaired learning and social adjustment, maturation, or both. The de-

grees of retardation are classified according to Intelligence Quotient (IQ) level as follows:

Borderline	68–83
Mild	52–67
Moderate	36–51
Severe	20–35
Profound	under 20

Psychoses Associated with Organic Brain Syndromes

Conditions in which the mental functioning is sufficiently impaired to interfere grossly with the capacity to meet the ordinary demands of life, and may result in a serious distortion in the capacity to recognize reality, hallucinations or delusions, profound alterations of mood, or severe deficits in perception, language, or memory. The types of psychoses are:

Senile and pre-senile dementia. The causes of both of these syndromes are largely unknown.

Alcoholic psychoses. These psychoses are caused by poisoning with alcohol, and the various types are marked by delirium tremens, hallucinations, memory impairment, disorientation, and jealousy.

Psychoses associated with intracranial infection. These are usually caused by syphilis of the nervous system, but can also result from meningitis or from a brain abscess. Intracranial infections frequently result in paralysis.

Psychoses associated with other cerebral conditions. This is a large category that includes psychoses associated with cerebral arteriosclerosis, cerebral thrombosis, cerebral embolism, arterial hypertension, cardiorenal disease, epilepsy, intracranial neoplasm, degenerative disease of the central nervous system, or brain trauma caused by severe head injury or brain surgery.

Psychoses associated with other physical conditions. These psychoses are caused by general systemic disorders, and are distinguished from the *cerebral* conditions previously described. The category includes disorders caused by endocrine, metabolic, or nutritional disorders; complications of diabetes; disorders such as pneumonia, typhoid fever, malaria, or rheumatic fever; drug poisoning; and pregnancy or the post-partum period.

Nonpsychotic Organic Brain Syndromes

This category is for patients who have an organic brain syndrome, but are not psychotic. Intracranial infections, drug poisoning, simple drunkenness, brain trauma, circulatory disturbance, epilepsy, degenerative disease of the nervous system, intracranial neoplasm, or disturbances in metabolism or nutrition can cause the onset of mental disorders.

Psychoses Not Attributed to Previously Noted Physical Conditions

Schizophrenia. This category includes disorders characterized by the following: disturbances in thinking, mood, and behavior; alterations of concept formation, misinterpretation of reality, delusions, or hallucinations; inappropriate emotional responsiveness, loss of empathy with others, self-protectiveness; insidious reduction in external attachments and interests, apathy, impoverishment of interpersonal relations, mental deterioration; unpredictable giggling, frequent hypochondriacal complaints, violent motor activity and excitement, stupor, grandiose delusions, excessive religiosity; hostility and aggressiveness, confusion, emotional turmoil, fear, autistic behavior, withdrawal, or gross immaturity.

Major affective disorders. These are characterized by a single disorder of mood, either extreme depression or elation, which is responsible for a loss of contact with the environment. Symptoms include worry and anxiety, severe insomnia, feelings of guilt, irritability, talkativeness, flight of ideas, perplexity, stupor, illusions, hallucinations, and delusions. Included among these disorders are involutional melancholia and manic-depressive illnesses.

Paranoid states. In these, delusion, generally persecutory or grandiose, is the essential abnormality.

Neuroses

Anxiety is the chief characteristic of the neuroses. They are marked by the fact that the individuals are aware that their mental functioning is disturbed. The types of neuroses are:

Anxiety neurosis, characterized by anxious overconcern extending to panic.

Hysterical neuroses, marked by an involuntary psychogenic loss or disorder of function. Symptoms usually occur during emotionally charged situations, and, in the conversion type, include blindness, deafness, or paralyses.

Phobic neurosis, in which faintness, fatigue, palpitations, perspiration, nausea, tremor, or panic occur.

Obsessive-compulsive neurosis, characterized by a persistent intrusion of thoughts, urges, or actions.

Depressive neurosis, manifested by an excessive reaction of depression due to an internal conflict or to an identifiable event.

Neurasthenic neurosis, marked by chronic weakness and exhaustion.

Depersonalization neurosis, in which the individual is dominated by a feeling of unreality and of estrangement from the self, body, or surroundings.

Hypchondriacal neurosis, characterized by a preoccupation with the body and presumed diseases.

Other neuroses, which include occupational ones.

Personality Disorders and Certain Other Nonpsychotic Mental Disorders

These are characterized by deeply ingrained, lifelong maladaptive patterns of behavior. This category includes personality disorders, sexual deviations, alcoholism, and drug dependence. Abnormal personality types include the following:

Paranoid personality, characterized by hypersensitivity, rigidity, unwarranted suspicion, jealousy, envy, excessive self-importance, and a tendency to blame others.

Cyclothymic personality, whose behavior pattern is manifested by recurring and alternating periods of depression (worry, pessimism, low energy, and sense of futility) and elation (ambition, enthusiasm, optimism, and high energy).

Schizoid personality, manifested by shyness, oversensitivity, seclusiveness, and eccentricity.

Explosive personality, marked by gross outbursts of rage, aggressiveness, an overresponsiveness to environmental pressures, and an inability to control such outbursts.

Obsessive-compulsive personality, characterized by an excessive concern for conformity and standards. Individuals in this group are marked by rigidity, an inability to relax, and excessive conscientiousness.

Hysterical personality, characterized by emotional instability, excitability, overreactivity, and self-dramatization.

Asthenic personality, marked by low energy level, incapacity for enjoyment, lack of enthusiasm, and oversensitivity to stress.

Antisocial personality, with gross selfishness, an inability to learn from experience, a tendency to blame others, a low frustration tolerance, and an inability to be loyal to individuals, groups, or social values.

Passive-aggressive personality, marked by obstructionism, pouting, procrastination, intentional inefficiency, or stubbornness. The behavior often reflects hostility that is not expressed openly.

Inadequate personality, characterized by ineptness, inadequateness, poor judgment, social instability, and lack of stamina.

The *sexual deviations* in this category include sexual orientation disturbance (homosexuality), fetishism, pedophilia, transvestitism, exhibitionism, voyeurism, sadism, and masochism.

Alcohol and drug dependence are considered to be nonpsychotic disorders if alcohol consumption damages the health or functioning of the individual, is necessary for his functioning, or is episodically excessive, habitual, or addictive; or if drugs such as opium, morphine, barbituates, hypnotics, sedatives, tranquilizers, cocaine, hashish, marihuana, hallucinogens, or amphetamines are used habitually and with a clear sense of need and dependence.

Psychophysiologic Disorders

This group of disorders is characterized by intense and sustained physical symptoms caused by emotional factors that the individual may not be aware of. They may be manifested as skin disorders, musculoskeletal disorders (such as backache, muscle cramps, and tension headaches), disturbances of the respiratory system (asthma), the cardiovascular system (hypertension), the hemic and lymphatic system, the gastrointestinal tract (ulcers, gastritis, colitis, or constipation), the endocrine system, or the sense organs.

Special Symptoms

This category is for the occasional patient who exhibits a single specific symptom, and includes speech, feeding, or learning disturbances, enuresis, encopresis, and cephalalgia.

Transient Situational Disturbances

This category includes transient disorders that occur in individuals without any apparent underlying mental disorder. They represent an acute reaction to overwhelming environmental stress, and often recede as the stress diminishes. These disorders include adjustment reactions of infancy, childhood, adolescence, adult life, or later life.

Behavior Disorders of Childhood and Adolescence

Characteristic manifestations of these disorders include overactivity, inattentiveness, shyness, timidity, overaggressiveness, a feeling of rejection, seclusiveness, a short attention span, chronic anxiety, excessive and unrealistic fears, nightmares, self-consciousness, immaturity, lack of self-confidence, hostile disobedience, aggressiveness, destructiveness, lying, running away, stealing, or delinquency.

Conditions Without Manifest Psychiatric Disorder and Nonspecific Conditions

This category covers people who are psychiatrically normal, but who must cope with problems that could precipitate a mental disorder. It includes people who exhibit maladjustment in marriage, social change, or occupation; or dyssocial behavior, such as that exhibited by racketeers, dishonest gamblers, dope peddlers, or prostitutes.

Schizophrenia accounts for about half of all serious cases of mental disorders, frequently taking its toll among younger people. In some of its primary forms it is probably never cured. Psychoses generally result in moderate to severe disability, but other mental disorders cause little or no significant impairment, with less than 30 percent resulting in disability. The neuroses and personality disorders account for a relatively small proportion of hospital admissions; however, they require the use of a large proportion of available ambulatory mental health services.

It is of interest that a much earlier classification of mental disorders developed by Kraepelin in Germany established three principal subdivisions: organic psychoses, endogenous psychoses without known structural pathology, and deviation of personality and reactive states.

Similarly, mental disorders have been classified into three major categories by the U.S. Department of Health, Education, and Welfare (HEW):

The Psychoses or Insanities

These may be acute or chronic illnesses. Ordinarily, they require intensive treatment in a hospital setting for a period of several months, and in some instances require follow-up care.

The Neuroses or Psychoneuroses

These are less severe emotional disturbances that in many cases can be treated in the psychiatrist's office or a clinic. In the main, the neurotic differs from the psychotic in the following way: The former is aware of his environment and is able to recognize and identify it, although he or she may not be able to deal with it satisfactorily; the latter has lost the ability to cope with the real world. Neurotic illness is most common in the early adult years.

The Personality Disorders

These are adjustment problems that manifest themselves in disturbed behavior, including chronic alcoholism, drug addiction, delinquency, and psychosomatic disorders.

One examination of the subject at the University of Chicago, however, has developed five classes of mental disorders:

Psychiatric and social maladjustment, including insomnia, depression, neuroses, psychoses, alcoholism, nervous breakdowns, brain damage, senility, and mental retardation.

Ill-defined conditions, which display symptoms with no obvious physical basis, such as migraine headache, disorders of the digestive system or the heart, and such chronic conditions as tiredness, low blood pressure, obesity or underweight, or vague pains.

Psychosomatic illnesses, possibly including hypertension, hyperthyroidism, peptic ulcer, colitis, asthma, neurodermatitis, and rheumatoid arthritis.

Physical illness, such as diabetes, cancer, heart diseases, stroke, fever of unknown origin, and bone fractures, which are not included in the foregoing categories.

A *residual category,* which consists of diagnostic disorders.

The following categorization has been proposed by Dr. Solomon H. Snyder of Johns Hopkins University:

Manic Depression

There can be two distinct types:

Endogenous depressions, which are psychoses arising from within the individual, or

Exogenous depressions, which are precipitated by some event in the environment (including success), which are neurotic in nature, and which frequently occur in those who have a long history of being mildly depressed.

Schizophrenia

There is no commonly accepted definition for this disorder, and it is not known whether it is a single disease or a group of diseases.

There are four types of schizophrenia, which have been classified as follows:

Catatonia, in which the patient develops severe tension, muscular immobility, and stupor, refuses to eat, and loses control of the bladder.

Hebephrenia, marked by a disturbance of thought processes and by inappropriate giggling (sometimes called the sad sillies).

Paranoia, marked by feelings of suspicion or persecution or by grandiose illusions.

Simple schizophrenia, which is often inconspicuous, but is marked by an impoverished intellectual and emotional life and a growing loss of interest in life.

Neuroses

These are marked by an emotional disability that impairs the normal life function. Included here are character disorders, hysteria, and phobia.

Psychopathic or Sociopathic Personality

This type is indicated by antisocial behavior, impulsiveness, a lack of meaningful relationships with others, and a desire to cause pain to others.

It should be evident that these various classifications have much in common with one another, and each serves to supplement, rather than contradict, the others.

One type of mental disorder not included in the APA manual is called traumatic neurosis. While there is a lack of agreement among psychiatrists concerning this diagnosis, the concept has become well established by the courts in workmen's compensation and personal liability cases. In addition, it is recognized by the military as shell shock, battle stress, or combat fatigue. One dictionary defines the disorder as:

> A functional disorder of the central nervous system usually manifested by anxiety, phobias, obsessions, or compulsions but frequently display-ing signs of somatic disorder involving any of the bodily systems with or without other subjective or behavioral manifestations and having its most probable etiology in intrapsychic or interpersonal conflict. . . .

The suspected causes of traumatic neuroses are noted in Chapter 5.

Any attempts to apply these classifications to real-life situations must proceed with caution. To begin with, one of the most difficult problems confronting the field of mental health is arriving at satisfactory definitions for the terms used by both lay and professional people. The differences of both definition and nosology (the classification of conditions) can result in a failure to reach agreement on the rubrics of nomenclature. As a consequence, there are those who feel that psychiatric classifications are frequently ambiguous and unreliable. Certainly, they are not matters to be engaged in by the untrained, any more than are physical conditions of any consequence.

Such concerns have led the Group for the Advancement of Psychiatry (GAP) to caution that overdependence on the diagnostic categories of mental disorders can become an obstacle to clear thinking on the subject. GAP has also expressed concern that the language used by psychiatrists can be used inappropriately, misused, and misinterpreted by those outside the field of psychiatry.

Beyond this there is the perplexing fact, discussed in earlier chapters, that mental or emotional disorders are not always readily identifiable conditions. As a result, professional opinion differs concerning the identification of disorders, to the extent that it has been said that psychiatrists rarely agree about the exact diagnosis of an individual patient. This is especially true for borderline cases that present knotty diagnostic problems.

At the root of the difficulty is the question of the distinction between normal and abnormal behavior, between sanity and madness. Since we all have our idiosyncrasies, when does one's behavior become deviant? Those in psychiatry and psychology admit that this distinction is fuzzy at best.

This situation has led to endless debate over the issue of whether psychiatric disorders are illnesses at all, whether they are behavioral problems, or whether they are actually social deviations. Thomas Szasz, a professor of psychiatry at the State University of New York at Upstate Medical Center in Syracuse, for example, holds that the lack of precision in psychiatry precludes any definition at all. "Mental illness," he says, "is a myth. Psychiatrists are not concerned with mental illnesses and their treatments. In actual practice they deal with personal, social, and ethical problems in living."

Where, then, does this leave the concerned individual, the troubled employee, his or her family, and the employer? Even though they may not know all the answers, reliance must be placed on the highly trained and experienced professionals in the mental health field. There are few, if any, alternatives available today. Lay attempts at diagnosis can only become confused, incorrect, and possibly dangerous.

BIBLIOGRAPHY

Anderson, Ronald, et al. *Psychologically-Related Illness and Health Services Utilization.* Center for Health Administration Studies, University of Chicago, August 1974.

Diagnostic and Statistical Manual of Mental Disorders. Prepared by the Committee of Nomenclature and Statistics. Washington, D.C.: American Psychiatric Association, 1968.

Follmann, J. F., Jr. *Insurance Coverage for Mental Illness.* New York: AMACOM, 1970.

Group for the Advancement of Psychiatry. *Medical Practice and Psychiatry,* 1964.

Leedy, Jack J., et al. *Compensation in Psychiatric Disability and Rehabilitation.* Springfield, Ill.: Charles C Thomas, 1971.

Snyder, Solomon H. *The Troubled Mind.* New York: McGraw-Hill Book Company, 1976.

Szasz, Thomas S. *The Myth of Mental Illness.* New York: Perennial Library, Harper & Row, 1974.

5

CAUSES
OF MENTAL DISORDERS

FOR the most part, the causes of mental disorders are not clearly known and remain at best conjectural. This is generally recognized by authoritative sources, including the Joint Commission on Mental Illness and Health, which, in 1961, took cognizance of the absence of definitive scientific evidence of the causes of mental illness.

It is true that for certain mental disorders, the etiology (the causes) have been established. In some cases there has been detectable damage to, or change in, the structure of the brain. However, for the vast majority of cases, there is no known cerebral damage. The cause of the disorder, then, is obscure, extremely difficult to determine, and quite speculative. A consequence of this is that despite the considerable progress that has been made in the conceptualization, identification, and treatment of mental disorders, questions about prevention and cures still persist. It must be noted that this situation is not unique to mental disorders. With many physical diseases or disorders similar problems exist. For example, the cause of diabetes is equally obscure and there is no known cure for the disease. Yet this does not mean that the disorder cannot be treated and brought under control if early detection of the condition occurs, followed by appropriate treatment and strict adherence to the prescribed regimen by the patient.

As a consequence, various theories exist as to the possible causative factors of mental, emotional, and personality disorders. Some search for causes in the genetic background of the individual or in his or her physiological makeup. Others attempt to find the cause in severe traumatic life experiences or in prolonged stress and strain. Still others investigate a variety of socioeconomic situations in relation to the individual, as well as the nature of work and conditions in the workplace as a cause. The question that remains unanswered is why, under a particular set of circumstances or conditions, one person will develop mental disorders of some consequence while another bears those same influences or pressures without serious or prolonged adverse effects, or perhaps even benefits from such life experiences.

This chapter presents a brief discussion of the various attempts to identify, to determine, the causes of mental disorders.

Injury, Pathophysiology, Heredity

A variety of biological factors have been identified as causing mental disorders. These include severe accidents resulting in brain trauma, particularly fetal injury and severe injury to the head resulting in brain damage. They include different types of infections, such as intracranial infection caused by syphilis, meningitis, or brain abscess; infections resulting from alcohol or drug poisoning; prenatal or postnatal cerebral infections; infections resulting from systemic diseases, such as hepatitis, pneumonia, rheumatic fever, rubella, malaria, encephalitis, pernicious anemia, complications of diabetes; and infections caused by the steroids used for the treatment of rheumatoid arthritis. It has recently been speculated that a slow-moving virus that is extraordinarily difficult to detect or destroy causes a rare brain disease called Creutzfeld-Jakon. The disease results in mental deterioration, memory loss, inability to coordinate motor activities, and sometimes death. It is not known how the virus is transmitted, but surgery is suspected to be one means.

In addition, thyroid or adrenal gland dysfunction, metabolic disorders, nutritional or iodine deficiencies, or certain circulatory disturbances can contribute to mental illness. Chromosomal abnormalities, congenital malformations, and other birth defects manifested in late childhood have been identified as causes, as well as brain tumors or lesions. Cerebral arteriosclerosis, thrombosis, or embolism have been found to be causative, and cardiorenal disease, intracranial neoplasm, or the degenerative diseases of the central nervous system can result in mental disorders. Senility has also been viewed as being causative, although the cause of senile dementia itself is not known.

These biological factors are usually the cause, although not the sole cause, of such disorders as the psychoses, the nonpsychotic organic brain syndromes, and mental retardation.

Many feel that there is overwhelming evidence that the cause of mental disorders lies in biological abnormalities or defects, or that it is genetic in origin. This is particularly the case for schizophrenia and depression, for the psychoses not attributed to physiological causes, and for other major affective disorders. The concept is that such biological or genetic factors can predispose the individual to respond abnormally to specific stresses in life; in other words, can make the individual more vulnerable to the onset of such disorders. This concept, however, does not have universal acceptance, and there are those who disagree with the premise.

Schizophrenia, a common and severe mental disorder, serves as an example of such differing views. Schizophrenia tends to run in families, and some have postulated that congenital defects exacerbate the condition. However, opinions differ, at times strongly, on the subject of family influences as a cause. There are those who argue that these do not fully explain the causation of schizophrenia, since no one appears to know whether schizophrenics suffer from a deprivation of external sensations, a bombardment of internal stimuli, or both. Others have suggested that the cause is a virus, a bacterium, or a faulty immune system. Still others suspect that it is caused by a vitamin B-complex deficiency, since many patients show positive response to B12 therapy. Essentially, the cause of schizophrenia is not known and therefore remains the subject of conjecture or speculation.

Depression serves as another example. Many are of the opinion that it often develops as a result of the genetic predisposition of the individual, and again there is a considerable body of opinion that severe depression is a familial, inherited disorder. For some, however, the suggestion that depression is genetically determined has not been proved, even though they agree that it can be passed down through family influence. The debate centers around the question of whether a genetic or biological abnormality creates a predisposition to the disease or whether it actually causes that disease. Many researchers are skeptical about the influence of inheritance and maintain that there is no specific chemical abnormality in depressives that could account for the presence of the disease. These people cite various other factors as being causative, including the home environment, disturbances in the early years of life, or physical dysfunctioning, which at times is found to accompany depression. Other researchers and physicians have noted that certain drugs, such as reserpine (used to treat hypertension), can sometimes bring on depression as a side effect. Others have observed a link between alcoholism and the onset of depression. As with schizophrenia, then, the causes of depression remain conjectural; however, genetic and other biological causes are highly suspect.

Past Experiences as a Cause

With such mental conditions as the neuroses, personality disorders, psychophysical disorders, and other nonpsychotic conditions without manifest psychiatric disorders, there are many who feel that the cause lies in the individual's past experiences, usually traumatic ones. Such experiences can cover a wide range, from the adjustment reactions to infancy, childhood, and adolescence, to the experiences of adult life.

Included in such experiences can be the loss of a loved one, disturbances in the child/parent relationship, rejection, neglect, desertion, deprivation, cruelty, abuse, and brutality; living in an unhappy home, the presence of unbalanced parents who are subject to drunkenness; a broken home; illegitimacy and adoption; and the effects of the rearing process, with excessive strictness at one extreme, excessive permissiveness at the other, and an irresponsible, erratic swing between the two.

Also included in conjectures of the causative factors are such experiences as the problems of growing up and entering a real world. This can lead to a sense of inadequacy and inferiority, a feeling of not measuring up to one's peers or to family expectations, and problems of self-identity. Gradually having to do for one's self, accepting responsibility, becoming self-sufficient, and coping with the anxiety, the uncertainty, the fear, and even the guilt that are all part of becoming a mature person can lead to self-doubts and a sense of insecurity. Today there is concern over the effects of protracted immaturity and the failure of some people to develop an adequate sense of responsibility, which can accrue from the combination of an affluent society and an emphasis, perhaps an overemphasis, on higher education. The concern is that in some individuals this can produce a sense of irresponsibility, a lack of ambition, and a withdrawal from the real world, which, in turn, can bring about the development of consequential neuroses and emotional or personality disorders.

There are many, however, who ask why some individuals who had such life experiences develop mental, emotional, or personality disorders, while many others do not. Again, the question of the presence of an underlying biological predisposition to such disorders is raised, and the opinion is that such past experiences simply serve as contributing factors or triggering events. As before, the search for causative factors continues, and the answers to key questions remain obscure.

The Effects of Trauma and Stress

Trauma and stress can, in the opinion of some professionals, contribute to the following conditions: those without manifest psychiatric disorders, psychophysiological emotional disorders of which the individual might not be aware, certain types of depression, transitional situational disturbances with no apparent underlying mental disorder, and personality disorders.

The traumatic experiences generally recognized as either a cause or a triggering catalyst for the onset of such disorders can run the gamut. Included are accidents, particularly those resulting in the loss of a limb, blindness, or long-term disability; traumatic experiences such as the threat of physical violence, rape, or witnessing a catastrophe; and the consequences of physical shock, of extreme or repeated vibrations, or of sudden or repeated noises. For those with a long history of mild depression any of these traumatic events can result in manic depression.

In addition, the daily stresses of life that we are all subject to are suspected to cause several types of mental, emotional, or personality disorders. Such situations might range from added responsibilities at home or on the job, financial worries resulting from changes in economic stability or the accumulation of debts, and emotionally charged situations occurring either at home or on the job. They include the problems of adjusting to marriage, sex, or bringing up children; the deterioration of physical health; and the problems exacerbated by the aging process. A person's lifestyle, or a family background that emphasized the accumulation of worldly goods as symbols of success, can also be contributing factors. The way people perceive themselves in relation to others can lead to unfavorable comparisons that may make them anxious, selfish, or greedy. In any case, for some people these stresses are overwhelming and can either cause or trigger the onset of a mental disorder.

That such events can have consequences of serious proportions is evident from studies of depressed patients, which found that the following were the principal events in the lives of people who were suffering from depression (in the order noted): increasing arguments with the spouse, moving or relocating, a change in working conditions, marital separation, serious illness of a family member, serious personal illness, starting a new type of work, a death in the immediate family, a new person in the home, major financial problems, pregnancy, and unemployment. Such studies conclude that a strong relationship is evident between stressful events in the life of an individual and the onset of depression.

Studies of clerical workers, skilled and unskilled factory workers, and construction workers by George W. Brown (London, 1970) showed that similar events brought about depression. He also reports that the onset of schizophrenia was triggered, probably where a predisposition existed, by the following events: tense and difficult situations at home or at work, job change, a necessary change of residence, change in a person's physical health, marital separation (by death or otherwise), a life-threatening illness to someone close, major material losses, or disappointment forcing the individual to reassess his or her life. Brown concluded that whether the causal link between life events and the onset of mental illness differs for schizophrenic or depression patients remains a matter for further research.

Many feel, however, that such trauma or stress, experienced to some degree by everyone, do not cause mental disorders, but serve as contributing factors to trigger latent conditions that might be pathophysiological, nutritional, or hereditary in origin. They point out that some mental disorders occur in the absence of external events, as in endogenous depression. Traumatic and stressful life events as causes of mental disorders, per se, remain a matter of speculation.

Socioeconomic Causes

Based on the observation of an increase in certain mental disorders among various socioeconomic groups, the cause of mental disorders is being increasingly sought today in socioeconomic factors and events. This is particularly true for neuroses, conditions without manifest psychiatric disorders, and transitional situational disturbances that have no apparent underlying mental disorders.

Under consideration are the effects of socioeconomic deprivation and poverty, which can result from economic recession, with its resultant unemployment, layoffs, and economic instability; the effects of immigration, including language and economic barriers; and the effects of ethnic and minority status, including racial and religious prejudice.

Various studies have indicated that a correlation between such socioeconomic factors and the incidence of mental disorders exists. However, proof of actual causation is hindered because the unfortunate victims of such circumstances frequently do not seek or obtain the care they need, and therefore cannot be accounted for. In addition, the nature of the relationship is obscured because adults who are mentally ill tend to drift downward in the socioeconomic scale, even though the cause of the illness is not poverty. Children of the poor are frequently said to have a greater chance of being psychologically impaired. Factors that can influence the development of mental disorders among the poor may include a sense of hopelessness, powerlessness to control or significantly alter their situation, inadequate prenatal care, malnutrition, disruption in the family life, and a high rate of job turnover with resultant insecurity. These factors can contribute to the occurrence of personality disturbances, chronic neurotic and psychotic reactions, psychosomatic disorders, and hypochondriacal syndromes. What confuses the subject, however, is the fact that children of affluent families can suffer from neglect and deprivation and can be afflicted by mental illness.

In 1977 the Joint Economic Committee found "that a strong, direct link exists between rising unemployment and increases in stress-related illnesses" such as strokes, heart diseases, and kidney diseases, and that there was an increase in the hospitalization of the mentally ill in state institutions. Similarly, Elmer A. Gardner et al., in studies at the University of Rochester School of Medicine and Dentistry, found that hospital admission rates for schizophrenia and personality disorders decreased as they proceeded from the inner city outward, and that mental disorders were more prevalent among lower-income groups and among nonwhites. They attributed these trends to the class structure of our society, although they acknowledged that their conclusions have not gone undisputed.

With respect to foreigners in America, Locke et al. found evidence that the incidence of insanity among immigrants is higher (by up to 50 percent) than it is for those born in this country. However, the evidence is not always consistent. In studies conducted in Minnesota, Massachusetts, and Ohio, immigration was found to influence mental health. A study in New York State, however, concluded that there was little difference in the relative incidence of mental disorders between foreigners and domestic citizens that could not be accounted for on the basis of environmental and age differences. Most certainly, language barriers and lower levels of income could account for the correlations mentioned above.

It was found by the American Jewish Committee that Jews have a lower rate of psychiatric disorders than others in the population studied, perhaps because of the greater material assets and greater interest in psychiatry, and probably because of better outpatient treatment. Italian-Americans also have a lower rate of hospitalization for mental disorders than other groups. This has been attributed to strong family ties, a low divorce rate, and the general climate of social stability. The inconsistent and inconclusive results of the studies discussed above indicate that ethnic or minority status, as such, cannot be cited as a cause of mental disorders, and there is psychiatric opinion that ethnic and minority status, in fact, can reduce the incidence of mental illness.

Certainly a great many victims of various socioeconomic factors do not experience serious mental disruption, and in fact a substantial number rise above their unfortunate circumstances to achieve important functional and social positions. Again, the question of whether such circumstances are causative in nature or whether they simply serve to propel the onset of an illness to which the individual is already predisposed remains unanswered.

Work and the Workplace as a Cause

Of particular interest to the troubled employee is, of course, the degree to which work and the workplace can cause any of the various types of mental disorders. Again, it must be recognized that there is the question of whether such factors are causes or whether they simply serve to trigger the onset of such disorders.

One of the causes of mental disorders commonly mentioned these days is the concept called the Protestant work ethic. Just what this means is anyone's guess. Since the Reformation did not occur until the sixteenth century, and since, for thousands of years, men, women, and children of all religious beliefs had to work extremely hard, it is difficult to understand what the concept means. In contrast, it was not until the late nineteenth century in Western Europe and America, after Protestantism had become well established, that laws were enacted that limited the work day and the work week, restricted or prohibited child labor, and provided benefits for workers. This resulted in increased security and a higher standard of living. The fact is that the availability of food, housing, clothing, transportation, medical care, and education, as well as works of art, literature, and music, which we so readily take for granted, could not exist unless a great many people (regardless of their religious concepts) had been willing to work, and to work extremely hard.

It is difficult to believe, then, that work, in and of itself, can be a cause of mental disorders. To the contrary, the process of work is known to have a salutary effect on the functioning of the human mind. It is work that, for most people, gives their life a purpose, a sense of usefulness and productivity, and a feeling of independence, of being master of one's own destiny. This is certainly not said to the exclusion of other elements in our lives, but it is important that the concept of work not be overlooked: Sigmund Freud asserts that work is man's strongest tie to reality.

Certainly it is recognized that there are aspects of the work process, whatever the type or level of work, that can exacerbate the onset of mental disorders. Ambition, an overzealous attitude toward work, excessive conscientiousness, a strong desire to get ahead, and a zest for power, when out of balance, can be the cause of trouble. This is particularly so if the process results in continued overwork, or in jealousy or greed. The outcome may be an unhealthily strong desire to achieve the American dream, whatever that is, and to acquire the so-called good things in life to the exclusion of all else. When combined with an inability to relax, trouble at home, or financial worries, mental distress can become a problem. In short, there is nothing wrong, and a great deal good, with working as long as it is not permitted to become all-consuming.

Beyond the concept of work itself, it is not infrequent to find conditions in the workplace that have been identified as causes of mental, emotional, or personality disorders. For example, a study titled *Work in America,* prepared by the U.S. Department of Health, Education, and Welfare in 1972, reported that various aspects of work cannot only account for physical diseases and accidents, but are also highly correlated with symptoms of mental disorders. The study, while recognizing that we are largely ignorant of the nature of the causative factors, demonstrated that the correlations, along with the case histories of workers and anecdotal evidence, all of which indicate a causal relationship, are too convincing to be dismissed.

Unfortunately, despite the considerable amount of speculation on the relationship between the role of the workplace and the development of mental, emotional, and personality disorders, we know too little about this subject. This becomes particularly evident when it is observed that those findings that do exist are frequently conflicting. Beyond that, it is not known whether such employment-centered factors cause such disorders or whether they act as catalysts in susceptible people.

It is undeniably evident, nonetheless, that psychiatric consequences (including traumatic neurosis) can result from experiences at the workplace. These events include accidents that result in injuries, such as burns, shock, and the loss of limbs, sight, or hearing. They include psychological reactions to the terror that accompanies fires or explosions, or to witnessing a catastrophe to fellow workers. The consequences can be depression, personality change, the development of obsessions or compulsions, nightmares, fatigue, blackouts, insomnia, a loss of appetite, headaches, dizziness, or anxiety. Another unfortunate consequence can be a distinct fear of returning to the job.

There appears to be general agreement among psychiatrists and psychologists that any given individual's psychological reaction to such traumatic events depends on a complex of interrelated factors, including the personality of the individual, his or her history of coping with stress or loss, tolerance levels, attitudes toward life, and past experiences. There is disagreement over whether the particular pattern of emotional complications that develops should be labeled mental illness or simply a reaction to the circumstances. Regardless of this problem, courts of law are making more and more awards under workers' compensation programs in cases of traumatic neurosis.

Closely related to the foregoing are the traumatic stresses that may be present under certain working conditions. These can result from repeated vibrations, sharp noises, or a continuous high level of noise; from the presence of noxious odors, fumes, dusts, or toxic substances; from temperature extremes, inadequate ventilation, or either glaring or insufficient lighting; or from physical hazards in the workplace that, despite modern safety precautions, can strike fear in some workers.

The modern industrial process has also been identified as a cause of mental disorders. Mechanization, automation, and computerization are becoming more prevalent in both industrial and office work, and their effects on the worker are a cause for concern. Mass production, assembly-line operations, job obsolescence, technological development, and increasing job specialization can lead to impersonalization, dissatisfaction and boredom. Undue demands for conformance, rigid work schedules, a reduction of individual responsibility, and the absence of any opportunity for the employee to exercise initiative can all exacerbate such conditions.

Today there are many who consider such aspects of work to at least contribute to the onset of mental disorders. In turn, their effect can be intensified when an individual's makeup is not properly considered in relation to job placement, or if excessive overtime, work overload, or other forms of pressure are permitted to develop.

As reasonable as these concerns may seem, their actual effects are not yet clearly known. For example, several studies have shown that matters such as discomfort on the job, long working hours, or layoffs rarely result in disability. A study of workers in an automobile plant by a research team at Johns Hopkins Hospital in Baltimore also indicated that, contrary to what was expected, 95 percent of the plant's employees were satisfied with their jobs and 71 percent found no part of their work to be tiring or upsetting. Most of the workers did not report feeling lonely or having the "blue collar blues." The researchers speculated that this might be attributable to the stability and security in the lives of these workers, including longevity on the job, a steady growth in income, and infrequent moves to other job locations. These advantages may be accounted for, at least in part, by the presence of a strong union.

The workers also exhibited a sense of satisfaction as a result of off-the-job hobbies and other pursuits. The job was not a central focus nor the source of meaning for these workers; rather it was the means of achieving security and having the opportunity to enjoy other endeavors. One can speculate from this study's findings on the astounding degree of plasticity that the human mind exhibits and on its impressive ability to adapt to and cope with life.

The large size of many modern places of employment, whether they are private businesses, universities, or government agencies, can lead to increasing impersonalization, which can make employees feel they are lost in an organizational maze and are invisible to the powers-that-be. When combined with mergers, diversification of interests, or changes in the organizational or management structure, the effects can be compounded. Other consequences of these developments can be disordered leadership, ambiguity of assigned responsibilities, revisions in supervisory structure, and transfers to new locations. Employees may feel alienated from the productive process as well as from management, and it can happen at all levels of employment.

Such events and their consequences were recognized in a report of the Congressional Committee on Labor and Public Welfare in 1972, which noted that alienation is prevalent not only among blue, but also among white collar workers, and in a 1973 report of the U.S. Department of Health, Education, and Welfare. Alienation is also becoming increasingly recognized by industrial managers.

Meanwhile, those at the upper management and executive level can suffer the stress of bearing the burden of authority and of the decision-making responsibility rested in them. Omnipotence and loneliness can accompany their positions, and sometimes unpleasant choices must be made between work priorities and family priorities. In his book *Job Stress and the Psychosocial Pressures of Change*, Dr. Alan A. McLean, a consulting psychiatrist at IBM, discusses a study of 865 employees at three levels of management in one unidentified company. It was found that managers who experienced an increase in symptoms of anxiety perceived both their job and their place of employment to be stressful, with a resultant dissatisfaction in the job. The context of the work environment, then, loomed large as a factor in the development of anxiety. This study also mentioned an increase in the number of physical health problems among this group. However, the matter of individual vulnerability to anxiety as a result of underlying causes was not investigated. Interestingly, such matters as the degree of satisfaction with their salary, the number of hours worked, or the amount of time spent traveling from home to work did not correlate with the degree of anxiety experienced. Clarence Randall, a former Chairman of Inland Steel, has also noted that responsibility breeds isolation; after an executive reaches the top he is seldom seen in public and seldom heard.

Occupational stress, however, has been defined differently by different students of the subject. Attempts to measure it have been made at the Karolinska Institute in Stockholm. It is generally recognized that such stress reactions, however they are defined, originate from deep in the unconscious of the individual and are difficult to assess or even understand. The emotional aspects of either the job or the work environment can certainly be important in triggering the onset of such conditions as anxiety, depression, or alcoholism.

The fact is that anyone who works must at times face stressful conditions that, to say the least, are unpleasant. The junior management individual passed up for promotion after working his hardest, the lathe operator or the clerk doing repetitive tasks day after day, the businessman who spends a considerable part of his life commuting, the actor who is either "at liberty" or else has been playing the same role for years, the professor who must cope with interdepartmental jealousies as well as the "publish or perish" dicta, the bartender forced to listen to the troubles of others ad nauseam, the advertising copywriter doing his eleventh commercial for a cure for constipation, the lobbyist who must endlessly entertain those same dull people, athletes and dancers facing advancing age, or painters and sculptors with unwanted works: all are under stress that could potentially result in the onset of mental disorders.

The psychological effect of work or the workplace on employees has become a subject of increasing interest to employers and labor unions. Dr. McLean has commented that the tendency to hold the workplace responsible for mental health problems deserves critical examination. He feels that standards for psychological exposure like the ones that presently exist for physical exposure are needed. Recognizing that the issues involved in job stress are exceedingly complex, he suggests that much more discussion of and research in the subject are required before adequate solutions will be found.

According to Dr. McLean, two factors can help determine whether or not a specific type of stress will produce symptoms of mental disorders. One is the external context in which an interaction takes place. This can be as broad as changes in the national economy, which may threaten a person's economic security, or as limited as the attitude of management toward workers. The second factor is the vulnerability of the individual, including biological and genetic susceptibilities, personality characteristics, age, educational level, and occupational status.

There are a great many current studies probing the effects of employment on the onset of mental, emotional, and personality disorders. These cover a wide range of workers and jobs. The National Institute of Mental Health has sponsored studies that run the gamut of mental health issues. The following represents a cross section of topics under investigation:

Occupational Stress and Physical and Mental Health
Physical Deviance and Occupational Mistreatment

An Analysis of Job Satisfaction by Age
Occupational Experience and Attitude Change
Urban Household Work and Mental Health
Stress, Ownership, and Pathology in Urban Dirty Work
Transitory Urban Workers and Occupational Identity
Exploratory Study of Industrial Life Styles
Inter-disciplinary Studies of Urban Blue-Collar Life
Economic Change and Individual Psychological Functioning
Impact of Inflation–Recession on Families in Cities
Family Adjustment to Unemployment in an Urban Setting
Urban Growth and Mental Health
Comparative Study of Personnel Practices in Private Firms

The findings of studies such as these should prove to be of considerable interest to employers, employees, unions, and psychiatrists.

BIBLIOGRAPHY

American Public Health Association. *Report of the Joint Economic Committee on the Nation's Health.* January 1977.

Asher, Janet, and Jules Asher. "Psychological Consequences of On-the-Job Injury." *Job Safety and Health,* March 1976.

Bommarito, Peter. "We'd Really Rather Stay Healthy." *Viewpoint,* AFL-CIO, Third Quarter, 1978.

Brown, George W. *British Journal of Psychiatry.* London, 1970.

Follmann, J. F., Jr. *Insurance Coverage for Mental Illness.* New York: AMACOM, 1970.

Freedman, Alfred M., et al. (eds.). *Comprehensive Textbook of Psychiatry.* Baltimore: Williams and Wilkins, 1975.

Gardner, Elmer A., et al. "A Psychiatric Dilemma—The Lower Socioeconomic Class." Rochester: University of Rochester School of Medicine and Dentistry, undated.

Group for the Advancement of Psychiatry. *The Welfare System and Mental Health,* 1973.

Institute on Pluralism and Group Identity of the American Jewish Committee. "A Report," 1976.

Joint Commission on Mental Illness and Health (report). New York: Basic Books, 1961.

Levi, L. *Society, Stress, and Disease.* London: Oxford University Press, 1972.

Levinson, Harry. *Emotional Health: In the World of Work.* New York: Harper & Row, 1964.

Locke, Kramer, and Benjamin Pasamanik. *Immigration and Insanity.* Public Health Reports, Vol. 75, No. 4, April 1960.

McLean, Alan A. "Job Stress and the Psychosocial Pressures of Change." *Personnel,* January-February, 1976.

——— (ed.). *Mental Health and Work Organizations.* Rand McNally, 1970.

Navarro, Vincent. "The Underdevelopment of Health of Working America." *American Journal of Public Health,* June 1976.

Randall, Clarence. "Business, Too, Has Its Ivory Towers." *The New York Times Magazine,* July 8, 1962.

Robbins, Lewis L. "Implications of a Changing Hospital Population." Long Island Jewish–Hillside Medical Center, 1977.

Schneck, Harold M., Jr. "A Deadly Virus Apparently Transmitted by Surgery." *The New York Times,* May 9, 1977.

Siassi, Crosetti, and Spiro. "Loneliness and Dissatisfaction in a Blue Collar Population." *Archives of General Psychiatry,* February 1974.

Snyder, Solomon H. *The Troubled Mind.* New York: McGraw-Hill, 1976.

U.S. Department of Health, Education, and Welfare. *Mental Health in Appalachia.* Public Health Publication No. 1375.

U.S. Department of Health, Education, and Welfare. *Work in America,* 1972.

Watts, Glenn E. "The Work Ethic Is Alive in America." *Viewpoint,* AFL-CIO, Third Quarter, 1978.

6

WHO NEEDS HELP?

A salient question to the troubled employee, to his or her family, employer, and union (if he or she is a union member) is: Who needs help? How is one to know when help should be sought?

As was noted earlier, certain signs of mental, emotional, or personality disorders or disturbances are evident in everyone, to varying degrees. We all have anxieties, suffer from frustrations and denials, and become depressed, impatient, or nervous. We have our own particular quirks and eccentricities. We become indecisive and confused. Most of us are ambitious and desire some form of status, and we can force ourselves to work under pressure, if necessary. Many of us feel guilty, envious, jealous, or greedy. The historian Arnold J. Toynbee has said that thinking is as unnatural and arduous an activity for human beings as walking on two legs is for a monkey.

Yet most people somehow find a way to bounce back and reestablish their sense of balance and normalcy. Or so they hope.

The problem, then, is that of determining when such matters should be taken seriously and when psychiatric diagnosis and treatment should be sought. Unfortunately, there are no precise answers, nor are there adequate guidelines on which the layman can rely.

Consequently, no one can say definitively the point at which help should be sought except when the obvious symptoms of serious mental disorders are clearly present.

When the behavioral, functional, or physical symptoms are persistent, profound, or extreme; when there has been a recent onset or intensification of serious symptoms that go beyond what might be considered reasonable cause; or when the individual is suffering intense emotional pain, then the seeking of help is necessary. Also, when suicidal tendencies are apparent, help is certainly needed. Another warning sign can be the exhaustion by the individual of his or her inner resources for dealing with the stresses encountered. In addition, the magnitude of regression or depression can become intolerable to the individuals or to those with whom they come in contact.

Still other signs are the point at which the processes of thinking, emotions, or behaviors adversely affect the normal or customary functioning of the individual, or inhibit such functioning to the point of disability; when they become destructive, rendering the individual incapable of movement or of getting control of the problems with which he or she is faced; or the point at which reactions to such circumstances of life as grief or reversals become abnormal in the sense of being unduly protracted and identifiable overreactions to subjective feelings. In other words, when the individual has reached a point where the mental functioning becomes sufficiently impaired that it grossly interferes with that person's capacity to meet the ordinary demands of life, help is needed.

Symptoms of Mental Disorders

Here it is of value to briefly take a look at some of the common symptoms of the various forms of mental disorders, certain of which were noted briefly in the discussion of the classification of mental disorders.

Symptoms of Manic Depression

One of the more serious and most common of the psychotic mental disorders is manic depression. It is marked by an introversion, an emptiness, a loss of affection, a lack of purpose, and a sense of futility. Manic-depressive people suffer from a strong sense of guilt and despondency, and suicidal or self-destructive tendencies can be prompted by the sense of pessimism, worthlessness, desperation, and hopelessness that permeates their lives. They may become overwhelmed by such feelings, which can make them frightened, anxious, or even panic-stricken. Disturbances in thinking, loss of memory, alterations in concept formation, or even gross disorganization or disorientation can result in confusion, indecisiveness, and an inability to work. Manic-depressives may also experience hallucinations or delusions. Physical symptoms can include insomnia, headaches, dizziness, constipation, loss of appetite, tremors, excessive perspiration, and sexual dysfunction.

Manic-depressives are conscious of what is happening to them, but unable to control the situation. At the same time, they are subject to profound alterations in mood, going from enthusiasm, elation, and exuberance, when they are agitated, energetic, and talkative, to pessimism, depression, and lethargy. They may become wildly extravagant and run into debt.

Oddly enough, depressed people may have been, in the past, quite self-reliant, conventionally well-behaved, well-organized, outstanding at their work, and even quite successful. When the symptoms of manic depression become severe and extend beyond a transient feeling of inadequacy, help is needed. Today, anti-depressive medication and electroshock therapy are helpful to some manic-depressives, and a few can be fortunate enough to experience spontaneous recovery.

Symptoms of Schizophrenia

Schizophrenics have lost contact with reality, yet they retain their intelligence. The profound disturbances in their relationship to the real world cause a withdrawal, aloofness, or detachment reflected in all of their thoughts and feelings. Their behavior is typified by vague, incoherent, or unrelated statements; by inappropriate, distorted, or exaggerated emotional reactions to events; or by the expression of confused or meaningless ideas. These are shattered, disintegrated personalities: in fact, the word means split mind.

Schizophrenics experience weird, unreal, distorted, and frightening memories from childhood, wild hallucinations or delusions; they are extremely sensitive and are intolerant of frustration or stress; they often have trouble working with others and at times display a decided egocentricity. There is a self-disintegration, with intellectual and physical functions gradually diminishing, and a feeling of the self falling to pieces, although some schizophrenics display considerable reserve, and seem quite reasonable even though they lack logical coherence.

Schizophrenia is the most disabling and crippling of the mental disorders, and can even be lethal. In Chapter 4, the types of schizophrenia were described: catatonia is marked by muscular immobility, stupor, extreme tension, contortions of the face or body, loss of appetite, and an inability to control the bladder; hebephrenia is symptomized by disturbances in thinking and complete withdrawal from reality; and paranoia is marked by auditory hallucinations, feelings of persecution, and grandiose delusions. When these symptoms are persistent, help is needed. Without help, the individual stands little chance of improving.

Symptoms of the Neuroses

When an inner conflict impairs mental or emotional functioning, this may indicate that a person has become neurotic. The principal symptom of neurosis is extreme anxiety: individuals become so concerned over their situation that panic sets in. Other symptoms can include chronic weakness (to the point of exhaustion), obsessive-compulsiveness, paranoia, tension, depression, hypochondria, or hysteria to the point of paralysis of the body. A feeling of unreality, an estrangement of self, or a distortion or misinterpretation of things seen or heard are typical in neurotic people. They feel inadequate and inferior, avoid others, are irritable, restless, or openly hostile. They may become overprotective, develop exaggerated notions of their abilities, or become inflexible and stubborn. Neurotic behavior has been described as inappropriate, inadequate, ineffective, and infantile, and results in a subjective or objective discrepancy between psychological potential and actual performance. If the condition goes untreated, nervous breakdowns can result.

Symptoms of Personality, Emotional, or Character Disorders

The symptoms associated with these disorders are less likely to cause emotional pain than those described for the neuroses or the psychoses. The borderline separating these two conditions is, however, a blurred one.

Personality might be described as the conceptualization of the person as a whole: what he or she has been, is, and hopes to be. It embraces that person's mind, body, memories, habits, impulses, motivations, abilities, and shortcomings. No two personalities are ever the same. Personality determines how much or little self-control people exhibit, how they react to external stimuli, the nature of their interpersonal relationships, their patterns of adjustment, whether they can maintain a sense of balance, and the way people approach work, love, recreational activity, and relaxation.

When personality, emotional, or character disorders develop, they are marked by maladaptive patterns of behavior that generally originated early in life. A marked change in or even a disintegration of a person's personality may signal the onset of a disorder. Anxiety, nervousness, compulsiveness, an exaggerated sense of duty, an overcompliance with routine and ritual, and a philosophy of self-denial can indicate that a problem exists. The individual may become irascible, argumentative, and overdefensive, and can have difficulty adapting to change or dealing with problems. Difficulty in making decisions can be a consequence.

On the other hand, timidity, shyness, and an overdependence on others can become apparent, along with other signs of immaturity, such as impulsiveness, self-centeredness, exploitation of others, and a sense of inadequacy. Threats to personal security can become overwhelming, and reactions might take such forms as marked jealousy, suspicion, envy, or greed. Rationalization, overambition, or acquisitiveness are also symptomatic. Some people suffer from character disorders. The symptoms can be lying, cheating, or stealing (without feelings of guilt), or antisocial behavior, characterized by the feeling that everyone else is wrong.

The consequences for those suffering from such disorders are many and varied. They may lose status, fail to advance at the job, be demoted, or even be dismissed. The excessive consumption of tobacco, food, alcohol, or drugs can become apparent. There can be marital difficulties or extramarital affairs. There can be wanton spending, an accumulation of debts, and constant gambling.

Several different types of personality disorders have been identified, and these were noted in Chapter 4. These include cyclothymia, the paranoid personality, the obsessional personality, the psychopathic or sociopathic personality, and those who suffer from any of a variety of phobias.

The personality, emotional, or character disorders noted here are the types most frequently occasioned in a place of employment. Should such symptoms persist, help is needed. Since people who need help seldom seek it of their own volition, their family, associates, or employers may have to bring about a confrontation to ensure that help is sought.

Miscellaneous Symptoms and Warning Signs

Unnecessary risk-taking can be a characteristic of mental disorders. Behavioral scientists have been unable, however, to agree on an acceptable definition of risk-taking. Risk-taking is an integral part of human experience and personality growth, and throughout life we are all inclined to take risks of many types. But when risk-taking is brash and perhaps an unconsciously suicidal act, it is unnecessary and may indicate the onset of an imbalance.

Unnecessary risk-taking can occur on the job, when safety precautions are ignored or protective equipment is discarded. Some people may even actively seek dangerous work. If people flagrantly ignore their family medical history, neglect to take prescribed medication, violate automobile or motorcycle safety regulations, or are careless while swimming, boating, or hunting, they may be exhibiting some type of mental disorder.

The tendency to be *accident prone* is closely related to risk-taking. Repeated accidents can result not only from the compulsion to take undue risks, but also from inattentiveness, inability to concentrate, psychomotor retardation, or poor visual-motor coordination. Related symptoms can be overt hostility, inflexibility with a strong tendency to rigidity and perfectionism, low self-esteem, and the presence of psychogenic headaches. Indeed, the vast majority of those who are accident-prone have been found to suffer from some form of depression.

A *preoccupation with suicide* is another characteristic of mental illness, usually of depression. This subject is discussed in the final chapter of this book.

The Need for Early Diagnosis

Without proper attention and adequate care, the consequences of mental illness can be serious and even deadly. Troubled people may experience not only mental pain and anguish, but their physical condition can decline as well. They may have accidents, become ill, or suffer from disabilities. Their family life can become affected, and their spouse and children can experience untold agony. They may turn to alcohol or to a variety of drugs. Savings and assets can disappear and debts can accumulate. The costs of health care and of lost income as a result of disability, to the extent they are not protected by insurance or by health and welfare funds, can mount. Status can diminish, careers can be thwarted or ruined, and unemployment can occur. The possibility of long-term hospitalization might be imminent. And death may be the unhappy consequence, suicidal or otherwise.

To delay action—to put off diagnosis and treatment—can therefore have grave repercussions.

The key to avoiding these consequences is this: The troubled individual must seek diagnosis and treatment as early as possible following the appearance of the symptoms described in this and preceding chapters. In this way, the problem can be arrested before too much damage has been done.

One basic problem is knowing where to turn for help. Unfortunately, the general public, and even many professional people, are by no means well informed of the sources of help or the kinds of treatment available. Troubled people, and those trying to help them, can become understandably confused about where to turn for assistance. In subsequent chapters, the types of facilities and array of professional and paraprofessional personnel concerned with the diagnosis and treatment of mental disorders are discussed in detail, as are the diverse concepts for treatment.

Another basic problem lies in the variety of factors that impede the troubled employee from seeking early diagnosis and help. Public impressions of psychiatric treatment are at best hazy and are often scorned and ridiculed. Everyone dreads mental hospitals, and the mass media helps maintain that tarnished image. Some approaches to coping with mental disorders are viewed simply as ridiculous fads. Even when some knowledge of the subject is present, there is an honest concern over the unclear definitions, the identification of problems, and the absence of efficacious forms of treatment for certain problems.

However, the paramount deterrent to seeking early diagnosis and treatment is perhaps the public and social stigma that attaches to mental disorders and to their treatment. As was shown earlier, all too often a person waits until conditions become unbearable to all concerned before seeking diagnosis and treatment. By that time serious damage can already have been done.

Troubled employees are keenly aware of the social stigma. As a result, even after admitting that they might have a problem, those who need help may be afraid of treatment. The reactions of those around them, concern over costs of treatment and time lost from work, fear of the effects on their livelihood, career, and future employability will cause people to postpone seeking help. Matters can only become worse.

Certainly these concerns can differ among individuals, depending on socioeconomic status, educational levels, and type of employment. That they are real concerns is beyond any doubt. This was made readily evident in a recent study by Melvin A. Glasser of the United Automobile Workers Union. The study shed light on the opinions and attitudes of employed people toward the need for the treatment and the consequences of seeking such treatment. It also provided valuable insight into the perceptions of the providers of health care, including all types of community mental health practitioners, as well as local union officials, the clergy, school officials, and police personnel.

The study showed that one-fifth of the workers felt that young people who were always getting into trouble on the job did not need mental health treatment; about 13 percent did not feel that those who couldn't hold a job because they drank too much needed treatment. One-third felt that treatment was not necessarily needed for those who spoke to the machine they operated, or for those who constantly watched television at home and had little or no communication with their family. Three-quarters of the workers did not feel that people who refuse to ride elevators needed treatment. Eighty percent did not feel that a married couple having problems because husband and wife worked different shifts could benefit from treatment. Furthermore, one-half the workers expressed a strong fear of talking to a psychiatrist, and one-third were convinced that it would do no good. Half the workers felt that they could handle their own problems, and two out of five thought asking for help was a definite sign of weakness. However, three-quarters of the workers were convinced that most family doctors could help patients with emotional problems.

The powerful negative effect public stigma can have on the resolution of mental problems was clearly indicated by the following attitudes uncovered by the study. More than one-half the workers had a strong fear that others would find out that they needed help, were afraid that people would think they were crazy, and said they would be embarrassed by having to seek help. Further reflecting the sense of stigma, 87 percent of the workers felt that mental illness tends to repel most people, 43 percent felt that most people would not like to work next to a person who had been a mental patient, and 72 percent were convinced that if a patient were treated in a general hospital or in a clinic, there would be less stigma than if he were treated in a mental hospital.

As to the effects of seeking help on their working careers, almost one-half of the workers had strong worries about "what would happen" to their jobs as a result of seeking treatment, and over one-third feared that their jobs would be adversely affected. It is interesting to note that the workers were joined by both the referral sources and the mental health professionals in most of their concerns.

Even though a union-negotiated health insurance program had removed a substantial portion of the financial obstacles to mental health care, the insurance benefits were being underutilized by employees. The researchers felt this indicated the lack of an effective mental health care program in which problems are detected early and the appropriate recommendations made. Furthermore, the workers were not aware of the professional resources available to them, were largely unaware of their own insurance program, had negative attitudes toward mental health care, and were not likely to seek professional intervention early.

The people to whom a worker could turn, particularly union officials and the clergy, were not fully aware of the available treatment resources, and frequently did not recognize mental problems early enough—even when workers sought their advice. In addition, the mental health professionals appeared to contribute little in the way of disseminating information about the mental health services available in the community.

These findings are most valuable. Unfortunately, they are real facts of life that are present in any attempt to cope with mental disorders, especially among blue collar workers, but also among other levels of employment. They indicate formidable hurdles in the way of early identification and treatment of mental, emotional, and personality disorders.

BIBLIOGRAPHY

American Public Health Association. *Mental Health: The Public Health Challenge.* Washington, D.C.: 1975.
Eelkema, Robert C., et al. "Statistical Study on the Relationship Between Mental Illness and Traffic Accidents." *American Journal of Public Health,* March 1970.
Flach, Frederic F. *The Language of Depression.* The Life Sciences Advisory Group, 1970.
Follmann, J. F., Jr. *Alcoholics and Business.* New York: AMACOM, 1976.
Glasser, Melvin A., et al. "Obstacles to Utilization of Prepaid Mental Health Care." *American Journal of Psychiatry,* July 1975.
Leedy, Jack J., et al. *Compensation in Psychiatric Disability and Rehabilitation.* Springfield, Ill.: Charles C Thomas, 1971.
National Center for Health Statistics. *Selected Symptoms of Psychological Distress.* Series 11, No. 37. Washington, D.C., 1970.
Snyder, Solomon H. *The Troubled Mind.* New York: McGraw-Hill, 1976.

7

INCIDENCE
OF MENTAL DISORDERS

THE incidence or prevalence of mental, emotional, or personality disorders, either in American society as a whole or in places of employment, has never been satisfactorily determined. The estimates that are frequently cited are certainly not precise. Some figures have been exaggerated, while others suffer from under-reporting. There are many reasons for this.

To begin with, there are no universally accepted standards of what mental health is, and the criteria for identifying disorders are not clearly defined or consistent. In addition, diagnoses can differ among professionals. Such inconsistencies can only serve to impede any statistical gathering on the incidence of mental disorders.

Another problem is that many of those afflicted, for reasons discussed earlier, do not seek treatment, and therefore are not represented in the records. However, there are projections that include such people. Even after diagnosis and treatment, it is not uncommon for health professionals, who are fully aware of public prejudices, to slant their diagnosis in favor of an accompanying physical ailment. Or they may respect the confidentiality of the patient's records and not divulge pertinent information. This, too, will distort the data on the incidence of mental illness. Compounding this problem further is the fact that people receive treatment at more than one facility. For example, a person may consult a private psychiatrist who recommends hospitalization. Following hospitalization, the person may receive outpatient care at a community mental health center, a rehabilitation agency, or at other types of facilities. Because each treatment center maintains its own records, double counting is inevitable. Furthermore, patients may suffer one or more recurrences of a disorder, and additional treatment will be required. Or they may simply discontinue treatment, only to return at a later date. Again double counting occurs since records invariably do not follow the same person through the years.

In addition, there are people in public mental hospitals who may no longer need treatment but who, after perhaps years of care, are economically or psychologically incapable of becoming self-sufficient. Unwanted by their relatives, faced by a world that appears foreign or even hostile, these people are virtually homeless. They require simply custodial care, yet they continue to be counted among the mentally ill.

With the foregoing in mind, it can still be valuable to briefly review the various estimates of the incidence of mental disorders in both the entire population and among employed people. Such estimates can at least provide an appreciation for the proportions of the problem.

Within the Population at Large

In 1948, the then Federal Security Agency reported that 8 million people in the United States were suffering from mental illness and that one out of 20 Americans would require psychiatric care at some time during their lives. In 1951, the President's Commission on the Health Needs of the Nation estimated that 6 percent of the population were suffering from mental disorders and needed treatment. In 1957, the Commission on Chronic Illness estimated that 10 percent of the noninstitutionalized population were mentally ill and in need of treatment. This estimate excluded minor personality or behavioral disorders but it totaled, at that time, 17 million people. In 1961, the Joint Commission on Mental Illness and Health reported that 1.8 million Americans were being treated each year for mental conditions and that one in 10 needed treatment.

It is often said that 10 percent of the nation's population is afflicted with some form of mental disorder that requires treatment. However, only 10 to 20 percent of these (some 2.5 to 4 million people) are currently receiving care. The trend in the incidence of mental disorders among Americans is not known and certainly should not be deduced from the foregoing information.

Other indicators of the scope of the problem are often noted. For example, 2 million people were either rejected by, or discharged from, the armed services as a result of neuropsychiatric disorders during World War II, and 43 percent of all U.S. Army discharges have been related to mental illness. Of course, these figures include psychological problems that result from the consequences of war itself, including shell shock and battle fatigue.

The frequent estimates of the number of people who consult family physicians for primary or associated mental disorders can also help give us an indication of the scope of this problem. The President's Commission on the Health Needs of the Nation estimated in 1951 that one-half the people consulting a family physician had some form of mental disorder. Other estimates range from 6 percent, to 8 percent, to 15 percent, to 50 percent, depending on which conditions are included, as well as the physician's sensitivity to the problem. A 1970 estimate, however, is that 6 percent of those who saw physicians in that year had a psychiatric disorder, and that 11 percent were suffering from psychosomatic illnesses, however defined. Similarly, the Group Health Cooperative of Puget Sound found in 1971 that 822 of the 10,667 patients who had physical examinations over a six-month period suffered from significant emotional stress. The Community Health Center Plan at New Haven reported in 1978, however, that 15.7 percent of patients visiting the Center over the two-year period had emotional problems.

There is, then, no matter how evaluated, a considerable prevalence of mental disorders of various types among the general population, more so than is generally thought to be the case.

The incidence of such disorders has been found to vary with various types of demographic and socioeconomic factors. It has been found to increase in incidence with age, to be greater among women, unmarried people, nonwhites and ethnic minorities, unemployed people, and those who are economically disadvantaged. Not all findings are consistent, however. For example, one examination of the subject found no appreciable difference in the incidence of mental disorders among the races or among those of different income levels.

Another found only a small correlation between the incidence of the disorder and whether the place of residence was urban, suburban, or rural.

A study of Group Health Insurance, Inc., enrollees in New York City found that salaried professional workers and their families accounted for 25 percent of all psychiatric patients, even though they represented only 10 percent of the enrollees in the plan. That study also found that 42 percent of the psychiatric patients were college educated or came from homes where someone had a college education. In contrast, the National Center for Health Statistics found, in 1970, that psychological distress was more widespread among people who were less educated, who had low incomes, and who lived in rural areas.

The evidences of greater incidence of mental disorders among different population groups are therefore inconsistent. However, they can point to certain factors that accelerate the onset of mental disorders.

Another indication of the incidence of mental disorder is demonstrated by the number of people receiving treatment in hospitals and other institutions. In 1970, 447,000 people were reported to be in psychiatric hospitals, and these patients occupied one-half of all hospital beds. A decade earlier this number was reported to have been 672,000, the decrease in the intervening ten years being attributable, in large part, to the development of psychotropic drugs (to be discussed later) and to the development of community mental health centers and other out-of-hospital forms of treatment.

There are, however, different estimates available, and the discrepancies probably reflect which types of institutions were included in the counting. In 1973 it was reported that 750,000 people were hospitalized or institutionalized for mental disorders; 400,000 were in state or county mental hospitals, and some 111,000 were in institutions for the mentally retarded. In 1976, however, the U.S. Department of Health, Education, and Welfare reported that the daily resident population in public mental hospitals was 200,000.

As for the types of mental disorders and their incidence among the general population, again variations in the estimates occur. The figure for the number of neurotic people is variously stated at 5, 10, 50, and 75 percent of the adult population. Such wide differences unquestionably reflect how the terms used were defined, and many such estimates are considered unreliable. Two decades ago, the Midtown Manhattan study, conducted in New York City, reported that 36 percent of the adults studied had neurotic disturbances and 22 percent had moderately severe abnormalities. In other words, more than one-half of those studied were found to be clinically neurotic. In that study, 23.4 percent of those studied exhibited some degree of impairment to the life functioning processes as a result of mental disorders.

A 1970 survey conducted by the National Center for Health Statistics is of considerable interest. The findings of the survey were based on a self-reporting of selected symptoms of psychological distress among adults of all ages who were sampled on a scientific basis. It was found that nervous breakdowns had been experienced by 4.9 percent of those queried, with a rate of 4.7 percent among whites and 6.9 percent among blacks, and with women suffering twice as many breakdowns as men. For both sexes, the incidence of nervous breakdowns was considerably higher from ages 55 to 74 and lowest from ages 18 to 24. In addition, 12.8 percent of those queried had felt an impending nervous breakdown at some time, the proportion being 17.5 percent for women compared to 7.7 percent for men.

The National Center for Health Statistics also compiled figures on the incidence of a variety of other conditions that may be symptoms of psychological distress. A portion of that data is shown in Table 1.

Table 1. Incidence of distress signals.

	Total	Males	Females
Nervousness (tension)	58.5%	45.1%	70.6%
Inertia (inability to take care of things)	25.1	16.8	32.5
Insomnia	32.4	23.5	40.4
Nightmares	10.1	7.6	12.4
Trembling hands	9.0	7.0	10.9
Perspiring hands	19.3	17.0	21.4
Fainting spells or blackouts	23.3	16.9	29.1
Dizziness	9.1	7.1	10.9
Headaches	21.1	13.7	27.8
Heart palpitations	4.8	3.7	5.8

In all, the survey found that 78 percent of these adults had at least one symptom of psychological distress, 18.5 percent had two symptoms, 13.9 percent had three symptoms, 10.2 percent had four symptoms, and 14.8 percent had five or more of the symptoms identified.

These behaviors are, of course, much more common than the serious and disabling disorders. There is evidence, for example, that psychoneurosis occurs 12 times as often as psychotic disorders, and psychophysiological disorders are two-thirds as common as the neuroses. In 1969, a study of 31,179 admissions and 23,260 discharges (both outpatient and inpatient) at a variety of mental health facilities showed that 38.7 percent of the people treated suffered from neuroses; 18.1 percent were schizophrenics; 8.3 percent were alcoholics; 6.7 percent suffered major affective disorders, such as manic depression and involutional melancholia; 4 percent had personality disorders; 3.6 percent had transient situational disturbances; and the remainder was composed of smaller percentages of other disorders.

It is important to recognize that some mental disorders are much more disabling than are others. While only 8.8 percent of psychoneurotics and 7.3 percent of those suffering from psychophysiological disorders have been found to have some form of functional impairment, 90 percent of those suffering from the psychoses are so impaired. Depression is the most common of the serious and disabling disorders, while schizophrenia is said to afflict 1 percent of the population, and 5 to 10 percent of the population are thought to be borderline schizophrenics.

Such differences are also evident from the 1967 reports of the U.S. Department of Health, Education, and Welfare on the principal diagnosis of hospitalized cases for mental disorders. It was found that 44.9 percent of the resident hospital population were diagnosed as schizophrenic; 29.6 percent as suffering from other psychoses, usually depression or disorders relating to old age; and 8.8 percent as having chronic brain syndrome. Only 16.7 percent were diagnosed as psychoneurotic or as having some other form of mental disorder.

Rounding out the picture, there are reported to be some 9 million alcoholics in the United States; and from 5 to 7 million mentally retarded people, 90,000 of whom suffer from profound retardation, 210,000 from severe retardation, 360,000 from moderate retardation, and 5.3 million from mild retardation.

Finally, it should be noted that the mortality rates among those with mental disorders have also been shown by several sources to be in excess of those for the general population. This might be due to a variety of causes: if mental illness has been caused by metabolic disorders, neoplasms, cerebrovascular diseases, skull fractures, or intracranial injuries, these same factors will no doubt affect longevity. Death can result from accompanying violent behaviors, suicide, or unnecessary risk-taking. It can be a consequence of long-term institutionalization or of treatment procedures. It can result from alcoholism or drug abuse, or from the living arrangements or the lifestyles and patterns of behavior that may accompany mental disorders.

In summary, the incidence of mental, emotional, and personality disorders among the general population is quite high, and is certainly not as uncommon as people frequently choose to think.

Among Employed People

While there are no undisputed findings that indicate what the actual incidence of mental, emotional, and personality disorders is for those in the workforce, there are clear indications that the phenomenon is quite widespread. And with more than 90 million people in the workforce today, data on the incidence of these disorders is by no means irrelevant.

It has been estimated that 25 percent of the working population have some type of mental, emotional, or personality problem. In 1970, Stanley F. Yolles, director of the National Institute of Mental Health, said that 15 to 30 percent of employed people were handicapped by emotional problems. Similarly, the Cornell University New York State School of Industrial and Labor Relations has estimated that 20 to 25 percent of all industrial workers have the potential for emotional instability. On-the-job manifestations of mental illness run the gamut, from a preoccupation with details, poor work habits, inefficiency, chronic indecisiveness, and job dissatisfaction, to friction with fellow employees and customers, to an increase in the frequency of illnesses and accidents, accompanied by an increase in absenteeism. Another consequence can be alcoholism, estimated to afflict some 4 to 5 million employed people. An increase in labor turnover can be a consequence.

HEW's 1967 study of people being cared for in long-term institutions revealed that one-half the patients studied had been employed at some time, principally as operatives, service workers, clerical workers, craftsmen and foremen, laborers, and professional and technical workers. Once again, the troubled employee is found at any type or level of job.

The National Center for Health Statistics found that among people classified as professional/technical/managerial, clerical/sales, and operatives, the incidence of psychological symptoms was lower than for other employees. For those classified as farmers/farm managers, and private household and service workers, there was a higher incidence. Among craftsmen/foremen and related workers, nervous breakdowns, impending breakdowns, inertia, nightmares, perspiring hands, headaches, and heart palpitations were recorded with a relatively high frequency. The incidence of nervousness and nervous breakdowns was also high for people working in clerical/sales. For those in private household and service work, insomnia, trembling hands, and heart palpitations were frequent complaints, and among farm laborers dizziness and fainting occurred more often than among other groups.

The study showed that those in the agricultural, forestry, and fishing industries had the highest incidence of symptoms of psychological distress. People employed in mining and construction were prone to nervous breakdowns, nightmares, fainting spells, and headaches, but were less likely to suffer from nervousness and insomnia. For those working in wholesale and retail trade there was a higher-than-average incidence of nervous breakdowns, nervousness, and fainting, but a lower-than-average incidence of headaches, nightmares, and dizziness (this was not true for the women). Those in finance, insurance, and real estate exhibited a higher incidence of fainting and (for the men) nervous breakdowns and nervousness, and a lower rate of impending breakdowns, inertia, insomnia, headaches, and dizziness.

For those working in government, the incidence of nervous breakdowns, nervousness, and trembling hands was relatively high; but it was low for impending breakdowns, inertia, insomnia, nightmares, headaches, and fainting. In the transportation and communications industries and the public utilities the record was quite good, with a relatively high incidence only in cases of inertia.

Perhaps surprisingly, among employees in the manufacturing industry the incidence of all the symptoms of psychological distress was below average—the exceptions being headaches and perspiring hands and, in the case of white women, impending nervous breakdowns and inertia.

Most of the symptoms of psychological distress occurred more frequently among retired men than among those who were actively employed. The incidence of such symptoms was greater among those women who were keeping house than it was for those who held jobs.

Other researchers have found that mental, emotional, and personality disorders are among the principal causes of worker absenteeism and disability. For example, the Metropolitan Life Insurance Company made a most informative study of its own employees. In 1975, it was found that new cases of disability among office employees that lasted eight or more days and were diagnosed as psychoneuroses and psychoses occurred at the rate of 4.2 per 1,000 men and 5.1 per 1,000 women. Among the sales force, these rates were 2.0 and 3.1, respectively. For both sexes, the incidence of these disabilities increased with age.

While psychoneuroses and psychoses were not a common cause of disability, they ranked high as a cause of prolonged absence from work. Among working men of all ages, 453 days of disability (excluding the first seven days of each illness) per 1,000 people were reported to result from these disorders annually. For women, the corresponding figure was 492 days. For men the average number of days of disability per claim was 135.7 days, and for women it was 92.9 days. This reflects the higher average age of the men. The rate of hospitalization per 1,000 employees for psychoneuroses and psychoses for the years 1963–1967 was 2.6 for men and 2.0 for women. Hospital stays resulting from mental disorders were also longer than those for other causes of disability, averaging 19.8 days for men and 39.6 days for women.

Another insurance company, which writes long-term disability insurance coverage on groups of employed people, found that claims resulting from mental, psychoneurotic, and personality disorders accounted for 5.7 percent of all long-term disability claims. Of these, 55.4 percent were for psychoneurotic disorders, 18.5 percent for personality disorders, 12.3 percent for psychotic disorders, 7.7 percent for psychophysiological disorders, and 6.2 percent for chronic brain disorders. The company maintains that disabilities due to mental disorders account for between 10 and 20 percent of the total claims costs for long-term disabilities.

Mental disorders present one of the most vexing problems facing employers today. It has been demonstrated time and again that people at all types and levels of employment can feel the effects. Among employed people the occurrence of various types of disorders differs from that found in the population as a whole: Employed people usually suffer from neurotic, emotional, and personality problems. But any type of disorder can strike those in the workforce. The problem and how to approach it are discussed in subsequent chapters.

BIBLIOGRAPHY

Anderson, Ronald, et al. *Psychologically-Related Illness and Health Services Utilization.* Center for Health Administration Studies, University of Chicago, August 1974.

Avnet, Helen. "Psychiatric Insurance." New York: Group Health Insurance, Inc., 1962.

Blum, R. H. "Case Identification in Psychiatric Epidemiology: Methods and Problems." *Milbank Memorial Quarterly* 40.

Coleman, Jules V., and Donald L. Patrick. "Psychiatry and General Health Care." *American Journal of Public Health,* May 1978.

Commission on Chronic Illness (report). Cambridge, Mass.: Harvard University Press, 1957.

Ennis, Bruce. "Madness." Civil Liberties Union of New York, February 1973.

Federal Security Agency. *The Nation's Health.* Washington, D.C.: September 1948.

Follmann, J. F., Jr. *Alcoholics and Business.* New York: AMACOM, 1976.

――――. *Insurance Coverage for Mental Illness.* New York: AMACOM, 1970.

Gardner, Elmer. "Emotional Disorders in Medical Practice." *Annals of International Medicine,* October 1973.

Joint Commission on Mental Illness and Health. *Action for Mental Health.* New York: Basic Books, 1961.

Kramer, Martin. "A Discussion of the Concepts of Incidence and Prevalence as Related to Epidemiological Studies of Mental Disorder." *American Journal of Public Health,* July 1957.

Lerner, Monroe, and Odin Anderson. *Health Progress in the United States.* University of Chicago Press, 1963.

Metropolitan Life Insurance Co. *Statistical Bulletin,* April 1976.

National Association for Mental Health. *Facts About Mental Illness.* New York: 1954.

National Center for Health Statistics. *Selected Symptoms of Psychological Distress.* Series 11, No. 37. Washington, D.C.: 1970.

Shepherd, Michael B., et al. *Psychiatric Illness in General Practice.* London: Oxford University Press, undated.

U.S. Department of Health, Education, and Welfare, *National Survey of Institutionalized Adults,* H.E.W. Publication No. (SSA) 75-11803. Washington, D.C.: 1967.

――――. *Report of the President's Commission on the Health Needs of the Nation.* Washington, D.C.: 1951.

――――. *Research and Statistics Note, No. 3,* 1976.

――――. *What Is Mental Illness?* U.S. Public Health Service Publication No. 505. Washington, D.C.: 1957.

Yolles, Stanley F. Presented at the Institute of Management and Labor Relations, Rutgers University, June 10, 1970.

8

The Cost of Mental Disorders

THE measurement of the economic costs of illness is an extremely difficult task. The underlying concepts that enter into such measurements are complex, there is not always unanimity as to their details, and the available data is often sparse or incomplete.

For example, Dorothy P. Rice, currently head of the National Center for Health Statistics, has said:

> A variety of studies and figures relating to the costs of illnesses have been generated in the health field. The methods used range from broad statements of costs, with no apparent basis, to detailed, sophisticated economic analyses. . . . Costs are often estimated in gross terms: average earnings are applied to overall morbidity (or mortality) data, often with no adjustments for labor force participation and unemployment rates; age and sex differences in earnings may or may not be taken into account; public payments in the form of pensions or public assistance and taxes on earnings are sometimes incorrectly included in the total; and direct costs are a conglomeration of educated guesses and available statistics on institutional care, with noninstitutional costs neglected.

The so-called indirect costs of illness are particularly difficult to estimate. These include not only matters such as the potential income lost by people who become ill, but such difficult factors as the costs of production loss, inefficiency, damaged employee morale, impaired customer relations, and turnover. Mental disorders also involve costs to the law enforcement system and to the judicial system, and these costs are extremely difficult to estimate.

Within the Population at Large

In 1958, Rashi Fein at Harvard University estimated the economic costs of mental disorders to be $3 billion a year. One billion dollars of that was spent on the direct costs of care (at that time maintenance of people with syphilitic psychoses alone cost $50.2 million), the remaining $2 billion went for other expenses, usually referred to as the indirect costs. By 1963, the U.S. Department of Health, Education, and Welfare estimated that mental illness cost $7.3 billion, $2.5 billion of that representing direct costs of care. At the same time, the man-year loss due to mental retardation alone was estimated at 107,000 years at an economic cost of $494 million in lost earnings. By 1971, the American Public Health Association reported that the economic costs of mental disorders totaled $26.2 billion, of which $10 billion went for the costs of care and insurance.

Then, in 1974, the National Institute of Mental Health (NIMH) conservatively estimated the total economic cost of mental disorders to be $36.8 billion. Of this amount the direct costs of care were placed at $14.5 billion. Other economic costs, the indirect costs, were estimated to be $19.8 billion. Research, fellowships, the development of facilities, management expenses, and unallocated NIMH expenses accounted for the remaining costs. Interestingly, the money that was spent on the care of the mentally ill represented roughly 15 percent of the total amount spent on care for all types of illnesses—$140 billion in 1977, or 8 percent of the Gross National Product. Of the costs of care for people with mental disorders, more than one-third went for hospital care.

According to this estimate, however, the economic costs other than those for the cost of care were $19.8 billion. The principal elements of these indirect expenses were identified as the costs of disability, estimated to be $10.3 billion. The remainder were attributed to the economic costs of the death of the patient, principally the loss of earnings that results from premature death, placed at $5 billion, and those costs due to patient care activities, estimated to be $4.5 billion.

The substantial costs of mental health care can be catastrophic, overwhelming, and devastating for the patients themselves and for their families. They are also important to employers, labor unions, health and welfare funds, and insurers. They are important to government at all levels because of their effect on government-provided care, on public welfare programs, including Social Security and unemployment compensation, on the national economy, and on tax revenues. The manner in which these costs are financed is discussed in Chapter 11.

Among Employed People

The economic cost of mental disorders among employed people is most significant to troubled employees, their employers, and unions. The widespread occurrence of mental, emotional, and personality disorders among employed people was indicated in Chapter 7. It can be very expensive. For example, HEW has estimated that 87 percent of the costs shown earlier for the entire population are occasioned by people in the labor force. These costs are borne in many ways, as will be shown in Chapters 11 and 12, including by the troubled employee and his family; by employers and labor unions; by health and welfare benefit plans, or insurance programs; and by a variety of public programs established by all levels of government.

Unfortunately, all the aspects of these economic costs have not been clearly identified. Many of them, in fact, are unmeasurable by techniques presently available. There are many reasons why this is so. To begin with, many employees with mental, emotional, and personality disorders remain undiagnosed. It is impossible, then, to measure their economic costs, either to themselves or to their places of employment. Yet such troubled employees enter into statistics on the rate of illnesses and accidents in the workforce, on absenteeism, on disability, on lost production, on labor turnover, and on insurance costs. Beyond that, we do not yet have a means for evaluating such effects as poor employee morale, dissatisfaction, inefficiency, faulty decision making, or harmful customer and public relations. Yet these concomitants of the troubled employee can be very costly to employers.

Despite the fact that they are hard to measure, costs associated with mental illness constitute a large part of an employer's operating expenses. In the case of private industry or the various professions such costs must, of necessity, be borne ultimately by consumers as part of the price they pay for goods or services. Where academic institutions are concerned, they enter into the costs of education, regardless of how these are paid. In the case of public employment, the taxpayer will unquestionably bear the burden. Whenever the consequences of such disorders necessitate the additional use of publicly provided forms of health care, or of the welfare program, the taxpayer again must bear the consequences. If the result adversely affects production, the Gross National Product, or employment, society at large feels the impact.

For the troubled employee, mental health care may be so expensive that it results in personal bankruptcy. When diagnosis and treatment are sought, the cost, which is frequently accompanied by the inability to work for a period of time, can be extremely burdensome to the extent they are not otherwise paid for by insurance or other financing arrangements. Even if a person is not receiving treatment, time lost from work as a result of mental illness, or as a result of illnesses or accidents directly flowing from such mental problems, can be very costly, especially if the employee is paid on an hourly or piecework basis. In addition, there are the costs of unrealized potential that accumulate when an employee is skipped over for a pay increase, is demoted, or actually loses the job. The resultant period of unemployment may be lengthy.

These costs to the troubled employee have never been satisfactorily measured. More than a decade ago, the National Association for Mental Health estimated that loss of earnings due to mental disorders exceeded $1.5 billion each year. More recently, the National Institute of Mental Health estimated that the loss of earnings by people in mental hospitals alone exceeded $1 billion, and that lost earnings resulting from absenteeism from work by those who were not hospitalized exceeded $60 million yearly.

Several attempts have been made to estimate how much troubled employees cost their employers. Recognizing the serious difficulties with the formulation of such estimates, they are nonetheless helpful in indicating the scope and seriousness of the problem.

In 1960, *Time* magazine reported that the economic loss resulting from mental disorders was some $3 billion a year. Several years later, the Opinion Research Corporation estimated that the cost to American industry ranged from $3 billion to $10 billion yearly. Then, in 1967, Ronald W. Conley et al. reported that the reduced marketability output that resulted from mental disorders cost $14.3 billion a year. One-quarter of this was attributed to the employee's inability to work, and three-quarters to absenteeism, unemployment, withdrawal from the workforce, inefficiency, poor employee morale, and job dissatisfaction, although the costs of the last three factors were admittedly speculative.

In 1970, Stanley F. Yolles, director of the National Institute of Mental Health, estimated the cost of mental disorders among employed people to be $20 billion. He expressed the opinion that 20 to 30 percent of all absenteeism could be traced to emotional factors, and that 65 to 80 percent of all discharges from places of employment were attributable to personal rather than technical reasons.

In 1974, the National Institute of Mental Health placed the annual cost of disabilities resulting from mental disorders alone to exceed $10 billion. Subsequently, the Cornell University New York State School of Industrial and Labor Relations estimated that absenteeism, personnel turnover, industrial accidents, and alcoholism related to mental disorders cost $12 billion a year. No matter how they are measured, the inescapable conclusion is that mental, emotional, and personality disorders are costly to employers, and can have a substantial effect on the national economy.

Since a characteristic of the troubled employee is not infrequently that of alcoholism or excessive drinking, estimates of these costs to employers are pertinent. In 1974, this cost was estimated at $8 billion a year, or $32 million for each working day. The yearly wage loss alone has been placed at $432 million. The goods and services lost, poor productivity, faulty decisions, and personnel turnover resulting from alcoholism have been estimated to cost from $1 billion to $2 billion yearly.

Some specific examples may help illustrate the magnitude of the problem. The North American Rockwell Corporation, with 100,000 employees, has placed the cost of alcoholism to its operation at $250 million, or $50,220 per year per alcoholic employee. Gulf Oil Canada, Ltd., with 11,000 employees, has estimated that alcoholism costs the company $400,000 annually. The United California Bank of Los Angeles, which employs 10,000 people, has estimated the cost to be $1 million a year. The Kennecott Copper Corporation employs 8,000 people, 7 percent of whom suffer from alcoholism—this costs the company an estimated $500,000 annually. The Scovill Manufacturing Company estimates that the average cost of an alcoholic employee exceeds $4,550 a year for absenteeism alone. In 1964, the Illinois Bell Telephone Company calculated that wage replacement cost $418,500 for the 155 cases of sickness disability caused by emotional illness, mostly alcoholism.

The U.S. Postal Service estimated that each alcoholic employee costs the service more than $3,000 a year, with a total annual cost of $168 million. The U.S. General Accounting Office has placed the cost of alcoholism among federal civilian employees at from $275 to $550 million annually.

Another aspect of the economic costs of mental disorders to places of employment relates to the costs of various types of insurance programs. While this subject is discussed in more detail in Chapter 11, certain aspects are germane here. When treatment is required, the costs are reflected in the health insurance programs that cover such treatment. Should such treatment require time off from work, or if there is a protracted period of disability, the accruing costs are reflected in the disability insurance program or in the salary continuance program. If treatment or disability is judged compensable under workmen's compensation insurance, the costs are reflected in the cost of such insurance.

As a result of their mental, emotional, or personality problems, troubled employees are more likely to become ill or have accidents than other employees. This will place a greater burden on health programs established for the benefit of employees.

Today, the costs of various insurance and employee benefit programs are very largely paid by employers. The cost of workmen's compensation insurance is borne entirely by the employer. In addition, more than 21 million employees today are entitled to benefits from salary continuance programs. The annual cost exceeds $3.6 billion, $2.8 billion of which is paid for by private industry.

Employer contributions to group health insurance premiums for the medical expenses of their employees and their dependents have increased steadily and appreciably since World War II. As a result of wartime wage–price freezes and the subsequent ruling of the National Labor Relations Board, health insurance became an important issue during collective bargaining. Employer contributions to premiums were a tax-deductible business expense. For employees the benefits constituted, in effect, tax-free wages.

Today it is not infrequent to find that the employer pays 100 percent of the health insurance premium cost. By 1970, an unpublished survey of the Health Insurance Association of America revealed that more than one-half (52.2 percent) of the employees and their dependents with group health insurance protection had the entire premium paid by the employer. For one-quarter (24.7 percent) of the insured employees, the employer paid from 75 to 99 percent of the premium. For 16.3 percent of the insured employees, 50 to 74 percent of the premium was paid by the employer; for 6.2 percent of employees the employer paid from 25 to 49 percent of the premium cost. The employer made no contribution to the premium cost for only 0.6 percent of the insured employees surveyed. The magnitude of these costs to large employers was illustrated by a report of the General Motors Corporation in 1975. In that year, the cost of health insurance for each worker averaged in excess of $100 a month, and the annual cost for all General Motors employees in the United States and Canada was $1 billion.

Since group health insurance premiums total some $30 billion today, it is apparent that the contributions of employers represent a considerable portion of their operating costs. Added to this is the $3 billion annual cost of group disability insurance for the partial replacement of income lost as a result of disability.

While these insurance costs are total for all forms of health care and disability, they nonetheless include the toll taken by the troubled employee. Unfortunately, the proportion attributable to the troubled employee is not known, but certainly it is considerable.

The economic costs of mental, emotional, and personality disorders among employed people that have been discussed here do not reflect accurate measurements or total evaluations. However, their proportions indicate that this issue warrants far more attention and concern than has so far been focused on it. These expenses cannot help but be reflected in the personal finances of troubled employees and their families, in the operating costs of their employers, in the price of goods and services that the consumer must pay, and in our national economy.

BIBLIOGRAPHY

American Public Health Association. *Mental Health: The Public Health Challenge.* Washington, D.C.: 1975.

Blue Cross Reports. Blue Cross Association. Chicago: July-September 1964.

Conley, Ronald W., et al. "An Approach to Measuring the Cost of Mental Illness." *American Journal of Psychiatry,* December 1967.

Cooper, Barbara S., and Dorothy P. Rice. "The Economic Cost of Illness Revisited." *Social Security Bulletin,* 1976.

Fein, Rashi. *The Economics of Mental Illness.* New York: Basic Books, 1958.

Focus, "The Economics of Mental Health Care." Washington, D.C.: The Psychiatric Institute, December 1976.

Follmann, J. F., Jr. *Alcoholics and Business.* New York: AMACOM, 1976.

———. *The Economics of Industrial Health.* New York: AMACOM, 1978.

———. *Insurance Coverage for Mental Illness.* New York: AMACOM, 1970.

————."The Mentally Retarded and Insurance Protection." *The President's Committee on Mental Retardation.* New York: Free Press, 1976.

Health Information Foundation. "The Economic Costs of Absenteeism." *Progress in Health Services,* March-April, 1963.

Institute of Management and Labor Relations, Rutgers University. "A Community Venture in Mental Health." June 10, 1970.

Mueller, Marjorie S., and Robert M. Gibson. "National Health Expenditures, Fiscal Year 1975." *Social Security Bulletin,* February 1976.

National Institute of Mental Health. *The Cost of Mental Illness, 1971.* HEW Publication No. (ADM) 72-265. Washington, D.C.

————. *The Cost of Mental Illness, 1974.* Mental Health Statistical Note No. 125. Daniel S. Levine et al. Washington. D.C.: 1976.

9

Treatment and Rehabilitation:

Where and by Whom?

In recent years, a growing concern about, and interest in, the treatment of mental, emotional, and personality disorders has developed. The result is that the number of places providing care and the types of care available to troubled employees, their family, or their employer or union has been steadily increasing. Accompanying this development is a growing supply of professionals and paraprofessionals for the treatment of such disorders. This progress, coupled with the public awareness of the problems associated with mental disorders, offers more hope for the future than at any time in the history of human endeavor.

Unfortunately, these laudable developments are by no means universal. The availability of resources for the treatment of mental disorders is, to say the least, spotty. Many communities in America have no resources to which those concerned might turn. Others have some forms of treatment available, but to the exclusion of others that might well be of equal importance. This is a situation that can result in a host of untreated conditions which, had they come under treatment at an early stage, might have been prevented from reaching serious and destructive proportions.

Most certainly the seeking of treatment for mental disorders, difficult enough to be brought about in the first place, poses questions that are not easily answered. To what place or to which professional should one turn? What sources are available in the community? How is one to evaluate the different modalities for care and the different concepts of treatment? How worthwhile are the various approaches to treatment?

Types of Treatment Facilities

The types of facilities available for the treatment of mental disorders include inpatient facilities, such as the various types of hospitals; semi-institutional facilities, such as day, night, or weekend hospitals, halfway houses, and foster or boarding homes; and outpatient facilities, such as community mental health centers, health maintenance organizations (HMOs), clinics of various types, and the outpatient services of hospitals.

Inpatient Facilities

Each year more than 1 million people are admitted as inpatients to all types of facilities. Hospitals for the mentally ill are essentially of three types: publicly operated hospitals, psychiatric units in voluntary general hospitals, and private psychiatric hospitals. Diagnostic services and treatment are provided by all three types, but public hospitals provide a considerable amount of custodial care. In each instance they may or may not provide partial hospitalization (to be discussed subsequently), and they may be associated with other community mental health services. Patients are frequently transferred to, or received from, such services.

Almost one-half the total number of hospital beds in the United States are used for the treatment of mental disorders. Their geographic distribution, however, is quite uneven. For example, in 1976 the Mid-Atlantic States had 398 psychiatric hospital beds per 100,000 people, while the Mountain States had only 123 beds per 100,000 people. Rounding out the picture, inpatient care is also provided by nursing homes and by institutions for the mentally retarded.

Public hospitals are usually operated by state and county governments. There are 312 such mental hospitals in the United States with a patient population of 193,000 in 1975 (this total was 559,000 in 1955). They receive roughly 250,000 admissions each year, half of whom are repeaters. State and county hospitals are generally large institutions that provide the care for a very sizable proportion of the chronic, long-term cases of mental illness. Frequently, their patients have been transferred from other types of hospitals and treatment sources. As evidence of the fact that state and county hospitals predominantly receive the serious cases of mental illness, it has been reported that 25 to 50 percent of all admissions to such hospitals are diagnosed as schizophrenics, and another 25 percent as having cerebral arteriosclerosis. The remainder are principally cases of alcoholism, psychotic disorders other than schizophrenia, and psychoneurotic reactions, in that order.

Many of the patients, some 30 percent, are over age 65. Many are impoverished, with 33 percent paying no charges and 20 percent paying reduced charges. Not infrequently, the patients have been legally incarcerated because they were considered dangerous. Because of this situation, patients in such hospitals often receive no more than custodial care. A third of the patients work in the hospital; a fifth of these are paid.

As a consequence of these conditions, the average length of stay in such hospitals is long, averaging 9.1 years. More than 20 percent of the patients have been hospitalized for 20 years or more. However, for 11.7 percent of the cases, the stays are less than 4 months; for 6.8 percent, from 4 to 6 months; and for 5.7 percent, from 7 months to 1 year. Thanks to the use of modern therapy and drugs, today these hospitals can stress the early release of patients for treatment in their own community, although this practice has become controversial.

State and county hospitals have been criticized by many people because their isolated location separates patients from their families. In addition, they have been accused of being too large to provide individual care, of being so old that they present fire and health hazards, of being underfinanced and ineptly administered, and of having poorly defined goals. Many are said to be understaffed, with most employees engaged in custodial, clerical, or maintenance capacities. In addition, many are said to be insufficiently trained. These hospitals are looked upon as facilities to be used only by default, as dumping grounds and places of abandonment. They have been referred to as human warehouses.

The Veterans Administration (VA) also provides hospitalization for a considerable number of the mentally ill at public expense. The VA maintains 175 hospitals, 41 of which are solely psychiatric facilities, and provides the care for 119,000 veteran psychiatric patients.

Each year some 11 percent of all inpatient hospital admissions for mental disorders go to VA hospitals.

Psychiatric units in voluntary general hospitals have come to play an increasingly significant role in the treatment of mental disorders since World War II. In 1970, the American Hospital Association said that it "believes that all hospitals have an obligation to examine their present policies and practices in the light of the need to give care while caring" and "urges general hospitals to develop programs for the care of alcohol and other drug problem patients."

The psychiatric services provided by a voluntary general hospital can offer distinct advantages to the patient. A facility can be selected that is much closer to the patient's home and family, and this can be therapeutically beneficial. Furthermore, much less stigma is attached to being cared for in a general hospital. In addition, the general hospital will also have the means for caring for any physical ailments the patient may have.

Today more than 800 community general hospitals have psychiatric units, accounting for about one-quarter of all such hospitals. These units usually range in size from 15 to 31 beds, although some exceed 400 beds. Each year about one-quarter to one-half million psychiatric patients are admitted to these hospitals, about 18 percent of all inpatient admissions. In general hospitals, patients usually stay a relatively short length of time, typically from 13 to 30 days, since they are there primarily for diagnosis and for therapy aimed at rapid symptom remission and discharge. Because the general hospital is not equipped to provide long-term care, patients might be discharged to some type of a community psychiatric service or a public hospital. Readmissions to general hospitals are not too uncommon for mental health patients: Some hospitals record that 10 percent of their patients are readmitted one or more times. It appears to be generally recognized that the success or failure of psychiatric treatment in a hospital can depend on a variety of factors other than the patient's mental condition.

As we have seen, a person's home and family situation, and the socioeconomic and ethnic background, age, religious affiliation, and occupational status, can all impinge on behavioral attributes. It has been recognized that a psychiatric patient must be psychologically prepared for discharge from the hospital and for re-entry into the community. If the patient's way of coping with stresses has not been altered, the episode of hospital care may have been useless.

Depending on the needs of the community and the other types of services available, many general hospitals also provide outpatient services, which can serve a variety of purposes, including diagnosis and evaluation, consultation and education, care for those recovering from hospital treatment, provision of emergency services, and group therapy. In addition, these services may be taken right into the neighborhoods or outlying areas. Today, more than 700 voluntary general hospitals provide these outpatient psychiatric services, and over 1,250 make emergency services available. In addition, over 300 general hospitals make available partial hospitalization services. In this way, patients can receive hospital care each day and then spend their evenings at home; or they can work during the day and return to the hospital in the evening; or they can work each week, and spend their weekends at the hospital receiving intensive care.

Private psychiatric hospitals play very much the same role as do the general hospitals. There are reportedly 482 such hospitals, 180 of which are members of the National Association of Private Psychiatric Hospitals. These hospitals have some 80,000 admissions yearly, about one-quarter of all inpatient admissions for mental disorders. The principal diagnoses in such hospitals are said to be psychoses (about half of all patients), neuroses (about a third of all patients), and personality disorders (about one-sixth of all patients). The length of stay in private psychiatric hospitals averages 60 days, although this figure varies from hospital to hospital. About 6 percent of all patients are discharged to other facilities for care. In general, these hospitals are not large: many hold 42 to 75 beds; others, 100 to 240 beds.

The services provided by these hospitals vary widely, with some being essentially short-term acute-episode facilities and others providing treatment for longer periods. Many provide quite comprehensive services, including diagnosis and therapeutic treatment, family therapy, occupational therapy, geriatric care, children's programs, crisis intervention, rehabilitation, and treatment for alcohol and drug abuse. Many provide partial hospitalization services, and in response to community needs more and more outpatient services and community mental health centers have become available.

Nursing homes provide another source of inpatient care for people with mental disorders, usually for the aged. In fact, for 34 percent of nursing home patients the diagnosis is advanced senility. An additional 28 percent are diagnosed as senile without psychoses, and 17 percent have other mental problems.

Institutions for the mentally retarded are reported to provide care for some 193,000 mentally retarded persons.

Semi-Institutional Facilities

Semi-institutional facilities serve mentally ill patients who have been discharged from hospitals, but who continue to need supportive care during the transitional rehabilitation period. They are particularly valuable for patients who are homeless, jobless, or unable to provide for their basic needs. Such aftercare is provided by facilities of different types, many of which are associated with general and private hospitals, and in some cases, state and VA hospitals. Unfortunately, the availability of these services is extremely limited. The principal semi-institutional facilities are discussed below.

Day hospitals, which care for patients during the day, allow patients to spend their nights at home with their family. These services are usually provided by a hospital, although a few function independently. The specific availability of such facilities is not known, but they are not numerous or readily available in the United States. The lengths of stays in day hospitals varies considerably, from 2 to 4 weeks, to 2 months, to more than a year.

Night hospitals provide a service similar to that provided by day hospitals, except that in this instance patients are hospitalized at night and spend their days at work or in vocational rehabilitation. Again, such services are neither numerous nor readily available. However, both day and night hospitals are an important part of the rehabilitative process.

Halfway houses are intended as transitional domiciles for mental patients who do not require further hospitalization, but who are not ready to begin living independently. The nature of such facilities varies considerably, and they may or may not be connected with a psychiatric hospital. They provide residential arrangements under the guidance of a supervisor. Some halfway houses are treatment oriented, whereas others are work oriented: both are clearly concerned with the process of rehabilitation. In 1970, there were reportedly only 148 halfway houses in the United States, with a total patient capacity of 3,500.

Foster homes share a common goal with halfway houses—that of enabling the patient to return to the community while maintaining supportive assistance. It is not known how many foster homes exist to serve the needs of those recovering from mental disorders.

Outpatient Facilities

In 1973, the U.S. Department of Health, Education, and Welfare reported that of all patients receiving care for mental disorders, the large majority received such care on an outpatient basis. The greatest proportion of this care was provided by general hospitals, followed by state and county hospitals, VA hospitals, psychiatric clinics, community mental health centers, private-office psychiatrists, and private-office psychologists, in that order.

During the past quarter century, new concepts of care and treatment for troubled people have been developed on the basis of a system of community-oriented health services. They offer an alternative to confinement in public mental institutions. These concepts have been made possible by the introduction (in the mid-1950s) of tranquilizing and antidepressant drugs that have made it possible to employ a number of different therapies and to return patients to their communities. Interest in their development has been heightened by the recent emphasis on deinstitutionalization although, as was noted previously, that concept is currently being re-evaluated.

The enactment by Congress of the National Mental Health Act in 1946 and the Mental Health Study Act in 1955 helped foster these developments. Also in 1955, a Joint Commission on Mental Illness and Health was established by the American Medical Association and the American Psychiatric Association, which had an interest in the subject. Then, in 1963 Congress enacted the Mental Retardation Facilities and Community Mental Health Centers Construction Act. Its provisions were subsequently extended by amendments made in 1967, 1968, and 1970, and in 1975 it was completely redrafted.

As a consequence, there has been a large increase in the number of people with mental disorders who are receiving treatment and care outside the hospital: roughly three-fifths of all mental health patients are receiving care through these means today. In addition to the outpatient and emergency services provided by hospitals, discussed earlier, alternatives to institutionalized health care may take any of several forms.

Psychiatric clinics today reportedly provide one-fifth to one-quarter of the care received by psychiatric patients. In 1973, there were reportedly 1,123 freestanding outpatient psychiatric clinics in the United States. Their geographic distribution, however, is very uneven, with half located in Northeastern cities, and the rest in the larger communities in California, Florida, Illinois, Michigan, Ohio,

Virginia, and Wisconsin. The clinics, which are of various types, frequently provide special services, such as child guidance, family counseling, or alcohol and drug abuse treatment. Some clinics are devoted entirely to providing aftercare, and others operate on a part-time basis only. Psychiatrists are reported to provide 32 percent of the man-hours of care at psychiatric clinics; clinical psychologists, 24 percent; psychiatric social workers, 37 percent; and other professionals, 7 percent.

Patient turnover in the clinics is relatively rapid; for most patients services terminate after a few visits. In fact, one study indicated that 20 percent of the patients made only 1 visit and 60 percent made fewer than 5. However, 8 percent of the patients returned for more than 25 visits. Although diagnostic evaluation is received by 80 percent of clinic patients, only 30 percent are treated. One-fifth to one-half the patients are referred elsewhere for treatment, and one-fifth the patients terminate clinic services. Of those clinic patients who have been diagnosed, one-quarter had personality disorders, and another one-quarter had psychoneurotic disorders. A relatively small proportion have been diagnosed as having psychotic disorders.

Community mental health centers have developed recently thanks to the Congressional actions that commenced in 1963. They are designed to be community-based services that can help relieve the costly hospital patient load. Their objective is to make continuity of care possible and to foster a positive mental health climate in the community by bringing about the early recognition and treatment of mental disorders. That these lofty expectations have not been entirely fulfilled bears evidence to the fact that good intentions, slogans, fads, the fine art of grantsmanship, and great pronouncements are not enough.

Community mental health centers are largely (73.6 percent) financed by public funds, principally by state (32.5 percent) and federal (29.7 percent) governments. Patient fees and insurance provide only 14.3 percent of the financing, and Medicare and Medicaid only 5.6 percent. A variety of other sources provide the remainder.

In order to receive public funds, a center must make available inpatient and outpatient services, partial hospitalization, emergency services, consultation and education to community agencies, and alcohol and drug abuse treatment (unless they are otherwise available in the community). Since 1975, new requirements include special services for children and the elderly, follow-up care after hospitalization, transitional services, and screening for state facilities. Such centers may also provide diagnostic and rehabilitation services. Within these guidelines, the purpose and goals of the centers, the scope of the services they provide, and the population they serve can vary.

Today, community mental health centers number 600, despite the fact that the 1963 legislation anticipated the number to be 2,000. Their geographic distribution is very erratic. These centers apparently account for about 6 percent of all psychiatric inpatient admissions and 21 percent of all cases of treatment provided. Three-quarters of the services are provided on an outpatient basis. The patients served are largely those with lower incomes; 64.3 percent have yearly incomes of less than $5,000, and 27 percent have incomes between $5,000 and $10,000. More than one-half do not have high school diplomas, and only 16.2 percent are college educated. The principal diagnoses of the patients are: psychoneurotic disorders (17.9 percent), other personality disorders (11.9 percent), and schizophrenic reaction (14.2 percent). Other disorders include alcoholism, depression, brain syndromes, and drug addiction, with 20.1 percent classified as other mental disorders and 2.6 percent without mental disorders. The average number of visits to these centers is reported to be 5.3 per patient.

Almost 20 percent of the staff of such centers have clerical, accounting, or maintenance duties, and another 20 percent are nursing aides. Psychiatrists make up 8.2 percent of the staff; psychologists, 5.8 percent; physicians, 1.7 percent; social workers, 10.3 percent; registered nurses, 11.1 percent; vocational rehabilitation workers, 1.3 percent; therapists, 4.9 percent; other professionals, 12 percent; and other nonprofessional workers, 6.6 percent. In many instances the centers suffer from insufficient manpower and inadequate funds. In 1977, the American Public Health Association said that the centers were fighting for survival.

Health maintenance organizations (HMOs) and prepaid group practice plans can also play a mental health role. Until relatively recently, however, this role was negligible or nil. However, principally as a result of insurance coverage provided by the United Automobile Workers, this role has recently become a more active one.

Studies conducted at certain HMOs indicated that physicians reacted to psychiatric conditions and their treatment in much the same way that physicians in private practice did. However, since HMOs are devoted to the concept of health maintenance, and since physical examinations are included without additional cost to the patient, they are in a position to detect the presence of emotional disturbances and to make adequate referral for treatment. Increasingly this appears to be the case, at least in the larger HMOs.

In 1977, there were 175 HMOs or prepaid group practice plans with some 6 million members. Of this membership, 64 percent were on the West Coast, primarily because of the size of the Kaiser Health Foundation Plan.

Since HMOs and prepaid group practice plans are an arrangement for health care on a prepaid basis, they are discussed in somewhat more detail in Chapter 11, which deals with insurance arrangements.

Others. Although they are not mental health facilities, public, private, and vocational schools, police departments, and the judicial system can all play an important mental health role. In addition, employers are providing more and more services that troubled workers can take advantage of. These will be discussed in detail subsequently.

Professional and Paraprofessional Services

In addition to the care provided in the various facilities, a considerable proportion of treatment for troubled and mentally ill people is provided by various professionals and paraprofessionals. Included here are psychiatrists, clinical psychologists, personal physicians, psychiatric nurses, psychiatric social workers, psychiatric aides, and members of the clergy. During the years since World War II, there has been an unprecedented growth in the numbers of such personnel. However, their distribution is geographically very uneven, with concentrations in the metropolitan areas, as pointed out in the following section.

At the outset, it should be noted that, as with personnel of all types, a great many are employed in various types of facilities. The American Public Health Association reports that of those so employed, 60 percent are employed in state and county hospitals, more than 10 percent are employed by the VA, 8.2 percent work for general hospitals, and 5.7 percent work for private psychiatric hospitals. Community mental health centers employ 6.6 percent of these personnel, freestanding outpatient clinics employ 4.2 percent, and residential treatment centers 4.5 percent.

In the United States there is one mental health worker for every 700 people. This is the highest ratio for any nation in the world.

Psychiatrists

A psychiatrist is a physician who specializes in mental illness. A psychoanalyst is a psychiatrist schooled in the procedures of psychoanalysis. In 1976 there were reportedly 27,000 psychiatrists in the United States, some 10,200 of whom were in full-time private practice. The remaining 16,800 practice solely in hospitals, outpatient clinics, social agencies of various types, or at places of employment. Some teach exclusively. The geographic distribution of psychiatrists is extremely uneven, however, with large concentrations in New York, Pennsylvania, Illinois, Massachusetts, and California, and only a few choosing to set up practice in Montana, Nevada, Idaho, Wyoming, and Alaska. Some 3,000 counties in the United States have no psychiatrist living in the county, while one-half of all psychiatrists are centered in 15 urban centers.

Despite this, psychiatrists in full-time private practice are reported to provide the care for 41 percent of the patient population under psychiatric care at any given time. Visits to the psychiatrist are higher among people under age 45, among females, and among those of higher socioeconomic and educational level. Customarily, a psychiatrist in private practice averages about 8 patient visits a day. Direct patient care is said to consume 66 percent of a psychiatrist's time, 41 percent of which is spent in private office practice, 18 percent in hospitals, and the remainder in clinics, centers, and other places for care. Administration of hospitals and health care programs consumes 15 percent of psychiatrists' available time, and 7 percent is spent in consultation, frequently with employers or employees. Teaching accounts for 8 percent of the psychiatrist's available time, and research for 4 percent.

Recently a group of psychiatrists at the Peninsula Hospital and Medical Center in Burlingame, California, formed a center that operates on a fee-for-service basis. The center provides inpatient, outpatient, and emergency services, including group psychotherapy and milieu therapy. This is one way that psychiatrists in private practice can help meet community mental health needs.

There is, however, a short supply of psychiatrists in the United States as a whole. In 1977, Dr. Paul J. Fiske of the Jefferson Medical College in Philadelphia alerted the President's Commission on Mental Health to this situation. He asserts that unless appropriate corrective measures are taken, there will be a shortage of 10,000 psychiatrists by 1980.

Clinical Psychologists

Clinical psychologists also play a significant role in the mental health field and have developed an increasing degree of professionalism.

Clinical psychologists are trained in the evaluation and modification of abnormal behavioral problems with the goal of enhancing the health, effectiveness, and productivity of the individual. They frequently function as members of a therapy team that collaborates with psychiatrists. The treatments administered include psychotherapy, group therapy, milieu therapy, and situational modification.

In 1976, of the 45,000 members of the American Psychological Association, 14,150 were reportedly clinical psychologists working in the mental health field. Roughly half of these are in full-time private practice. The other half provide consultation and services for a variety of institutions, including hospitals, community mental health centers, schools, and places of employment. In such cases, the psychologist may or may not engage in private practice on a part-time basis. As with the other mental health professions, the geographic distribution of clinical psychologists is quite uneven, with concentrations in the Northeast, and in California, Illinois, Colorado, and Kansas. Clinical psychologists are either licensed or certified in most states and in some Canadian provinces. Where licensure does not exist, the profession has established a self-licensing or certification procedure.

Viewpoints often differ between psychiatrists, who are M.D.'s, and clinical psychologists, and this can lead to strained relationships between the two professions. Psychiatrists, for example, insist that for treatment such as psychotherapy, a medical function exists and therefore the psychologist should function only under the direction of a psychiatrist. Their position is reinforced by a similar requirement in many forms of insurance coverages. Here it is of interest that the World Health Organization has recently reported that in all European countries the psychologist, as a health professional without a medical qualification, is barred from assuming ultimate responsibility for a patient and must be subject to the supervision of a psychiatrist.

It should further be noted that the clinical psychologist is specifically trained to conduct psychological testing. Testing is used for evaluation, prediction, and reassessment; for the measurement of aptitudes, abilities, achievement, and intellectual functioning. Psychological testing is used by a great many sources, including places of employment and the educational system. There are those in the mental health field, however, who do not think highly of psychological testing; some even maintain that results can be faked.

Physicians

The significant role of the family physician in relation to mental disorders cannot pass unnoted. The physician is frequently the first professional that a disturbed patient comes in contact with. Furthermore, a sizable proportion of people receiving care from a general practitioner or an internist are generally recognized to have a significant emotional, personality, or psychological problem. Thus the physician can play an important and valuable role in the early detection of mental disorders.

Several examinations of this relationship of the physician to the mental health field, however, have shown that many physicians have a sense of inadequacy when dealing with neurotic patients, despite the fact that patients often feel that the physician should meet their emotional needs. This appears to be the case, particularly where medical specialists are concerned. Certainly physicians, who consider that they already have more than enough to do, can feel frustrated with, or confused by, the disturbed patient. In some instances they may even dislike these patients or feel that emotional problems should not be a responsibility of medical practice. To some extent such reactions are natural, and may reflect the education and training that physicians have received.

Further compounding this situation is the fact that many physicians lack confidence in the discipline of psychiatry. They may have difficulty understanding the psychiatric approach. They might even be antagonistic toward the ambiguity that pervades psychiatry, or perhaps because they have become disappointed or disillusioned with the concept. In other instances, physicians may not have received full cooperation from psychiatrists, who may fail to keep the physician informed after referral has taken place; this happens in 70 percent of the referrals, according to one study. Apparently, the two professionals have difficulty communicating with one another, with the result that cleavage between the two develops, even in hospitals and health centers where they function in close proximity to one another.

The result of this situation can be a refusal on the part of the physicians to refer patients for psychiatric treatment. This accounts in part for the relatively low referral rate to psychiatrists. At the other extreme the physician might prematurely refer the patient without sufficient preparation simply to be rid of the disturbed patient. In either instance severe harm to the patient may result.

Nevertheless, physicians have increasingly developed an interest in mental disorders and have a growing tendency to observe and refer disturbed patients for psychiatric surveillance. This is particularly true if the patient recognizes the presence of an emotional problem.

In addition, there is growing recognition that the inclusion of mental health services as an integral component of primary health care offers a very feasible means of substantially improving the distribution of mental health services for the entire population. There are those professionals who feel that the separation between psychiatric and medical services excludes large numbers of our population who are in need of mental health care. Others urge that psychiatric appraisals be included as part of physical examinations. Two factors argue for these suggestions: the ready availability of family physicians, and the fact that no stigma is attached to visiting such physicians.

To bring about these changes physicians must receive their mental health education not only through medical school training and internship, but also through postgraduate courses or continuing education sponsored by psychiatric associations. In this way, physicians can learn to recognize the symptoms of mental disorders and become more knowledgeable with respect to referrals. Unfortunately, present efforts toward achieving this goal are considered by some to leave much to be desired.

Parallel needs are improved communication and liaison between the two professions, which could lead to a greater degree of understanding and collaboration. This is not easily accomplished, unfortunately, since both physicians and psychiatrists are inclined to protect their own prerogatives. However, the recognition of this need is important, since the mental health of many people depends on the realization of this objective.

What is said here, it must be noted, is not applicable to those physicians who are qualified neurologists trained in the treatment of disorders of the brain and nervous system.

Psychiatric Nurses

Specially trained psychiatric nurses are important professionals in the treatment of mental disorders. In 1976, there were 37,860 registered psychiatric nurses in the United States. However, the vast majority of these, some 85 percent, worked in hospitals of various types.

Public health nurses play a valuable role in the identification of patients in need of referral for psychiatric treatment, in administering medication, in counseling, and in filling the needs of convalescent mental patients and their families. However, there is a paucity of cooperation on the part of psychiatrists, and psychiatric nurses need to have more information about the condition and prognosis of the patients, as well as about the drugs prescribed.

Psychiatric Social Workers

In recent years, psychiatric social workers have become more and more important in the treatment of emotional and mental disorders. In 1976, it was reported that there were 29,500 social workers in the United States. Of these, however, only one in five, some 6,000, are in the mental health field, 60 percent of whom are employed by governments at all levels. Some, however, function in private practice.

The efforts of psychiatric social workers are generally directed toward the alleviation of crises. They function under the guidance of a psychiatrist or psychologist, usually in a hospital or community mental health center, and their aim is essentially that of bringing about an improvement in the social functioning of the patient. Because a clear-cut definition of their role is lacking, other professionals do not always take full advantage of the services that psychiatric social workers can provide. Social workers nonetheless provide an important bridge between patients and many types of community and social programs that can provide supportive assistance to them and between patients and their families. By putting patients in touch with the services available to them, social workers can be a great help to mentally disturbed individuals.

Support Personnel

In 1976, there were reportedly 148,430 psychiatric aides and 29,495 other professionals or paraprofessionals working in the mental health field. Included are laboratory technicians, occupational and speech therapists, vocational counselors, homemakers, housing service aides, child care aides, and community action aides. In most instances they work to facilitate the processes of rehabilitation.

The Clergy

Before leaving this discussion, the role of one other profession must be noted: that of the clergy. Throughout history, and in religions of all societies, the clergy, high priests, witch doctors, and men of faith have been concerned with mental disorders. For a great many people, the concept of religion gives meaning to their lives, protects them from despair, and offers them faith, belief, and hope. That religion reinforces social cohesiveness, solidifies family and community life, and links the faithful to the world in which they live has been recognized by many professionals in psychiatry. In addition, religion has been credited with aiding character formation, and the confessional has long been noted for its therapeutic effects.

Many in psychiatry, however, have sincere concerns about the influences of religion, since it often appears in actual manifestations of mental illness. These critics observe the characteristics of excessive religiosity and become concerned that religion can feed the depressive's deep sense of guilt and need for punishment, or the schizophrenic's tendency to become detached from the world. Aspects of religion, such as prohibitions, obedience, repressions, guilts, and punishments, have come under close scrutiny, as have the myths, illusions, and vows associated with particular beliefs. Conversely, there are members of the clergy who consider psychiatry an atheistic and amoral profession, and who consequently distrust it.

These cross purposes are indeed unfortunate. In spite of their lack of professional competence in the field of mental illness, clergymen are in a position to observe the onset of a mental disorder and to refer the individual for treatment. A mutual understanding and appreciation must develop between members of the two professions if they are to help one another combat mental illness.

The clergy must cultivate a knowledge of psychiatry and how it functions. On the other hand, psychiatrists and psychologists cannot ignore the evidence indicating that the incidence of mental disorders, including alcoholism, appears to be lower among people with strong religious affiliations—particularly among the conservative Protestant sects, the Mormons, and the Muslims. It is not known whether the religion itself or the nature of religious people is responsible for this phenomenon. However, the facts cannot be ignored.

Rehabilitation Services

Rehabilitation of the mentally ill is crucial if they are to once again become functional, productive, and useful people. The rehabilitation services play a role of importance in helping the patient avoid recession of a disorder and avoid the necessity of returning to treatment. The purpose of these services is to aid patients in reestablishing their former relationships and vocations, or perhaps in adjusting these when indications so dictate. For example, a patient might be advised to change his type of job, but to stay with the original employer, or indications could suggest that a change of employer would prove beneficial.

Today, places of employment are becoming increasingly interested in psychiatric rehabilitation, since the courts have extended the concept of workmen's compensation insurance into the area of psychiatric disabilities. This development will be discussed in Chapter 11, but suffice to note here that the adjustment of a worker to the loss of a limb, to the fear of returning to the same job, or to the effects of certain working conditions can prolong the period of disability beyond the time required for physical ailments to heal. Efforts to overcome such occurrences are therefore of growing interest.

Just as for physical rehabilitation, psychiatric rehabilitation should commence early in an episode of hospitalization. The process of rehabilitation can include: (1) medical follow-up, particularly where psychotropic drugs or physical therapies are involved; (2) personal adjustment counseling, which covers such matters as family and social relationships or finances; (3) vocational services, to encourage motivation toward work, to establish discipline, and perhaps to retrain the individual for another type of job; (4) family counseling, so that the family can be fully involved in the period of readjustment; and (5) residential services, if the establishment of a suitable home is necessary. In some cases, it might be necessary to obtain financial assistance during the period of rehabilitation. This might come from such sources as the disability insurance benefits available from the Social Security system, veterans benefits, public assistance, or general welfare programs.

The needs for and types of rehabilitation services to be used can vary from case to case depending on a great many factors. These can include the psychiatric history of the patient, the type of mental condition involved, the family structure, and the socioeconomic and vocational status of the patient. The pre-existing personality characteristics of the patient can be most relevant, as can the patient's maturity, degree of independence, and age. Compulsive personalities do not respond well to rehabilitation, nor do those suffering from depression, who often exhibit psychomotor retardation, inattentiveness, poor visual–motor coordination, and a low sense of self-esteem, all of which can slow the recovery process. The aged have also been found to respond poorly to rehabilitation. For the psychoses, particularly schizophrenia, the functional process can be impaired, and the patient suffers from disorganization and disorientation. Thus rehabilitation can be prolonged and difficult. Beyond these factors, rehabilitation can be difficult if the patient is malingering, because supportive financial benefits are available.

Rehabilitation services are available through hospitals, community mental health centers, outpatient services, foster family care, rehabilitation centers, and home care services. The professionals and paraprofessionals who administer these services include psychiatrists, psychologists, family physicians, psychiatric social workers and, in some cases, volunteer workers. In addition, vocational rehabilitation agencies (usually operated by state governments), sheltered workshops, state and private employment agencies and, of course, private and public employers provide a variety of rehabilitation services.

A problem inhibiting complete success of the rehabilitation process is the lack of coordination among the various services and professions. This indicates the need for a comprehensive approach to the rehabilitation of the psychiatric patients that will assure continuity of the helping process. Another beneficial development would be a greater supply of sufficiently trained personnel in the various agencies concerned with rehabilitation.

When the rehabilitation process is well handled, however, not only does the patient benefit, but so does the employer who has recovered a skilled employee and who has experienced reduced insurance costs.

Some Persistent Problems

Throughout this chapter, many of the problems facing mental health care and the administration of services have been mentioned. One pervasive problem is the *shortage of personnel and services,* and particularly their uneven distribution, which means that many troubled people are deprived of the help they need and could benefit from. Correction of this problem is by no means easy. Improving the geographic distribution of services is particularly difficult. No one has found an adequate solution, either here in the United States or throughout the world.

The *lack of cooperation and coordination* among the various types of services is another important problem discussed earlier. Not only does this situation impair public confidence in such services, with the result that people who need treatment fail to seek it, but the very much needed follow-up treatment and continuity of care may also suffer. Correction of this problem should be possible through action programs on the part of the various professional societies working together to achieve this goal. It is a form of action that is sorely needed.

Closely related to the foregoing is the need for a greater degree of standardization in structuring the *medical records* of people treated for mental disorders. As a patient moves from one type of treatment to another, these records must be comprehensible to all recipient professionals and should be continually maintained so that the patient's history is always available. In this way the ever important continuity of care can be enhanced.

Also needed is a measurement of the *cost-effectiveness* of the various types of services for those with mental disorders. The cost of such services in relation to the results achieved needs to be assessed. This matter is critical to the troubled employees and their families, to employers and unions, and to insurers. The information is also necessary whenever public funds are involved. Certainly the determination of the cost-effectiveness of any type of health service or program is a difficult matter involving techniques that are only just beginning to evolve. Nonetheless, the relationship between the unit or per diem cost of a particular service and the patient's ultimate gain is well worth investigating. Much has been said about the savings that can be generated by certain types of services when compared to others, yet very little if anything is actually known when the entire history of the patient is taken into consideration, as he moves from one form of care to another, or as he suffers relapses and requires further care.

Another basic problem is that of *evaluating the various mental health services*. Once again, these evaluations are not easily arrived at by professionals and are next to impossible for laymen. One reason for this is that the requirements for both facilities and professional personnel under the state licensure laws vary from state to state. Correcting this discrepancy could help ease the difficulty facing people who recognize that they need help, but who have no idea where to turn. It would provide at the least a floor on which the individual's decisions could be based. Furthermore, public confidence in the various mental health services would be enhanced if the process of licensure were made more uniform, and therefore more meaningful.

Beyond that, there is need for the means of evaluating the various mental services in terms of their efficacy. Granted, this is no simple matter, but it is important. This fact was recognized by Congress when the Community Mental Health Centers Amendments of 1975 were enacted. Funds were allocated "for a program of continuing evaluation of the effectiveness of its programs in serving the needs of the residents of the catchment area and for a review of the quality of the services provided by the center."

One problem in attempting to evaluate the various forms of treatment for mental disorders is that such treatment involves highly complex judgments. Professional differences of opinion can be strong. Furthermore, there is a fear among professionals that any evaluative process would inhibit or discourage innovations, experimentation, or new techniques. This can lead clinicians and hospital or center administrators to react to evaluative attempts with ambivalence, if not complete negativism. Yet the public recognizes that they need criteria to provide a basis for their decision making.

One of the most important evaluations that must be made is an assessment of the effectiveness of each type of treatment. This would include the accuracy of the clinician's diagnosis and of the expected outcome of treatment, as well as the extent to which recovery has been achieved, or the degree to which relapses or transfers to other forms of care occur.

Closely related is the need to evaluate the reactions of the patient/consumer to any particular type of treatment. Even though it may be unclear whether the results observed are attributable to the treatment or to extraneous conditions, it is still important to know how far patients have come in their ability to function personally, socially, or vocationally. The means for acquiring such measurements exist today, and include the Psychiatric Status Schedule, the Psychiatric Evaluation Form, the Global Assessment Scale, the Family Evaluation Form, the Goal Attainment Scaling, the Brief Psychiatric Rating Scale, the Self-Rating Symptom Scale, the Taylor Manifest Anxiety Scale, the Consumer Satisfaction Scale, and the MAUT Evaluation Paradigm, all of which were developed since 1970.

In addition, measurements of the financial efficiency of mental health practices, including the means by which their costs and charges are arrived at, the utilization of available staff time, and the degree of the utilization of the various services for care, still require rigorous evaluation.

Naturally, any such evaluations would have to take into consideration the type of person being treated, including his or her age, level of education, and socioeconomic status, as well as the disorder afflicting that person.

While much has been written on the subject of evaluating mental health services, the efforts to date have been described as diffuse, random, unintegrated, and unsynthesized. The paucity of people trained for this type of evaluation has also been recognized, and the field is certainly very young. There is no large, scientific body of knowledge to draw upon when measuring how successful the delivery of mental health services has been. Yet the pressures for increased accountability have provided an emphasis on the need for useful evaluation.

A final problem concerns the relationship between mental illness and the *processes of law,* particularly the controversy surrounding the compulsory hospitalization of certain individuals with mental disorders. This is a difficult problem to resolve, partly because it is based on a concept that has prevailed for hundreds of years. However, it is clear that such practices denigrate the concept of mental health hospitals and confuse the efforts of psychiatrists. In many cases, irreparable harm can result to patients by forcibly removing them from their family, job, and community, and making them permanent hospital residents. The situation has been further complicated by professional criminals who are quite knowledgeable about how to feign psychiatric symptoms in order to avoid a prison sentence.

Many people feel that any publicly imposed form of hospitalization or restriction of personal liberty that is based on the mental state of an individual should be critically re-evaluated. Others are less tentative and feel that any type of compulsory treatment is improper and should be abolished. Among other things, such incarceration creates confusion as to whether the individual is being deterred in order to protect other citizens, in order to punish him (which may be the case for alcoholics and drug addicts), or in order to administer treatment. Meanwhile, the courts must deal with this issue in the absence of professional agreement on the behavioral criteria upon which decision can be based. It is obvious that this problem needs much more attention than it has been receiving before it will be satisfactorily resolved.

BIBLIOGRAPHY

American Hospital Association. *Mental Health Services and the General Hospital.* Chicago: 1970.

Avnet, Helen H. *Psychiatric Insurance.* New York: Group Health Insurance, Inc., 1962.

Coleman, J. V., and D. L. Patrick. "Integrating Mental Health Services into Primary Medical Care." *Medical Care,* August 1976.

Community Mental Health Centers. Report prepared by the U.S. House of Representatives Committee on Interstate and Foreign Commerce. Washington, D.C.: U.S. Government Printing Office, March 1973.

Department of Health, Education, and Welfare. Publication No. (SSA) 76-11701.

Fink, Raymond, Sam Shapiro, and Sidney S. Goldensohn. "Family Physician Referrals for Psychiatric Consultation and Patient Initiative in Seeking Care." *Social Science and Medicine,* Vol. 4, undated.

Follmann, J. F., Jr. *Custodial Care.* New York: Health Insurance Association of America, 1973.

————. *The Economics of Industrial Health.* New York: AMACOM, 1978.

————. *Insurance Coverage for Mental Illness.* New York: AMACOM, 1970.

Freeman, H. E., and O. G. Simmons. "Social Class and Posthospital Performance Levels." *American Sociological Review,* June 1959.

Galvin, Ruth M. "Psychology: There Are Other Therapists at Work." *The New York Times,* August 14, 1977.

Gardner, Elmer A. *The Use of a Psychiatric Case Register in the Planning and Evaluation of a Mental Health Program.* University of Rochester School of Medicine and Dentistry, 1967.

Gibbon, Robert W. "Resolving the Health Crisis: Is the Psychiatrist Expendable?" *Journal of the National Association for Private Psychiatric Hospitals,* Fall 1970.

Group for the Advancement of Psychiatry. *Administration of the Publc Psychiatric Hospital.* New York: July 1960.

————. *Medical Practice and Psychiatry.* New York: 1964.

————. *Psychiatry and Religion.* New York: 1960.

————. *The Psychic Function of Religion in Mental Illnesses and Health.* New York: 1968.

Klarman, Herbert E. "Characteristics of Patients in Short-term Hospitals in New York City." *Journal of Health and Human Behavior,* 1962.

Kogan, W. S., and Kira Carey. "Exploration of Factors Influencing Physician Decisions to Refer Patients for Mental Health Service." *Medical Care,* January-February 1971.

Lieberman, E. James. *Mental Health: The Public Health Challenge.* Washington, D.C.: American Public Health Association, 1975.

Markson, E. W., and D. F. Allen. *Trends in Mental Health Evaluation.* Lexington, Mass.: Lexington Books, 1976.

Myers, J. K., L. L. Bean, and M. P. Pepper. "Social Class and Psychiatric Disorders: A Ten Year Follow-Up." *Journal of Health and Human Behavior,* Summer 1965.

National Institute of Mental Health. *Financing Mental Health Care in the United States.* Washington, D.C.: U.S. Department of Health, Education, and Welfare, 1973.

Reed, Louis S., et al. *Health Insurance and Psychiatric Care: Utilization and Cost.* Washington, D.C.: American Psychiatric Association, 1972.

————. *Health Insurance and Psychiatric Care: Utilization and Cost.* Unpublished supplementary paper.

Rensberger, Boyce. "How Good Are Today's Hospitals?" *The New York Times,* March 19, 1978.

Roberts, Steven V. "What About the Halfway Home Idea?" *The New York Times,* March 19, 1978.

Rosenzweig, Simon. "Compulsory Hospitalization of the Mentally Ill." *American Journal of Public Health,* January 1971.

Taylor, James Bentley. "The Organization of Physician Attitudes Toward the Emotionally Disturbed Patient." *Journal of Health and Human Behavior,* 1963.

Williams, Richard H. "Psychiatric Rehabilitation in the Hospital." *Public Health Reports,* November 1953.

Wolff, Ilse. "The Public Health Nurse Serves the Mentally Ill and Their Families." *Pass It On.* Connecticut Public Health Nursing Agencies, June 1959.

World Health Organization, *Working Group on the Role of the Psychologist in Mental Health Services,* Document EURO 5428 I. Geneva: 1973.

10

TYPES OF TREATMENT

It should be obvious that the treatment of personality, emotional, and psychiatric disorders will differ in form or intensity depending on the type of disorder involved in an individual case, who the therapist is, and whether treatment is administered in a hospital, at a center or clinic, or by a psychiatrist in private practice. Furthermore, different concepts of treatment prevail among professionals, and this will have a great influence on which type of treatment is prescribed.

The principal approaches to treatment are discussed here briefly. It should be clear that these are not necessarily, in theory or in practice, mutually exclusive (for example, psychotherapy might include drug therapy).

Psychotherapy

Individual Psychotherapy

Individual psychotherapy predominates over all other forms of treatment in the United States. This one-to-one or "talking cure" approach is emphasized in the vast majority of programs and enjoys the greatest prestige, although it is not always well understood. It includes any systematic attempts to change behavior through the development of increased self-awareness. The objective of individual psychotherapy is to alter thoughts, feelings, and behavior patterns by eliminating the underlying problems.

In all of the many approaches to psychotherapy, the doctor–patient relationship is of primary importance. The goal of treatment is always to provide symptomatic relief, to ease distress, and to enhance the functional capacity of the patient. Although it is not yet clearly understood why such therapeutic practices work, for many people they do achieve results.

There are two primary approaches to psychotherapy in use today. In the *directive approach,* in which the therapist plays a more active role, he or she structures the therapy, attempts to have patients understand why they do what they do, and explains why those thoughts or behaviors can be harmful. In the *evocative approach* the patient's past is explored. Patients are encouraged to spill their guts while the therapist listens. In essence, this is a do-it-yourself form of therapy.

Psychoanalysis is, in a certain sense, the basis of individual psychotherapy, but it is not a do-it-yourself form of therapy. It attempts to help the patient examine his or her thought and behavior patterns, to develop an awareness of what is or is not rational, and thereby to rebuild the personality structure. Its language and concepts have permeated modern society and are reflected in our novels, films, plays, and TV shows. Terms such as ego, id, and paranoia are used regularly by those who have little or no knowledge of their meaning.

Psychoanalysis is derived, for the most part, from the theories and concepts of such men as Freud, who investigated the influence of childhood experience on adult behavior. Freud probed the guilts and self-defenses that we all acquire in an attempt to render the unconscious conscious. In this way, he revealed the conflicts, repressions, rationalizations, and projections of his patients. Freud theorized that mental disorders result when people fail to deal with one or more of the stages in their development, with the result that they then become oversensitive to the stresses of life.

During therapy, patients are encouraged to talk about themselves, about their childhood memories (which some consider unreliable), about their relationship with parents (which some consider illogical), and about their dreams (which some consider to lead to fanciful interpretations). The psychoanalytic process results in an emotional catharsis that is very draining to the patient. The therapist thereby attempts to make the patient aware of, and through this awareness responsible for, his or her actions. Other schools of thought on psychoanalysis derive from the work of Jung, Adler, Erikson, Horney, and Reich.

Psychoanalysis can be a very lengthy process, involving as many as four or five sessions each week during a period that may range from 1 to 6 years. Consequently it is very expensive, the cost of treatment frequently ranging from $15,000 to $50,000. However, it can be very rewarding.

The increasing amount of criticism that psychoanalysis has received is probably responsible for the drop in the number of people seeking treatment during the last 20 years. There are those who maintain that there is no way of knowing whether the approach is valid. Some feel that the evidence is quite strong that mental disorders are biologically based, and therefore that psychoanalysis is of dubious effectiveness. Others think that it inaccurately describes the nature of the psyche and is a wildly fanciful approach to treating mental illness. There are also those who recognize that evaluation is difficult if not impossible, and consider analysts neither better nor worse than others, including witch doctors, faith healers, or clergymen. Thomas S. Szasz, a professor of psychiatry at the Upstate Medical Center of the State University of New York at Syracuse, has cautioned that "it is imperative that all of us—professionals and nonprofessionals alike—keep an open and critical mind toward all psychiatric intervention and, in particular, that we do not accept or approve any psychiatric intervention solely on the ground that it is now officially regarded as a form of medical treatment." Szasz is critical of its aims and practices, describing it as "torture rather than treatment," and maintains that psychiatry can be harmful. Martin L. Gross is a critic of psychiatry, maintaining that it offers a "mass belief, a promise of a better future, opportunity for confession, unseen mystical workings and a trained priesthood of helping professionals devoted to serving the paying-by-the-hour communicants."

In spite of these criticisms, psychoanalysis appears to be successful in less severe cases of emotional, personality, and mental disorders. Mildly neurotic, intelligent, and highly motivated people respond better to this form of treatment than do those who are less intelligent or unmotivated. Clearly, some patients will benefit from this treatment process, whereas others will not. Schizophrenics apparently do not show much improvement after psychoanalysis, nor do manic-depressive psychotics. In these cases, drugs elicit more favorable results. Patients with character disorders (especially psychopaths), exogenous depression, biologically based illnesses, psychosomatic diseases, and severe neuroses are also said to profit little from psychoanalysis. What is important is to treat the right condition with the right form of therapy. Unimpressive results are not necessarily a reflection of this form of therapy as such.

There are many other types of individual psychiatric treatment, most of which are closely related to the foregoing. They include *psychodynamics* (which, in contrast to organic or behavioral approaches, attempts to relate personal history and subjective experiences to a patient's present problems), *transactional therapy* (which relies on insights into here-and-now interactions, rather than analysis of past issues), *behavior modification* (a relatively new short-term approach based on rewarding desirable behaviors while extinguishing undesirable ones that is most successful in treating highly specific symptoms, such as those associated with phobias), and *milieu therapy* (which attempts to cope with the environmental factors that produce stress and lead to neurotic or psychotic breakdowns).

Convulsive Therapy
Convulsive therapy includes electroshock therapy and insulin-produced coma. The former is used to treat schizophrenia and is one of the most effective means of dealing with severe cases of depression. The practice dates back to ancient Rome, with precursors during the Middle Ages that came to be looked upon as barbarous and cruel. Shock treatment can cause serious side effects, such as amnesia, confusion, or even permanent brain damage. Generally, this therapy is used as a last resort and is employed only when other approaches to treatment have failed. Although patients may benefit from it, electroshock therapy is often avoided in favor of administering drug therapy. It is always used in conjunction with other forms of psychotherapy.

Crisis Intervention
Crisis intervention is a form of emotional first aid. It deals with a specific acute emotional disturbance, such as a suicidal drive, and attempts to help the individual regain his or her equilibrium and return to a functional state. Crisis intervention is used by most psychiatric units of general hospitals and by clinics and private psychiatrists. It is no panacea to the onset of mental disorders and of little or no value to neurotics.

Family Therapy

Family therapy emerged in the 1950s and is still in the process of development. However, it has been gaining increased acceptance and popularity in this decade. Functionally, it has much in common with individual psychotherapy, but in this case the couple or entire family is considered "the patient." The family is treated as a system whose members are interdependent, the actions of each affecting the others. Those who embrace this concept of therapy feel that mental or emotional problems are based on a dysfunction of the family system as a whole. The therapist's goal is to help the family understand its patterns of behavior and the maladaptive interactions between its members. This is accomplished by modifying the present, not by exploring the past.

Group Therapy

This form of psychotherapy usually involves six to ten patients who meet once or more a week. The principles or variations of the principles that shape the structure of individual psychotherapy are applied to group therapy. In this case, the group members relate their experiences and hear those of others.

Some troubled employees may be able to take advantage of any group therapy programs established by their employers, usually as part of an industrial health program. In some cases, services are available to all employees. In others they are limited to alcoholics, and in still other cases only managers or executives have access to them.

One advantage of group therapy is that patients are often more comfortable as members of a group than they would be if they were undergoing individual psychotherapy. Patients often feel that less stigma is attached to group treatment than would otherwise be the case. Furthermore, group therapy makes more efficient use of the psychiatrist's time and that of other psychiatric personnel, both of whom are always in short supply. As a consequence, it costs about one-half as much as individual therapy.

A type of group therapy called *Gestalt therapy* attempts to deal with the present difficulties of group members. Its aim is to foster the mental and emotional growth of participants. In striving for a release of feelings, or in learning to experience the here-and-now, some groups have engaged in unconventional practices. Massage sessions and nudity are two recent forms of group therapy. A criticism of Gestalt therapy is that anyone can be called a therapist, regardless of the qualifications (or lack of them).

The controversial *encounter group* is also a popular form of group therapy that has been highly publicized. Encounter group participants learn to listen and respond to each other with feeling in order to help improve their own psychological condition. There are many types of these groups, and the competence of their leaders is said to vary widely. The psychiatric community has been critical of encounter groups because they are often unstructured and uncontrolled. In fact, in many groups patients are not properly screened, and the groups simply enhance the "awareness" of participants without addressing either their individual problems or the cures for them. The results of encounter group therapy have not been rigorously evaluated, but there are reports of patients suffering ill effects from their experiences in encounter groups.

There are many other forms of group therapy, including *therapeutic communities in mental hospitals, psychodrama groups, transactional analysis groups, play therapy* for children, *evocative group therapy,* and *Esalen* for interpersonal relationships. In addition, there are special purpose forms of group therapy, such as the very effective groups for alcoholics (*Alcoholics Anonymous* and *Al-Anon*), for obese people (*Weight Watchers*), and for those who smoke excessively (*SmokEnders*).

The results of group therapy appear to be mixed. One evaluation has indicated that one-third of the patients gained insights into themselves and became better able to function. However, other patients have reacted negatively to the strong criticism and judgment of their group, to their own rejection by the group, and to the group's inadequate leadership. Consequently, one in ten felt worse as a result of the therapy, 9 percent were severely affected psychologically, some became severely depressed, some suffered from insomnia, and one patient committed suicide. There is evidence that group therapy can be ineffective or even detrimental for patients who are shy or who feel inferior; for those who are highly emotional or antagonistic; for those who become dependent on the psychiatrist; or for people who have difficulty relating to others. Unfortunately, knowledge of the results of group therapy is very limited.

Many people are openly critical of group therapy, calling it a cheap substitute for individual psychoanalysis. It has also come under fire because there is rarely any follow-up care, and because it can be dangerous, since it is often conducted by people who are not trained in psychotherapy. Some forms of group therapy have been criticized by Martin L. Gross as promoting self-indulgence and gratification in the form of "doing your own thing" or "letting it all hang out."

Surgery

For certain types of serious, unyielding mental disorders, particularly those with a physiological base, psychosurgery or brain surgery may be recommended. Frontal lobotomies may be performed, although their benefit is doubtful and there is evidence that the patient's psychological health may be permanently impaired. The efficacy of psychosurgery remains to be proved.

Drug Therapy

Since the 1950s, drugs have become increasingly important in the treatment of mental disorders. The number of prescriptions for such drugs increased from 45 million to 80 million per year between 1964 and 1970 alone. Generically known as psychotropic drugs, these chemical compounds can be used in conjunction with other forms of therapy, and play an important role in the rehabilitation process. Not every patient receives drugs, however, and some patients have an adverse reaction to them.

As a result of psychotropic drugs, the number of patients who have to be placed in isolation or under physical restraint has dropped, and there has been a reduction in the number of hospital admissions and in the length of hospital stays. The patient population in mental health hospitals has decreased by 50 percent since 1955, and this has been attributed in large part to the use of the drugs that have now become available.

Drugs do not cure mental illness, but they can ameliorate symptoms and thus facilitate the management of mental and emotional disorders. By relieving symptoms, they make it easier for patients to live with their problems. In essence, drugs have a salutary effect on the central nervous system, particularly the brain, although in most cases the mechanisms by which this is achieved are not precisely known.

According to the Pharmaceutical Manufacturers Association, the following drugs are prescribed most frequently:

Valium
Empirin compound with codeine
Darvon compound
Achromycin (tetracycline)

Lasix
V-Cillin K (penicillin)
Percodan
Librium
Lomotil

These include the drugs prescribed for symptoms of psychological disorders. Valium and Librium, both of which are tranquilizers, are the most commonly prescribed drugs for the treatment of mental or emotional disorders. Darvon, a painkiller, is often used to relieve psychologically related symptoms of pain. Psychiatric drugs fall into two broad categories: tranquilizers and antidepressants.

Tranquilizers
Essentially, tranquilizers calm and soothe people who are anxious and hyperactive. The major tranquilizers are very potent psychiatric drugs frequently used in very high doses to treat seriously disturbed psychotic patients. They also help control delusions and hallucinations.

Drugs used to treat schizophrenic conditions include phenothiazines, chlorpromazine (Thorazine), and the antihistamines. The manic phase in manic-depressive states is treated with haloperidol, Valium, or Librium, and there are others that can help prevent the recurrence of depression.

In lower doses, these drugs are used to treat less severe neurotic and psychosomatic conditions (anxiety, agitation, stress, disorientation, nausea, and vomiting), and to reduce pain. A new drug, called MHPG for short, is now being used in the diagnosis of depression.

Weaker tranquilizers are used in the treatment of disorders that are not severe. They have a calming, sedative-like effect on anxiety, apprehension, stress, and tension, but are not effective in the treatment of psychoses.

Antidepressants
Antidepressants (tricyclics, lithium carbonate, imipramine, amitriptyline, MAO inhibitors, and Valium), unlike tranquilizers, stimulate the central nervous system. These drugs help patients quell flights of mania, control extreme emotional states, regain their optimism and alertness, counteract lethargy, and deal with despair, dejection, and feelings of guilt.

The major antidepressants are potent drugs that are prescribed for seriously disturbed neurotic or psychotic patients. They do not cause startling changes in behavior, but they do relieve the symptoms of depression and can counteract suicidal tendencies. Some patients respond to these drugs quickly, in a week or so, whereas others may take much longer. Some patients show no response at all.

The minor antidepressants, such as amphetamines, are often used to treat situational depression, a mild form of depression that usually stems from a particular situation or event. The drugs help patients to once again become alert, interested, and able to function and work. They may be used in conjunction with tranquilizers and have also been effective when coupled with electroshock treatment.

In the use of psychotropic drugs, as with other medicines, it may be necessary to adjust the dosage for each individual patient until the desired effect has been obtained. It is particularly important that patients cooperate fully by taking the exact dosage that has been prescribed. Taking too much can be very dangerous, and patients have become addicted to therapeutic drugs. On the other hand, patients who are neglectful about taking medicine can suffer from a regression of symptoms.

Psychotropic drugs cause a variety of adverse effects, many of which are difficult to anticipate. Some patients can develop a tolerance for a drug they have been taking for a period of time, and to maintain its effectiveness the dosage must be continually increased. Some people are hypersensitive to certain drugs, and may suffer from severe allergic reactions. Minor reactions, such as drowsiness, fainting spells, diarrhea, constipation, dry mouth, lack of coordination, double vision, blurred vision, dizziness, and skin inflammation, can be unwelcome side effects of particular drugs. Other reactions, however, can be quite serious, causing trembling, muscular rigidity or spasms, fever, changes in blood pressure, or adverse effects on the blood. Liver disease, cardiovascular disease, hypertension, glaucoma, or overactive thyroid can be aggravated by certain drugs. Whenever any of these reactions are reported, a change in the prescription or the dosage may be in order.

Alternative Approaches

Other approaches used in the treatment of mental illness are discussed briefly in this section. Some of these are considered fads, and others are not successful in the treatment of serious psychotic disorders.

Biofeedback is a process used to treat stress. It is a system for monitoring electrochemical signals of muscular tension and stress through the use of machines such as the electromyograph (EMG) and the electroencephalograph (EEG). The concept originated in the late 1950s at Rockefeller University, and a breakthrough occurred in 1972 as a result of work at the Menninger Foundation. Therapists use the information gleaned from biofeedback to determine the most effective treatment to employ.

Patients suffering from chronic anxiety, insomnia, tension, migraine headaches, primary Raynaud's disease (a disease of the nerves), bruxism or other muscular disorders, or lack of bowel control appear to respond well to biofeedback therapy. Biofeedback also appears promising in alleviating menstrual pain, asthma, colitis, cardiac arrhythmias, and sexual disorders. Some 20 to 30 percent of the patients, however, do not respond well, particularly those suffering from depression or paranoia. Biofeedback is being used more and more by employers in their health care programs. At the Equitable Life Assurance Society, for example, there is reportedly a $45.gain in increased productivity and reduced illness for every $15 spent on teaching employees relaxation techniques.

Sociocultural intervention techniques offer another alternative to drug therapy. These techniques involve the functional use of the community in problem solving, in improving attitudes and values, and in raising people's self-esteem and enabling them to take control of their lives and return to the real world. People are seen as part of a social network and are thought of synonymously with their environment. The aim is to alter the context in which patients function so they can develop positive self-concepts, roles, and communication patterns. The rationale is that a change in the social context will help bring about changes in the patient. Community organizations and social action and self-help groups contribute to this effort. This approach is directed toward people who have minor personality and emotional disorders. The outcome of sociocultural intervention techniques is not yet known.

Other concepts related to mental health care have been employed with varying degrees of success. *Transcendental Meditation* (for which Lefkowitz, Elgart, Inc., a New York advertising agency, offers to pay 80 percent of the cost for its employees), *reflection, yoga, Bioenergetic Analysis, reality therapy, Primal Scream therapy, Rolfing* (a physically oriented therapy), *relaxation–response therapy* (found to work significantly for less than 20 percent of 500 New York Telephone Company employees), *cognitive therapy, hypnosis,* and *activities therapy* (including planned outings, recreation, sports, camping, and gardening) are among them.

It might be noted here that *self-help techniques* can play a useful role in preventing and relieving minor mental disorders. The practice includes attention to one's physical condition and sleep and relaxation needs and avoidance of tobacco, alcohol, or drugs. People are encouraged to become orderly and neat, courteous, self-disciplined, punctual, to improve their skills, and to keep busy. Self-help techniques are designed to foster the development of a strong sense of self-esteem, an optimistic outlook, and an enthusiastic and interested approach to life. It can mean a realistic and philosophic view of the stresses in one's life and an acceptance of serious losses of whatever nature.

With respect to the *treatment of alcoholism* it is important to note that studies have shown that the alcoholic frequently suffers from depression, far more so than other members of the general population, and exhibits a suicidal tendency or actually attempts suicide more often. Loss of self-esteem is an accompanying symptom. In other cases, a paranoid pattern, characterized by marked aggressiveness or defensiveness, is exhibited. Alcoholics usually drink to relieve stress or to overcome worries. Yet in alcoholism treatment programs, psychiatric symptoms are sometimes overlooked and therefore go untreated. Such oversights can significantly alter treatment results and can lead to the development of more serious mental disorders. In a few cases, alcoholism programs have used work therapy, which offers the patient remuneration in order to encourage a sense of self-esteem, social acceptance, identity, and accomplishment. The results have been very favorable. This approach makes good sense because for patients who return to the outside world ill-equipped for employment the possibility of recidivism is all too likely.

For all these concepts and approaches to psychiatric treatment, some of which have been accused of being fads or the work of charlatans, it can well be asked: Where is the troubled person to turn for help? Recognizing that different approaches can be of varying value for different types of people and disorders, the troubled individual should seek informed counsel. This subject is discussed in Chapter 16.

BIBLIOGRAPHY

American Public Health Association. *Mental Health: The Public Health Challenge.* Washington, D.C.: 1975.
————. *The Nation's Health.* Washington, D.C.: February 1977.

Culligan, M. J., and Keith Sedlacek. *How to Kill Stress.* New York: Grossett & Dunlap, 1976.

Follmann, J. F., Jr. *Insurance Coverage for Mental Illness.* New York: AMACOM, 1970.

Gross, Martin L. *The Psychological Society.* New York: Random House, 1978.

Kovel. *The Complete Guide to Therapy.* Pantheon, 1976.

Selzer, Melvin L. "Treatment-Related Factors in Alcoholic Populations." *Alcohol Health and Research World,* Spring 1977.

Slobogin, Kathy. "Stress." *The New York Times,* November 20, 1977.

Smith, Howard K. *"Madness and Medicine."* American Broadcasting Corporation, television show, May 26, 1977.

Smith, Kline, and French Laboratories. *Treating Mental Illness with Drugs.* Philadelphia: 1968.

Snyder, Solomon H. *The Troubled Mind.* New York: McGraw-Hill, 1976.

Szasz, Thomas S. *The Myth of Mental Illness.* New York: Perennial Library, Harper & Row, 1974.

———. *The Myth of Psychotherapy.* New York: Doubleday–Anchor, 1978.

Thomas, Sam D., et al. "A Cooperative Program for Funding and Administering Work Therapy." *Alcohol Health and Research World,* Spring 1977.

11

FINANCING
THE TREATMENT
OF MENTAL DISORDERS

As has been shown, the treatment of mental, emotional, and personality disorders can be a lengthy process, and it can be costly. Not only is the cost of treatment involved, but the time lost from work during periods of hospitalization, disability, and episodes of treatment, or in caring for the needs of the family when a member is suffering from such disorders can also be costly.

The drain on personal or family resources in such cases can be burdensome at the least, and can be catastrophic, devastating, and bankrupting to the extent that such costs are not borne by a variety of public programs, or by insurance or other types of benefits provided by, or made available through, the place of employment. The economic costs resulting from mental disorders discussed in Chapter 8 clearly indicate the scope of the problem.

According to the National Institute of Mental Health, $14.5 billion was spent in 1974 for the treatment of mental disorders. Three-quarters of these expenditures were for inpatient care in state and county mental hospitals, Veterans Administration hospitals, nursing homes, general hospitals, private psychiatric hospitals, and other health care institutions. The remaining 25 percent of expenditures went for outpatient care and drugs. Treatment by psychiatrists in private practice accounted for 8.6 percent of the expenditures, and treatment in clinics or community mental health centers accounted for 8.8 percent.

Most of these expenditures are financed with public funds, estimated anywhere from 50 percent to 75 percent of the total. State and county governments account for the greatest outlay of such public expenditures, which are directed mainly toward the operation of mental institutions. Federal funds are used for the maintenance of VA hospitals, for community mental health centers, and for such forms of treatment as the Office of Economic Opportunity and Model Cities clinics. What is left of the costs is shouldered by individual patients and their families, by private insurance programs, by employers or labor unions, or by various philanthropic organizations. Earned income lost as a result of mental disorders is borne in essentially these same ways, although the proportions are not known.

Today there are many types of programs, both public and private, that can help employees or their family members when mental, emotional, or personality disorders require treatment. Their availability and the extent of the support provided differ from case to case. Employees faced with the costs of such treatment for themselves or for a member of their family, or with lost time from work, can do nothing more positive than examine the various sources of support available to them, determine their eligibility in relation to each, and then apply for those benefits that are applicable in their particular case.

There are two important aspects of all mental health programs. First, their nature and their presence (or absence) can affect the type and duration of the treatment provided, or even whether or not a person in need of care will seek treatment. Second, such programs have specified limits on the benefits they can provide. These limits can take several forms: (1) time limits on the duration for which benefits are available or payable; (2) dollar limits on the benefits, either on a per-unit basis or in the form of a maximum amount payable; or (3) a requirement that the patient share in the cost of treatment.

Financial arrangements vary from program to program. Dr. Hugo J. Zee believes that limits to financial support have a salutary effect on both the treatment process and on the patient. Zee maintains that limits provide the means to counteract what he calls "the procrastination and regressive resistances that are most likely to occur in an open-ended approach." As for the patient, Dr. Zee is of the opinion that time limits give the patient "some hope in the short-term venture, bring to the task some degree of motivation," and produce the "esteem-enhancing and pain-reducing effects of having the patient participate in planning his transfer out of the system." The various sources of financial support to individuals are discussed here.

Publicly Established Programs

There are several types of publicly established programs that can help people with mental, emotional, or personality disorders get the care they need, cover the costs of treatment, and partially replace lost income. The following discusses the various types of publicly provided programs available to the troubled employee.

Medicare

The Medicare program was enacted in 1965 and became effective in 1966. Its purpose is to finance medical care, within limits, for most people age 65 and over. Administered by private health insurers, the program is divided into two parts. The hospital portion of the program (Part A) is financed by a federal tax levied equally on employers and employees. The medical care portion of the program (Part B) is paid for in equal amounts by a monthly premium from the aged person and by a subsidy from the federal government that comes out of general tax revenues. At present, Part A is a compulsory program and Part B is voluntary. Both portions of Medicare function under the Social Security system.

Part A   Hospitalization. Provision is made for inpatient psychiatric hospital services and is limited to 190 days of such care during a person's lifetime. The care must be provided in a hospital approved by the Medicare program and accredited by the Joint Commission on the Accreditation of Hospitals. More than 330 participating public and private psychiatric hospitals are covered by the Medicare program, accounting for nearly a third of a million beds. General hospitals with psychiatric units also participate in the Medicare program. For these, the customary Medicare limits for general hospital care are applicable. The program also covers 100 days of care in a nursing home, but the patient must share in the costs after the first 20 days. Custodial care is not covered by Medicare. The extent to which the Medicare program pays for hospital treatment for the mentally ill is not known, although psychiatric hospital care was responsible for only 2 percent of the total hospital costs of the program in 1973, most of this for care in general hospitals.

Part B   Medical Care. Medicare provides for care by physicians, including psychiatrists, and for certain treatment services in outpatient clinics, but by and large treatment in community mental health centers is not covered by the program. The benefits are limited to 50 percent of the charges, or to $250 in any calendar year, whichever is less. The extent to which outpatient treatment of the mentally ill is covered by the program is not known, although it is certainly minimal.

Whereas Medicare benefits for hospital and medical care were originally limited to over 65s, in 1973 the program was extended to provide these same benefits to workers who became totally or permanently disabled and who were eligible for the Disability Insurance (DI) benefits discussed in the following section. Therefore, the hospital and medical benefits provided by Medicare can benefit the troubled employee who becomes totally, and presumably permanently, disabled as a result of mental disorders, and who is otherwise eligible by virtue of work experience.

Social Security Disability Benefits

In 1956 the Disability Insurance (DI) program was established by Congress to provide Old Age and Survivorship Insurance OASI (Social Security) income benefits for seriously disabled workers aged 50 to 65. In 1960 the cutoff at age 50 was removed, and in 1965 the Social Security Amendment changed the definition of disability to the "inability to engage in any substantial gainful activity by reason of any medically determinable physical or mental impairment which can be expected to result in death or has lasted for a continuous period of not less than 12 months." Monthly payments similar to Social Security payments are payable after the first five months of disability and are discounted if workmen's compensation benefits are being paid. The DI program is financed by designated taxes on employers, employees, and the self-employed.

Eligibility for benefits under the DI program depends on the work experience of the individual, but certain employed people (such as domestics, farm workers, employees of nonprofit organizations, and public employees) are not included in the program. Nearly 90 percent of employees are said to be covered by the program, however.

The employee who becomes disabled as a result of mental disorders, who otherwise qualifies by work status, is entitled to basic disability insurance benefits. Furthermore, the program makes provision for the vocational rehabilitation of eligible beneficiaries. For example, trial work periods are permitted without interference in the benefits, provided this is part of a rehabilitation program.

The amount or proportion of DI benefits paid for cases in which mental illness is the cause of disability has not been established, although indications are that 10.3 percent of the recipients of these benefits in 1971 were disabled as a result of mental disorders, including mental retardation.

As has been noted, such DI beneficiaries are also entitled to the benefits of the Medicare program.

Medicaid

The Medicaid program (Title XIX of the Social Security Act), established in 1965, provides federal funds to the states to finance the costs of medical care for needy and medically indigent persons. By July 1977, every state had its own Medicaid programs. Eligibility of recipients varies from state to state, but anyone who is eligible for public assistance programs set up for the totally and permanently disabled, for families with dependent children, and for the aged and the blind must be included in the Medicaid program. The types of medical care for which payment will be made (subject to certain basic requirements) are also determined on a state-by-state basis, as are the amounts to be paid for such services and the duration of time over which they will be paid. Variations among the states are considerable. Health care providers are free to accept or decline Medicaid patients.

The treatment of mental disorders is covered by the Medicaid program in 35 states. For persons under age 65, however, care for mental disorders in mental hospitals or nursing homes usually is not covered, and care provided by community mental health centers is covered only in some cases. In 30 states the care provided by free-standing clinics is covered, as is the care provided by psychiatrists.

While employed persons usually have other resources available to them, including insurance benefits, serious mental disorders can be financially devastating, so that, to the extent that care is not received from publicly provided facilities, Medicaid could conceivably play a role for the mentally ill employee. The extent to which this occurs is not known.

Temporary Disability Benefits

Temporary disability benefits are compulsory in five states: California, Hawaii, New Jersey, New York, and Rhode Island. Under these laws, certain, but not all, employees (usually about 70 percent) are provided fixed cash amounts while they are temporarily disabled for more than 7 days and up to 26 weeks. Disabilities caused by occupational accidents or diseases are excluded, since these are covered by workmen's compensation. The benefits are financed by the employer–employee contributions and are insured either by insurance companies or by state funds, or are self-insured by employers.

These benefits, in conjunction with private disability insurance plans discussed later in this chapter, can provide basic financial support to the troubled employee who is temporarily disabled.

Workmen's Compensation

In 1911 all states and the federal government came to enact workmen's compensation legislation for longshoremen, harbor workers, railroad workers, and employees in the District of Columbia. Coverage is elective on the part of employers in 19 states. All other states have compulsory coverage. Some 84 percent of the civilian workforce today are protected by such legislation. States differ as to which types of employees they will agree to cover, the benefits they will provide, and the type of insuring mechanism employed, which might be an insurance company, a state fund, or self-insurance. In any instance, the employer bears the entire cost, which averages about 1.2 percent of the payroll.

None of the workmen's compensation laws covers all employees. Those who are usually exempt from coverage are farm workers, domestics, casual workers, and those working for small businesses whose staff consists of less than three employees.

Workmen's compensation benefits pertain to occupational accidents and occupational diseases and differ from state to state. They include disability benefits to partially replace income lost as a result of such occupational accidents or diseases up to specified limits (generally 330 to 550 weeks, if the disability is of a permanent nature); medical care benefits (usually the reasonable and necessary costs without limits or exceptions); and survivor benefits, in the case of fatal injuries.

While the original intent of the workmen's compensation laws was to limit the benefits to physical accidents and diseases, in recent years the courts have come to expand the concept to include, at least to some extent, occupationally related mental disorders that have a causal relationship to work or that result from a traumatic injury suffered at the workplace. The line of demarcation becomes increasingly blurred. This extension of the concept of occupational hazard is the subject of considerable debate and is discussed more fully in Chapter 12. Suffice to say here that the troubled employee today might be held to be entitled to benefits under these laws.

Veterans Administration Program

The Veterans Administration program can play a significant role with respect to mentally ill employees who are veterans of the armed forces. Under this program, medical care and disability compensation are provided for veterans with service-connected disabilities and for veterans who are in need and who are permanently and totally disabled by virtue of diseases or injuries without regard to service, including mental disorders.

In 1972 there were 29 million veterans. Of these, 31,000 were psychiatric patients in VA hospitals and 110,000 were receiving psychiatric outpatient care. In either instance the care is without limits and no patient payments are permitted by law. Psychiatric care under the VA program accounts for almost one-third of the total costs of health care. The VA employs more than 1,600 psychiatrists on a full-time or part-time basis, more than 1,700 full-time or part-time psychologists, and upwards of 2,200 social workers.

The disability payments under the VA program vary according to the income and resources of the patient, but in any case they are minimal. These benefits are limited to service-connected disabilities only. One report indicates that about one-fourth the veterans who receive disability benefits under the VA program are receiving care for neurological or psychiatric disorders.

Public Assistance Programs

Public assistance programs of various types could conceivably play some role in helping mentally ill workers, although the extent to which this is so is not known. The medical care aspects of public assistance programs have been discussed under the Medicaid program. Beyond that, public assistance programs provide income for people at the subsistence level. These programs are categorized as follows:

Old Age Assistance
Aid to the Blind
Aid to the Permanently and Totally Disabled
Aid to Families with Dependent Children
General Assistance

In all cases, the intent of the program is to assist needy persons. Such programs unquestionably would benefit mentally ill workers who had been employed in occupations where no protection is offered by workmen's compensation, who do not qualify for benefits under the Old Age Survivorship and Disability Insurance program, or whose resources have become exhausted.

Reportedly 53 percent of the severely disabled on public assistance were employed at the onset of their disability. Furthermore, most public assistance recipients, including those who are severely disabled, had never applied for disabled-worker benefits, and most did not have the required work experience under OASDI to be insured for disability. It would appear, therefore, that the public assistance programs do not play a very significant role for mentally ill workers, but they can be of some value for those who qualify.

Public Provision of Care

The previous discussion has centered on several types of publicly provided care for people suffering from mental disorders. Among these are the state and county mental hospitals, the VA hospitals, and the community mental health centers; clinics of various types, including those for the treatment of alcoholism and drug addiction; and institutions for the mentally retarded. In toto, these publicly provided forms of care play a significant role in the treatment of persons with mental disorders—including troubled employees or members of their families.

The extent of the importance of the public provision of care for mental disorders was indicated at the beginning of this chapter. It should be noted, however, that private funds also pay part of the costs of care provided in public institutions and facilities. This takes the form of charges levied on patients or their families, and the amount of such liability varies considerably from state to state.

In 37 states the maximum legal charge is based on patient costs for the preceding year; in others it is a fixed amount. Charges can also differ with the age of the patient and whether the patient or his family is paying the charges. Some states decide each case on an individual basis; others have a maximum period of time for which charges are made. In most states, unpaid charges accumulate as legal claims against the estate of the patient, and in 21 states the same is true for relatives who are liable. However, the proportion of patients who are levied the maximum charge is extremely small in most states, the more notable exceptions being Nebraska, Illinois, Maryland, and New

Hampshire, where the proportions of such costs paid by patients or their families appear to run about 11 percent, 14 percent, 16 percent, and 17 percent, respectively. In other states the proportion of such costs paid this way varies from 0 to 28 percent, the median for all states being 9 percent.

The Question of National Health Insurance

The issue of national health insurance has been discussed in this country since 1912. During the 1940s the subject received considerable attention, but no action by Congress resulted, and interest subsided. Then in 1967, after the enactment of the Medicare program, Walter Reuther, then president of the United Automobile Workers Union, formed what is now known as the Committee on National Health Insurance. The result was that in 1968 a host of proposals for a system of national health insurance was placed before Congress, sponsored by such diverse groups as the AFL-CIO, the American Medical Association, the National Association of Manufacturers, and the Health Insurance Association of America. Proposals were also made by President Nixon's administration and by Senator Earl Long of Louisiana.

Since that time, each session of Congress has received a great many proposals for national health insurance, with amendments tacked onto the original proposals. By the 1972 presidential election, however, it was quite evident that public interest in the subject had waned once again, while other concerns had taken precedence. Since then, the subject has essentially lain dormant, but the issues are certainly not dead. President Carter indicated in 1977 that the issue would be reopened sometime in 1979.

This being the case, it would avail little to enter into a comparison of the various proposals placed before Congress, particularly since they are changed each year. Each would establish a system of national health insurance for practically everyone. Each would cover, to varying degrees, most health care expenditures as defined and to the amount specified. Under some, administration would be by the federal government; under others, private insurers would administer the program. Under most proposals, private insurers could supplement the benefits of the program. Under some the financing would be by federal taxation on employers, employees, and the general taxpayer; under others it would be by employer–employee premium payments, supplemented to some degree by federal tax funds.

A large question, pertinent here, is the degree to which any such program, if and when enacted, would provide benefits for the treatment of mental disorders. The answer, obviously, cannot be known in advance of any such enactment. The American Psychiatric Association (APA) recommended in 1972 that any national plan cover treatment of the mental disorders in all professionally approved facilities, public or private, that furnish active treatment for the mentally ill—all accredited hospitals, community mental health centers, outpatient or ambulatory care facilities, and intermediate care and nursing home facilities, as well as treatment by private physicians. Under a program providing limited coverage, according to the APA, there should be the same coverage of mental illness as of all other types of care. Under a program providing comprehensive coverage there should be full and complete coverage of mental conditions in general hospitals and in mental hospitals, both private and public, as well as full coverage of partial hospitalization, outpatient psychiatric care, and the cost of prescription drugs.

Private Insurance and Employee Benefits

Beyond the use of personal or family resources, several types of privately established programs play a significant role in financing the treatment of mental, emotional, and personality disorders and in partially replacing income lost as a result of such disorders. These include a variety of insurance and prepayment programs, health and welfare funds, as well as the forms of care provided by employers or labor unions, discussed in Chapters 12 and 13.

The discussion in this section turns to the various types of private health insurance programs, disability insurance programs, and salary continuance plans that can be available to the troubled employee and the role they can play in assisting the individual with mental disorders, be it an employee or a member of an employee's family, in financing the economic effects of such disorders.

Health Insurance

In the United States there are essentially three types of private health insurance plans which provide protection against the high costs of health care. Table 2 shows the types of such plans, the number of each, and the number of persons covered by each.

Table 2. Private health insurance plans in the United States.

Plan	Number (approx.)	Payment Basis	Millions of People Covered by Each	Percent of All Covered Persons
Insurance companies	1,000	Cash-reimbursement indemnity to the insured	111	58
Blue Cross plans	74	Agreements with most hospitals and physicians for direct payment	78*	38
Blue Shield plans	72			
Group practice plans, HMOs, and union/labor health centers	400	Prepaid care provided	6–8	4

*Figure for Blue Cross and Blue Shield plans combined.

In the vast majority of cases, coverage pertains to the individual and to the dependent members of the family. Today some 88 percent of the civilian population have some form of private health insurance protection, the benefits of which exceed $30 billion yearly. It should be noted that some employers finance health care on a self-insurance basis, acting, as it were, as an insurance company for employees and their dependents.

Eighty percent of insurance company coverages are written on a group basis, predominantly for groups of employed people. The remaining 20 percent are policies written individually for those who have no group affiliations or for those who wish to supplement other forms of protection. Most Blue Cross/Blue Shield plan enrollments are set up on a group basis, as are the enrollments in prepaid group practice plans or health maintenance organizations (HMOs).

The forms of protection offered by insurance companies and by Blue Cross/Blue Shield plans assume essentially two forms: basic coverages and major medical expense coverages. Under the basic coverages, the costs of in-hospital care, surgery, physician care in or out of hospital, and outpatient diagnostic and X-ray services can be covered.

The limits for hospital care are for the cost of semiprivate room care or for a fixed per diem amount for a limit that can range from 31 days to one year or longer. The costs of covered surgery can be paid according to a fixed schedule amount, or for the reasonable and customary costs of such care. Physicians' charges are covered on essentially this same basis by insurance companies and Blue Cross/Blue Shield.

Major medical expense coverages, on the other hand, cover practically all types of care in or out of hospital after the payment by the patient of a deductible amount which can range from $25 or $50 to $300 (although this amount may be zero for hospital care), and up to a maximum amount which can range from $5,000 to $250,000. For all covered medical expenses the insured bears a share of the cost, called coinsurance, which most usually is 20 percent of the costs of care (although this can decrease on a graduated scale where large maxima amounts are payable). Today more than 90 million persons have this form of health insurance protection.

Variations in these coverages occur in principally three ways. Blue Cross/Blue Shield plans are autonomous, with territorial limitations such as a state or a specific area within a state. Each determines for itself the nature and extent of the coverage to be offered the public. Each also offers more than one type of benefit pattern. The insurance companies, similarly, are each autonomous organizations and each determines for itself the benefit patterns to be offered the public.

In addition, group insurance coverages can be tailor made to meet the demands of individual group purchasers. As will be shown in the next chapter, the demands of these group purchasers vary widely and account for many of the variations found among insurance coverages. Pervading the entire picture, however, are the forces of competition which prevail among all types of health insurers and which exert a very strong influence on the patterns of health insurance coverages and the rates charged for those coverages. The costs of these coverages, as was shown in Chapter 8, are largely borne by employers.

As to the costs of the treatment of mental, emotional, and personality disorders, these private health insurers have come to play a role of increasing importance over the last two decades. In 1969, for example, the U.S. Department of Health, Education, and Welfare estimated that 126 million persons (63 percent of the population) had some degree of insurance protection against the costs of in-hospital treatment of mental disorders, and that 73 million (36 percent of the population) had some coverage for the costs of office visits for the treatment of mental disorders. In either instance the coverage would be subject to any special limits that had been established for mental illness.

Coverage for the treatment of mental disorders provided by insurance companies varies from company to company. Furthermore, coverage for employed groups of people can differ from plan to plan, depending on the wishes of the purchaser. As a rule, group hospital insurance covers the treatment of mental disorders, although practices differ with regard to the care provided in public hospitals. The vast majority of group major medical expense policies cover the in-hospital treatment of mental disorders on the same basis as for the treatment of other conditions. Out-of-hospital care today, however, has special limitations for the treatment of mental disorders under major medical expense coverages, most usually increasing the share of the costs to be borne by the patient to 50 percent, limiting the number of covered visits to a psychiatrist to 50 in a year, and limiting the dollar amount paid per visit to a specified amount such as $20.

For coverages written on smaller groups of employees, such as 25 employees or less, the coverage is most usually more restricted and might be limited to in-hospital care. The individual policies written by insurance companies are even more restricted, many excluding the treatment of nervous and mental disorders entirely and others restricting the coverage to in-hospital care for periods ranging from 30 to 365 days of hospitalization. The reasons for these special limitations or exclusions are essentially the possibility of adverse selection; that is, the people who know that they are experiencing a mental problem that requires treatment then go out and purchase a policy that will cover such treatment.

In 1975 the Blue Cross Association reported that 65 of the 74 *Blue Cross plans* provided coverage for the in-hospital treatment of nervous and mental disorders, with 66 percent of Blue Cross enrollees being covered for less than 120 days of care, and 27 percent being covered for 120 or more days of inpatient care. Outpatient care for these types of disorders was covered by 60 of the Blue Cross plans to the extent of 45 percent of Blue Cross enrollees, and 38 plans covered day or night hospital care for 33 percent of the enrollees.

Some plans excluded care in a private psychiatric hospital, while others reduced the coverage for such care, limiting it in some instances to 30 days. A few years earlier, Evelyn S. Myers of the American Psychiatric Association noted that less than half the Blue Cross plans covered care in a public hospital and that the most common coverage for the in-hospital treatment of mental disorders at that time was for only 30 days. As has been noted, Blue Cross coverage varies from plan to plan.

In 1971, Myers also reported that 63 of the 72 Blue Shield plans covered the in-hospital treatment of mental disorders by a physician, half of these providing the same coverage as for other conditions and half providing a more limited benefit, such as 10 visits. Many of these plans also cover in-hospital electroshock therapy and psychotherapy. For mental disorders, some Blue Shield plans also cover certain types of outpatient treatment, such as psychotherapy, psychological testing, the services of psychiatric social workers, and prescribed drugs. Once again, the coverage differs from plan to plan.

Prepaid group practice plans, or health maintenance organizations, provide or arrange for the provision of health care on a prepayment basis. The care provided is quite complete. There are, as has been shown, several hundred such plans in the United States, although their geographic distribution is very uneven. The Kaiser Foundation Health Plan is the largest prepaid group practice plan. In 1974, it provided more than 10 million office visits, 1.2 million patient days of hospital care, and a large volume of other services to its almost 3 million members. At the other extreme, some HMOs are relatively small and have experienced difficulties in becoming established and gaining acceptance by large numbers of employees and their dependents. In response to this problem, insurance companies and Blue Cross/Blue Shield plans have become actively involved in the formation and operation of health maintenance organizations in several areas. Others are sponsored by a variety of sources, including unions, employers, and community groups. Under many employee health plans, the employee can elect to have his or her benefits covered by an insurance program or to receive care through an HMO plan.

For many years, the prepaid group practice plans provided little or no treatment for mental disorders. Today the picture is changing. First, partly in response to the mental health insurance coverage contained in the health insurance programs for the federal government employees and for the membership of the UAW, and partly in reaction to the 1973 congressional legislation, which requires that in order for an HMO to receive support from federal funds it must provide mental health services of at least 20 outpatient visits a year for short-term evaluation or for crisis intervention, and must provide diagnosis and treatment or referral services for cases of alcoholism and drug addiction. The result is that today many such plans are providing mental health services to at least some of their subscribers, most usually in the form of short-term outpatient care and hospital care limited to 30 or 45 days of care.

For example, the Kaiser Foundation Health Plan entitles about .5 to 1 million of the almost 3 million subscribers to some treatment for mental disorders. Most of these subscribers are federal employees, UAW members, or members of the Retail Clerks Union of Los Angeles. The coverage for the treatment of such disorders differs from group to group, but generally includes hospital care, inpatient physician visits, and outpatient care subject to certain charges after the first 20 visits.

Another example is the Health Insurance Plan of Greater New York (HIP), which conducted a pilot experiment from 1965 to 1968 for the treatment of mental disorders, after which it made short-term therapy and family and group therapy available on an optional basis. By 1973, one-fourth of the 750,000 membership was eligible. The treatment does not include psychoanalysis, psychotherapy for organic psychiatric conditions, or the treatment of drug addiction. An additional premium is charged for this benefit. The goal of HIP is to return the individual to a functioning status as soon as possible.

Another large prepaid group practice plan, the Group Health Association in Washington, D.C. (GHA), now provides for the diagnosis of mental disorders and for short-term treatment administered by approved outside professionals. The coverage is for a maximum of 20 psychiatric visits up to a specified dollar amount, and for psychological testing. Care in a general hospital is limited to 30 days, but it does not include care provided in public facilities, where there is no obligation on the part of the patient to pay for the care received. The plan also provides for 40 sessions of group therapy.

Group Health Insurance (GHI) in New York, which does not provide care but pays for care provided by specified sources, conducted an experiment in 1959–1962 to test coverage for the treatment of mental disorders. As a result of this experiment, GHI now offers ambulatory care for mental disorders upon payment of an additional premium.

Other variations are the Group Health Cooperative of Puget Sound, where certain members receive ambulatory care for mental disorders, subject to specific charges, but they receive no hospital care. The Ross-Loos Medical Group at Palo Alto, California, provides in-hospital treatment for mental disorders subject to varying limits, and optional outpatient care subject to payment of certain charges. Another group, the Community Health Center Plan of New Haven, Connecticut, provides for 20 outpatient visits subject to copayment by the patient after the tenth visit and then arranges for any further necessary services from a community mental health facility or from other providers of care. The Los Angeles Medical Plans provide for private or group therapy on either an outpatient or an inpatient basis subject to a specified limit on the number of such therapy sessions and to charges to the patient after a certain number of sessions, with hospital treatment up to 30 days and patient charges after the tenth day.

How effective these various private insurance coverages are in paying for the treatment of mental disorders is a matter that would differ in individual cases, depending on the types of treatment received, the length of such treatment, and the nature of the insurance coverage in the particular case. However, one study of several thousand admissions and discharges at various types of facilities for treatment, both inpatient and outpatient, showed that the primary source of payment in 48.5 percent of the cases was group insurance, and that in 9 percent of the cases the source was individual insurance. Government programs were responsible for the major outlay in 18.7 percent of the cases, and individual and family resources were the primary source in 23.7 percent of the cases.

Other indications, reported by the American Psychiatric Association a decade ago, are that one-quarter of patients received some reimbursement for the private office treatment by psychiatrists, that 74 percent of mental patients in general hospitals had an average of 71 percent of the bill paid by insurance, and that 69 percent of patients in private psychiatric hospitals had an average of 58 percent of the total bill paid.

Over the past quarter-century, many comments and recommendations have been made with respect to health insurance coverage for the treatment of mental disorders. In 1952 a report to the President, *Building America's Health,* commented that private insurance plans "cannot be expected to cover the costs of prolonged hospitalization . . . for mental illness. These are already an accepted responsibility of government."

In 1960 the Joint Commission on Mental Illness and Health expressed the opinion that health insurance can play a significant role with respect to short-term care for mental patients in general hospitals, but that prolonged episodes of hospitalization would have to be provided at public expense. Two years later, the Council on Mental Health of the American Medical Association said that health insurance benefits for the treatment of mental illness should be expanded. In 1964 the AFL-CIO recommended that while private insurance can provide coverage for short-term care in a general hospital, basic benefits and long-term institutional care should be financed primarily with public funds.

That same year, the Health Insurance Association of America (HIAA) recommended that health insurers reappraise their role in financing the treatment of mental illness. Then in 1969 the HIAA recommended that private insurers take all possible steps to cover the costs of treating mental illness, including the treatment of alcoholism and drug addiction. Subsequently, HIAA's proposal to Congress for a national health insurance program included insurance coverage for the treatment of mental disorders in a hospital or nursing home, in the physician's office, or at other outpatient facilities, up to certain specified limits.

During this same period, the American Psychiatric Association developed *Guidelines for Psychiatric Services Covered Under Health Insurance Plans,* which called for psychiatric benefits "no more restrictive than for other illnesses covered," and the UAW collectively bargained for the inclusion of the treatment of mental disorders in its health insurance program (discussed in Chapter 13).

In this decade, several states have enacted legislation requiring that insurers offer to insured groups coverage for the treatment of mental illness. The conditions and limitations of the coverage differ from state to state, with minimum covered hospital care ranging from 30 days in Maryland and Oregon to 70 days in North Dakota. Coinsurance up to 50 percent is usually permitted for outpatient care (although New Hampshire requires full coverage for the first five visits, and 80 percent thereafter). Some states permit a maximum amount of benefit, ranging from $500 in New Hampshire and Oregon to $1,000 in Connecticut. Clearly, then, there is a growing interest in health insurance coverages for the treatment of mental disorders.

Meanwhile, in making protection available against the costs of treatment for mental disorders, insurers are faced with certain problems that serve to retard the more rapid expansion of such coverage. One problem has been the vagueness that at times pervades both the diagnosis and treatment of mental disorders, noted in Chapter 4. As

Lewis S. Reed et al. have commented: "The definition of mental disorders is often complex. In many cases the onset of a disorder is so insidious that one cannot state precisely the time at which a person is passing from a healthy group into an ill group." The problem is how to determine what constitutes mental disorders, as well as the indeterminate length of time over which the treatment process extends, often determined by the differences in treatment philosophies, which were noted in Chapter 10.

Still another problem involves the charging practices of public mental hospitals and several types of clinics and mental health centers. Where these are subject to variances due to the economic resources of the patient, insurers do not feel that they should be placed in a position of what amounts to being discriminated against.

Another problem faced by insurers is the question of what types of treatment services for mental illness are to be included or excluded from the coverage. In the absence of an accreditation program, the therapeutic value of certain types of clinics, centers, and other forms of outpatient treatment can be questioned. Questions also arise as to whether the services of psychologists, social workers, and certain non-professionals should be covered if they are not functioning under the direction of a psychiatrist. There are areas that, in the absence of professional guidance, insurers do not feel properly equipped to deal with. Thus, Norman R. Penner of the American Psychiatric Association has noted that a problem for insurers "is the gross variations in the treatment that may be used for the same diagnosed mental conditions," as well as "the absence of clear agreement about the most appropriate therapeutic modality or type of mental health practitioner who should be involved."

One problem of considerable importance to insurers and to purchasers of insurance as well is the cost of adequate coverage for the treatment of mental disorders. Such costs must reflect not only the charges for treatment, but also the degree to which such treatment services are used. Unfortunately, the absence of adequate data on the cost and utilization of such services has impeded progress in this area. Thanks to recent studies made by Helen H. Avnet at Group Health Insurance, Inc., in New York, by the Society of Actuaries, and by Louis S. Reed and coworkers for the American Psychiatric Association, headway is now being made in the development of such data.

Another aspect of the problem of insuring groups of employed people lies in the extreme variation of the utilization of mental health services experienced by different types of employees. Such factors as the age and sex composition of a group, its educational level, its socioeconomic status, and its geographic location are all known to have an effect on the utilization of mental health services. For example, wide variations in utilization and costs have been found among university faculties, scientific laboratories personnel, and advertising agencies on the one hand, and automobile workers, construction workers, and office clerks on the other.

Still another aspect of this problem is that extant cost and utilization data are primarily concerned with one episode of treatment. They do not follow the patient through the entire treatment process or as he or she experiences recurrences of the disorder.

The result of all this is that insurance costs and the utilization of benefits for the treatment of mental illness are not clearly known and vary quite considerably among insured groups and the sources of information. A study conducted in 1968 by the Health Insurance Association of America, however, indicated that 4.6 percent of all health insurance benefit payments were for the treatment of mental disorders, although there were instances of insured groups in which mental illness accounted for one-third of all claim costs. Interestingly, there is evidence that of all such claim costs, about 25 percent represent the treatment of alcoholism and drug abuse. There is also evidence that mental illness claims are lower among insured employees than among their spouses, and that they are highest for the treatment of dependent children.

The result of this paucity of sound data is a conservative approach taken not only by insurers in making coverage available for the treatment of mental disorders, but also on the part of those who purchase such coverage for employees. In both cases, they are faced with the indefiniteness of the costs involved.

A final and salient problem with regard to the extension of health insurance coverage for the treatment of mental disorders is the prevailing public attitude toward mental illness which, in turn, affects the public demand for such insurance coverages. Employees, their unions, and their employers often take a dim view of the subject of mental illness and of its treatment, with the result that there is little or no demand for insurance coverage for this type of treatment in many instances.

This problem was recognized by the National Institute of Mental Health in 1965, when it said: "There is convincing evidence that insurance plans are willing to adapt to changing patterns and needs. . . . However, change comes in response to demand." Similarly,

Norman R. Penner recently wrote: "The question comes down to what the public is willing to pay for," and that to increase insurance coverages for mental disorders calls for "an effective educational program and increased research efforts."

There is no question but that the proper and adequate solution of these problems would assist health insurers greatly in making the coverages for the treatment of mental disorders more meaningful and effective. What is needed is the forthright and thoughtful cooperation of the health professions.

Disability Insurance

Private disability insurance programs are made available by insurance companies for the partial replacement of income lost as a result of disability. This can be an important form of protection for employees, self-employed people, and professionals who become disabled.

Today insurance companies provide such protection for some 48 million workers on either a group insurance or an individual insurance basis. In either case, work-related forms of disability generally are not covered when they are included under workmen's compensation. Offsets are provided against the types of disability benefits made available by the government programs mentioned earlier. In addition, union-administered plans provide disability protection for some 550,000 employed people, and an equal number are protected through various employee benefit associations.

Short-term disability insurance. The majority of group disability insurance is written for *short-term disability,* usually for nonoccupational hazards. At one time, this type of coverage provided protection for disabilities lasting up to 13 weeks. Today, however, the predominant period covered extends to 26 weeks, and many plans provide protection for 52 weeks. Typically, benefits commence 8 days after the onset of the disability, although many plans commence benefits on the first day of disability, if the worker is hospitalized or if the disability is the result of an accident. The amount of the benefit is always wage-related. It is generally 50 to 80 percent of wages up to a maximum dollar amount, which can range from $50 to $125 per week.

The Conference Board study in 1974 showed that of the employers surveyed, two-thirds had such short-term disability coverages for their nonoffice employees, and 39 percent had this type of coverage for office workers. One reason for this difference is the fact that in many of the places of employment salary continuance or paid sick leave is provided, most usually for office employees. That study also found that 55 percent of the employers surveyed provided short-term disability benefits which continued for 26 weeks. In 17 percent of the plans coverage was for 13 weeks; and in 23 percent of the plans it was for 52 weeks. Benefits under these plans ranged from 50 to 70 percent of wages to maxima of $50, $75, $100, or $125 a week. Such benefits are not subject to income taxes and are therefore, in effect, tax-free wages.

In 1974–1975 the U.S. Department of Labor prepared a digest of the employee insurance benefits for 89 individual employers and 42 industry-wide (multiemployer) programs in a wide range of industries, including railroads, coal, clothing, furniture, taxicabs, hospitals, and retail trade. This survey found that most single-employer programs for short-term disability insurance as well as many such programs under collectively bargained multiemployer programs were limited to nonoccupational disabilities. However, a great number also covered occupational disabilities, with the benefits being offset by any workmen's compensation benefits payable.

The U.S. Department of Labor digest showed the following with respect to waiting periods. Most of the programs commenced benefits on the eighth day of any disability resulting from sickness, but paid from the first day for disability resulting from accidents. In some cases, the waiting period was made retroactive once disability became established or was waived if hospitalization was required. Other variations of waiting periods were shown to be four, six, or seven days. In a few instances, there was no waiting period.

With respect to the period of time for which disability benefits were payable, the survey found that the most usual period covered was 26 weeks. Some programs, however, covered 52 weeks of disability, while others were restricted to 13 weeks. The amount of the benefits for short-term disabilities was found to vary in almost every instance. Some programs paid stated dollar amounts, with a minimum and maximum amount depending on the wage level of the disabled employee. In a few instances, the benefit was stated as a flat percentage of wages, varying from 50 to 80 percent, and in some cases with a maximum dollar amount.

In combination, these two surveys provide an adequate profile of short-term disability benefits as they exist today.

Long-term disability insurance. Over the past decade, long-term disability insurance (LTD) has been a rapidly growing form of employee protection. Today it covers more than 18 million workers.

Under this form of protection, benefits are provided for income lost as a result of long-term or permanent disability, whether the cause is occupational or nonoccupational in origin, although some are limited to nonoccupational causes only. Offsets are provided for against benefits paid under workmen's compensation or under the Social Security DI program.

Some employee benefit programs provide LTD benefits for some, but not all, employees. Thus, the Conference Board found in 1974 that of the employers surveyed, 72 percent provided LTD benefits for managerial personnel, 62 percent for office employees, and 28 percent for nonoffice employees.

Under LTD programs, benefits commence in almost all cases either after the cessation of short-term disability or salary continuance benefits. The Conference Board found that the waiting period was one month in 5 percent of the places of employment surveyed, two months in 4 percent of the cases, three months in 23 percent of the cases, six months in 62 percent of the cases, and twelve months in 6 percent of the cases. Most plans continued benefits until age 65. Again, the greatest degree of variation among employee programs concerns the amount of the benefits paid, although it is generally 60 percent of wages up to a maximum dollar amount.

A related long-term disability benefit that is frequently provided are the *disability retirement provisions under pension plans.* Typically these provide disability coverage on the completion of a length-of-service requirement, such as 10 to 15 years, or attainment of a specified age, such as 45, 50, or 55, or both. The benefits in such cases are generally equal to the accrued normal retirement pension benefit, but with additional minimum benefit, which might be a flat dollar amount or a percentage of the wage level at the time of disability. The Conference Board study in 1974 showed that of the employers surveyed, 47 percent had such pension provisions for office employees and that 62 percent made such provision for nonoffice employees. In union-negotiated plans, 71 percent of the cases had provisions for disability pension.

The relevancy of these employee disability benefit programs to the troubled employee is that almost universally no distinction is made between mental disorders and other causes of disability. The degree to which earned income lost as a result of mental disorders is replaced by employee disability insurance is not known. Obviously, in an individual case it would depend on the length of disability experienced in relation to the size and scope of the benefits available.

Individually purchased disability income insurance policies offer a wide range of benefits, usually up to one-half or three-quarters of earnings, the choice resting with the purchaser. Benefits might be continued for anywhere from 2 years to age 65, or even for life, again depending on the preference of the purchaser. The unit cost is greater than for group insurance coverage as a result of increased merchandising, underwriting, and claims administration costs. Most such policies are now written on a noncancelable basis, but the prospective purchaser must give evidence of good health and sound credit standing. In cases of impaired health, substandard insurance is available at increased premium rates or for reduced benefits. Under the terms of these policies, coverage for disability resulting from mental or emotional disorders is usually excluded from the plan.

Salary Continuance Programs

Another form of benefit for employees that replaces, in whole or in part, income lost as a result of illness or injury is provided by salary continuance or paid sick-leave programs. Such programs exist both on a formal basis (in writing) and on an informal basis (not in writing and with the benefits determined on a case-by-case basis). In some instances, these benefits stand alone in the absence of any disability insurance benefits; in some cases, they precede the long-term disability insurance benefits; while in others they supplement short-term disability insurance benefits or workmen's compensation benefits if the salary continuance is applicable to occupationally related disabilities.

Not all places of employment make provision for salary continuance in the event of illness or injury, particularly if a disability insurance program has been established, or if the company is located in a state in which short-term disability insurance is compulsory under a temporary disability benefits law. It is estimated that more than 19 million employed people have protection under formal salary continuance programs, and that perhaps an additional 2 million have some protection under informal programs. This latter estimate is necessarily with little foundation and is probably ultraconservative, considering the large number of very small businesses not taken into account.

The variations among salary continuance programs seem to be infinite. Differences can pertain to matters such as the types of employees covered or not covered, the amount of the benefit, the duration of the benefit, the waiting period before benefits commence, the distinctions between occupational and nonoccupational causes of disability, and the relationship to such compulsory programs as temporary disability benefits and workmen's compensation. Although complete delineation of these differences would be too lengthy and would serve little purpose here, the following will serve to illustrate the differences and variations among the formal salary continuance programs. The information shown derives from two principal recent sources: The Conference Board *Profile of Employee Benefits* and the U.S. Labor Department *Digest of Insurance Benefits.*

One basic difference among salary continuance programs concerns those employees who are covered by the program and those who are excluded. In general, such programs are limited to regular full-time employees, often requiring some period of established service, such as six months or a year. It would be extremely difficult to administer such a program for casual workers, short-term workers, or part-time workers. Hence, the length of service of an employee is an intrinsic determinant in such programs, not only as respects eligibility for benefits, but also in determining the extent of the benefits. It has been found that 45 percent of employers required one year or less of service for eligibility, the remainder requiring one to ten years of service, and that the benefits under the vast majority of programs increase as the length of service increases.

Beyond this, differences exist as to the classes of employees covered by the program. The Conference Board survey, for example, found that 85 percent of the places of employment had such programs for office or salaried employees, this proportion dropping to 46 percent for nonoffice employees and down to 35 percent for employees covered by union collective bargaining agreements.

Benefits vary from program to program. For most, full pay is provided for a specified period, which can range from 1 to 78 weeks. In many instances, the time limit is related to the length of service of the employee. Under some programs, the period of full pay is supplemented by a further period of partial pay (e.g., 1 week full pay, 51 weeks 60 percent of pay; 4 weeks full pay, 52 weeks at half-pay; or 26 weeks full pay, 26 weeks half-pay).

In some instances, the salary continuance benefits are cumulative; in most they are not. In the large majority of reported cases, benefits are payable from the first day of sickness or injury. For others, there can be a waiting period of 1 to 14 days before benefits commence, although in some of these instances the benefit can be retroactive to the first day. Under some programs the benefit can be from the first day if hospitalization is required.

Regardless of these variations among salary continuance or paid sick-leave programs, they can be of significance to the troubled employee who loses time from work due to mental, emotional, or personality disorders or as a result of physical illnesses or accidents which are a direct consequence of such disorders. This is particularly so since, as has already been noted, the troubled employee has an above-average incidence of such work absences. In no known instance does a salary continuance program deny benefits for work absences that result from mental disorders.

BIBLIOGRAPHY

American Psychiatric Association. *APA Guidelines for Psychiatric Services Covered Under Health Insurance Plans.* Undated.

Avnet, Helen H. "Psychiatric Insurance—Ten Years Later." *American Journal of Psychiatry,* November 1969.

———. *Psychiatric Insurance.* New York: Group Health Insurance, 1962.

Blue Cross Association. *Annual Report of Enrollment by Benefit and.Coverage Classification.* Chicago: December 1975.

Blue Cross Consumer Report. *National HMO Census Data.* March 1977.

The Conference Board. *Profile of Employee Benefits.* New York: 1974.

Cummings, Nicholas A., et al. *Psychiatric Services and Medical Utilization in a Prepaid Health Plan Setting.* Oakland, Calif.: Kaiser Foundation Health Plan, September 1967.

Fink, Raymond. "Financing Outpatient Mental Health Care Through Psychiatric Insurance." *Mental Hygiene,* April 1971.

———. "Mental Health Services in Prepaid Group Practice." Presented before the Group Health Institute, June 1973.

———, et al. "The Filter Down Process to Psychotherapy in a Group Practice Medical Care Program." *American Journal of Public Health,* February 1969.

Follmann, J. F., Jr. *Alcoholics and Business.* New York: AMACOM, 1976.

———. "How National Health Insurance Developed." *Insurance Magazine Gold Book,* 1972.

———. *Insurance Coverage for Mental Illness.* New York: AMACOM, 1970.

———. *Medical Care and Health Insurance.* Homewood, Ill.: Richard D. Irwin, Inc., 1963.

Goldberg, Irving D., et al. "Effect of a Short-term Outpatient Psychiatric Therapy Benefit in a Prepaid Group Practice Medical Program." *Medical Care,* September 1970.

Group for the Advancement of Psychiatry. "The Effect of the Method of Payment on Mental Health Care Practice." New York: 1975.

Guillette, William. Presented before the National Association of Private Psychiatric Hospitals, November 1976.

Health Insurance Association of America. *New York Medical Economics Bulletins,* October 21, 1975; March 5, 1976; July 14, 1976; June 2, 1977.

———. *Statistical Bulletin* No. 10-74. September 23, 1974.

Health Insurance Institute. *Source Book of Health Insurance Data.* New York: Annual.

Locke, Ben Z., et al. "Psychiatric Need and a Demand in a Prepaid Group Practice Program." *American Journal of Public Health,* June 1966.

Myers, Evelyn S. *Coverage of Mental Disorders Under Insurance Plans.* Washington, D.C.: American Psychiatric Association, September 1971.

Myers, Robert J. *Medicare.* Homewood, Ill.: Richard D. Irwin, 1970.

National Institute of Mental Health. *Financing Mental Health Care in the United States.* Washington, D.C.: HEW Publication No. (HSM) 73-9117, 1973.

————. *The Financing, Utilization and Quality of Mental Health Care in the United States.* Washington, D.C.: April 1976.

Penner, Norman R. "Hospitalization of Adolescents: Insurance Coverage." *National Association of Private Psychiatric Hospitals Journal,* Vol. 9, No. 3.

The President's Commission on the Health Needs of the Nation. *Building America's Health.* Washington, D.C.: U.S. Government Printing Office, 1952.

RAND Corp. *Mental Health, Dental Services, and Other Coverage in the Health Insurance Study.* Santa Monica: November 1973.

Reed, Louis S., et al. *Coverage and Utilization of Care for Mental Conditions Under Health Insurance.* Washington, D.C.: American Psychiatric Association, 1974.

————. *Health Insurance and Psychiatric Care.* Washington, D.C.: American Psychiatric Association, 1973.

Schmeidemandel, Patricia. *Health Insurance for Mental Illness.* Washington, D.C.: American Psychiatric Association, 1968.

Somers, Anne R. *Medical Care Program.* New York: Commonwealth Fund, 1971.

U.S. Congress, House Committee on Ways and Means. *Disability Insurance Programs.* Staff report, July 1974.

U.S. Department of Health, Education, and Welfare. *Extent of Voluntary Health Insurance in the United States.* Washington, D.C.: Annual.

————. *Findings of the 1970 APTD Study.* Washington, D.C.: September 1972.

————. *Financing Mental Health Care Under Medicare and Medicaid.* Research Report No. 37, Washington, D.C.: 1971.

————. *Forward Plan for Health.* HEW Publication No. (OS) 76-50046. Washington, D.C.: August 1976.

————. *Illness, Disability, and Hospitalization Among Veterans.* National Center for Health Statistics Series 10, No. 14, Washington, D.C.: 1965.

————. *Independent Health Insurance Plans.* Research and Statistics note No. 21, Washington, D.C.: November 30, 1976.

————. *Mental Health Benefits of Medicare and Medicaid.* PHS Publication No. 1515, Washington, D.C.: 1971.

————. *The 1967 National Survey of Institutionalized Adults.* HEW Publication No. (SSA) 75-11803, Washington, D.C.

————. *Social Security Survey of the Disabled.* HEW Report No. 9, Washington, D.C.: June 1970.

————. *Veterans Health and Medical Care.* Series C-No. 2, Washington, D.C.: 1960.

U.S. Department of Labor. *Digest of Insurance Benefits.* Washington, D.C.: 1974, 1975.

Zee, Hugo J. "Influence of Funding on Course of Treatment." *National Association of Private Psychiatric Hospitals Journal,* 8:2, 1976.

12

THE ROLE OF EMPLOYERS

THE role of employers with respect to the troubled employee can be a debatable one. There are those who consider that a place of employment has a moral and ethical responsibility to the troubled employee. There are those who would deny this vigorously, among other things maintaining that the problems of the troubled employee have a deep-seated causative factor that has nothing to do with the circumstances of employment. While some consider the most expeditious way to handle troubled employees is to discharge them, others regard this type of action not only as inhumane, but as economically unsound.

Whatever the causative factors, the problem is one no employer can blithely walk away from. The incidence of mental, emotional, and personality disorders in the workforce shown in Chapter 7, and the economic costs of such disorders to places of employment shown in Chapter 8, are of such proportions that they cannot be ignored. The possible causal relationship between the workplace and the onset of such disorders, discussed in Chapter 5, is also a matter which cannot easily be overlooked.

In 1960 Dr. Ralph T. Collins, neurologic and psychiatric consultant to the Eastman Kodak Company, pointed out that among employed people mental disorders and emotional illnesses were responsible for more absenteeism from work than any other illness, except the common cold. In 1976 absenteeism alone was estimated to cost employers $12 billion a year. In addition, the inability to get along with people, which may well be caused by emotional disorders, is said to be the primary cause of all discharges. Labor turnover is a costly matter in the loss of experienced personnel and in the hiring and training of replacements. Added to this is the estimate that 80 to 90 percent of all industrial accidents may be attributed to some type of mental or personality problem that caused the worker to be careless, resulting in a loss of 15,000 lives and 2 million disabling injuries each year at an annual economic cost of more than $3 billion.

When you add to this toll the increases in the costs of health insurance, salary continuance programs, and disability insurance, as well as the cost of faulty managerial decisions, inefficiency at all job levels, impaired customer relations, job dissatisfaction, and poor employee morale, much of which can be seated in mental disorders, the costs can be staggering to a place of employment. They merit thoughtful attention.

A study was made of the rate of absenteeism among 1,297 female employees of the New York Telephone Company a quarter of a century ago, which was quite revealing. The study compared two groups of employees: those with a high rate of absenteeism and those with a low rate of absenteeism. It was found that one-third of the employees accounted for 80 percent of the days lost from work. The reasons for such high levels of work absences were many. The principal cause was found to be the various respiratory illnesses. Various disorders of the gastrointestinal system were also predominant, as were gynecological disorders, including menstrual abnormality, menopausal symptoms, and spontaneous abortions. Other disorders included those of the skin, the eyes, the ears, the urinary tract, bones and joints, as well as goiters and thyroid adenomas, hypertension, diseases of the cardiovascular system, headaches, palpitations, nervousness, sleeplessness, and fatigue. Many of these ailments fall within the group called psychoneurotic illnesses.

Employees in the high-absentee group also had a greater incidence of surgery, experiencing 13 times as many surgical operations as other employees. They also incurred 3.5 times the number of accidents, including fractured skulls, fractured bones, concussions, serious burns and lacerations, and severe contusions, which frequently resulted in prolonged disabilities.

At the same time, it was found that those employees with high rates of absenteeism were marked by insecurity, tension, stress, resentment, and anxiety, as well as those having compulsions and phobias. Many suffered from paranoid schizophrenia, conversion hysterics, psychoneurosis, and alcoholism. Many had experienced broken marriages. These employees were frequently defensive, suspicious, and unhappy, did not make friends easily, were discontented, somewhat hostile, given to complaining, and reacted adversely to job location or assignment changes. By and large, they were women with ambition who were not happy with their jobs.

It is readily apparent from this study that absenteeism is not simply a reflection of physical disability. Also evident is the fact that many physical illnesses and accidents are a result of a person's adaptive response to events or situations in his or her environment, or of the stresses in their lives.

In contrast, the women with a lower rate of absenteeism, who were otherwise similar to those with the high rate, were, as a rule, quite content, made friends easily, were outgoing, and were capable of diffuse emotional attachments. They had a profound sense of loyalty to their families, yet the loss of a loved one led to no prolonged behavioral disturbance. They had no unalterable goals, and many had refused promotions because they preferred a lesser degree of responsibility. They readily adapted to changes in job locations or job procedures, and were flexible.

This study is quite revealing in many ways and clearly indicates the effect of psychiatric disorders on a place of employment. The economic costs are apparent.

One further reason for the sensitization of employers to the effects of mental disorders is the trend that has been taking place on the part of judicial opinion as respects workmen's compensation claims, where causal relationship to mental or emotional disabilities is found, even in those resulting from willful misconduct. The courts have held that neurotic illness is not considered to be malingering nor a conscious disorder, and that neurotic suffering is considered a disease.

Workmen's compensation was originally conceived to provide benefits for occupational accidents and injuries and was not held to cover psychiatric impairment brought about by job-induced emotional stress. Today the courts grant benefits not only for psychiatric disorders precipitated by job injuries, but also for physical disabilities produced by stressful working conditions that need not be traumatic in nature, but that can result from cumulative pressures over a period of time. Examples of more recent decisions include cases of fatal brain hemorrhage produced by stress, and stress-produced coronary attacks, thrombosis, peptic ulcers, depression, suicides, migraine headaches, nervous breakdowns, and degenerative disorders. Involved have been such diverse occupations as statisticians, salesmen, plant managers, factory workers, clerks, librarians, construction workers, truck drivers, and railroad workers. Such decisions have been handed down even if a predisposition for the illness existed in the employee, provided that a causal link can be shown to exist between the emotional strain and the physical disability. The burden is on the employer to prove that the mental disorder was not aggravated by the work conditions.

Unquestionably this trend adds to the cost of production and administration at any place of employment. Thus Dr. Alan A. McLean at IBM has commented that "one motivating force for occupational mental health programs is workmen's compensation insurance." Noting that increasingly workmen's compensation benefits are provided to individuals with psychiatric or emotional disabilities caused by physical trauma or emotional stress, and that the courts are construing workmen's compensation laws "in such a manner as to relieve the employee of the burden of proving causal connection between his employment and his disability," thereby making the presumption that "the disability is employment related, unless substantial evidence is provided by the employer to the contrary," Dr. McLean feels that this alone is sufficient reason for employers to be concerned over the mental health of their employees.

This chapter deals with the attitudes of employers concerning the mental, emotional, and personality disorders of their employees; the relationship of mental health to an industrial health program; the relationship of insurance and employee benefit programs to mental disorders; and the problem of employing or re-employing the troubled employee. Later chapters discuss what is presently being done and what can be done in places of employment to help the troubled employee, who is doing it, and where help and guidance may be obtained to assist the troubled employee.

Employer Attitudes

Growing numbers of employers are developing real concern for their troubled employees. Not that this trend is by any means universal, for there are those to whom the troubled employee is a nuisance at best, and who furthermore have little or no confidence in psychiatric treatment, whatever its form. On the other hand, there are those employers who have a real concern and sympathy for the troubled employee, but who lack any depth of understanding of the subject and do not know where to turn for help and guidance. There are also those who, while recognizing the problem, are convinced that mental, emotional, and personality disorders are highly personal matters in which an employer should not attempt to intrude. Others are convinced that they do not have such problems among their employees. Yet others react that there is little evidence that professionals can help the troubled employee, that blue-collar workers could not benefit from treatment, that to recognize the problem would simply be to encourage malingering, and that mental illness is a problem for government, not for employers.

Despite such attitudes, the impressive number of conferences held on the subject in recent years attests to the fact that there is employer interest in the mental health of their workers. For example, in 1966 the National Association of Manufacturers sponsored a national Conference on Mental Health and the Business Community. The following year, Pennsylvania Mental Health, Inc., convened a conference on the subject of Emotional Health: An Industrial Problem. In 1972 and again in 1977 the Center for Occupational Mental Health at the Cornell University Medical Center sponsored occupational mental health conferences. In addition, ongoing interest is evident from meetings conducted by the American Psychiatric Association, the National Association of Private Psychiatric Hospitals, the American Medical Association, the National Institute of Mental Health, the National Health Council, the American Public Health Association, and the organizations concerned with occupational health.

A few statements made by corporate executives and medical directors will illustrate the attitudes on the part of some employers. Two decades ago, Dr. James H. Sterner, then medical director of the Eastman Kodak Company, in addressing the 1959 National Health Forum, said:

> There is increasing recognition of the importance of health to our well-being. But, at the same time, new threats to health, physical and mental, are to be found in new products, new forms of energy, and new patterns of production and distribution. To apply our increasing knowledge of preventive medicine to improve the health of people who work . . . are the tasks of occupational health.

A few years later, Kenneth H. Klipstein, president of the American Cyanamid Company, said:

> Good employee health is a universal industrial policy. In assuming responsibility for occupational health, industry only serves its own enlightened self-ir terest.

In 1968 Clifford A. Conklin of the St. Joseph Lead Company said:

> It is to industry's enlightened self-interest to do something constructive about the problem of mental illness. . . . At this stage, however, neither management nor labor in most companies is very knowledgeable concerning the needs of the mentally ill.

More recently, Dr. William Jend, Jr., of the Michigan Bell Telephone Company, commented:

> The physical and mental health of our employees is a major consideration in the ability of any business to provide good service or a good product. . . . The emotional environment of the workplace is also of increasing concern and the occupational physician, nurse, or other professional can do much to prevent emotional problems and provide counseling and first aid when they do arise.

John L. Fleming of the Aluminum Company of America said recently that there are two reasons why places of employment must be concerned with the emotionally troubled employee: (1) it is the right thing to do, and (2) it is pragmatic since people are a costly and valuable resource to a business organization. "To fail to recognize this," he says, "is poor management." And John Mullen of Johnson and Johnson has stressed the need for employees to be made aware of the available mental health resources in the community where they live and work. He also said that there is increasing emphasis in places of employment on the human relations aspects of supervisory duties and in counseling employees with "hang-ups." N. H. Collison of the Olin Corporation has said similarly:

> There has been much improvement in the human relations aspect of industry. The concept of industrial health . . . has moved slowly from "post facto" medical care to the beginning of a concept of preventive medicine. . . . A good medical program persuades the worker that management is sincere in its concern for him. It promotes mutual respect. . . .

> An industry has a bona fide interest in the health of its employees . . .
> their good health is good business.

That unanimity does not prevail is evident from the findings of a survey of 118 senior business executives published by the Conference Board in 1972. The survey found that a sizable majority of executives believed that social issues other than health care have equal or higher claim on their attention. These executives expressed an awareness of, and concern about, such matters as the importance of the prevention and treatment of disease and disability, the status of the health care delivery system, the escalating costs of health care, the shortages and maldistribution of a health workforce, and the inefficiencies that occur in the utilization of health services. Several executives urged the creation of joint occupational health facilities by groups of employers. Others, on the other hand, opposed the creation or the expansion of industrial health services, some on the grounds that "employees are suspicious of so-called company doctors." One in five, however, urged the creation or expansion of in-house health facilities, including several executives from the smallest companies (those with less than 500 employees) represented in the survey.

Negative opinions concerning industrial health programs, the survey showed, centered in such matters as the costliness of medical facilities, the lack of expertise in health affairs on the part of business management, the inefficiency that could result unless the employee population was sufficiently large and concentrated, and the employee dissatisfaction that could result if anything less than complete health care was provided. On the other hand, a number of executives stated the belief that the cost of health care could be controlled through direct provision of some health services by the company. The survey quoted an unidentified president of a rubber manufacturing company as saying, "The possibility of business doing in-house is probably the most effective brake on the escalating costs of outside health services."

The survey also revealed considerable sentiment that the community role of business must involve active participation in the functioning of hospitals, in the operations of voluntary health agencies, in the development of community health planning, and in the establishment of health maintenance organizations (HMOs).

These views on the part of business management as to the role of employers in the various aspects of employee health are revealing in many respects. Most certainly there is a diversity of opinion. Most certainly there are forward-looking concepts, although these might not always predominate. Furthermore, the question of what the role of the employer should be in relation to the health of employees is one that has not yet been resolved by a preponderance of opinion.

Dr. Alan A. McLean of IBM has aptly noted, "It has not been easy for management to accept the idea that work can adversely affect both the mental and physical health of many workers. Nonetheless, there is mounting interest in what has come to be called job stress." He takes cognizance of the fact that "Mental health in industry is a topic of enormous breadth and complexity." "Is it the responsibility of industry to enhance employee satisfaction through a sense of performing purposeful, productive work?" he asks. He then comments:

> No employer is really able to assume such a contractual commitment . . . the stimulation of mental health may be far from the minds of most employers . . . one could argue convincingly that industry should not be singled out for a particular responsibility for the mental disorders of its employees . . . the ultimate responsibility is with the individual and his family.

A final word is in order here. Employers frequently display concern over the availability and cost of health-care facilities and services. They make financial contributions to support such facilities, to train health manpower, and to promote research. Employers have made the services of their industrial health programs available to the community, have brought about the development of HMOs and, as in the case of Eastman Kodak, have developed home health services in their communities. How extensive such efforts are with respect to the treatment of mental disorders is not known, but most businesses could certainly play a very significant role in bringing about increased availability of facilities and services for the treatment of mental disorders.

Relationship to Industrial Health Programs

One aspect of the employer's role is the relationship of the industrial health program to the troubled employee. Basically, an industrial health program is concerned with the prevention of accidents and illnesses to the greatest extent possible and with the prompt treatment of those which do occur. As has been shown, occupational accidents and resultant disabilities can be related to the onset of mental disorders. The hazards leading to such accidents can include fires, explosions, inadequate space and clearance, faulty machine or equipment maintenance, and faulty construction or plant layout. Contributing factors can be inadequate lighting or ventilation, noise, and insufficient selection and training of employees. Age, ill health, or fatigue can contribute to accidents. Illnesses can be prompted by the presence of toxic agents, by noxious odors or fumes, and by repeated traumatic noises, vibrations, or pressure changes. Adequate protection against such hazards, based on the findings of periodic plant inspection and study of the employee health records, can play an important role in avoiding the onset of mental disorders. Several studies have identified the onset of mental and nervous disorders with such occupational hazards, as well as with such matters as job monotony and job stress.

An equal concern of an industrial health program should be those accidents and illnesses that occur off the job, deleterious lifestyles engaged in by employees, and any problems of concern to employees, whether job-related or not. All such matters can play a significant role in the onset of mental disorders.

The consequences of such hazards, whether occupational or nonoccupational in nature, are always the same: increased absenteeism, inefficiency, lost productivity, and unnecessary employee turnover.

The importance of these increasing interests on the part of places of employment have been pointed out by Dr. Robert O'Connor of U.S. Steel when he said:

> The only concerted, planned, large-scale, personal, adult health maintenance programs in this country today are in the occupational health programs of American industry. . . . The workplace is probably the ideal locale to practice real preventive medicine on a wide and effective scale.

Dr. G. H. Collings, Jr., of the New York Telephone Company, similarly takes the view that total health care is "composite and a continuum" and that industry is often better able to deliver primary care to its employees than are other services in the community. He notes that industry has medical records for many employees and is in a better position to achieve a more comprehensive view of understanding each patient, and that where industrial health facilities already exist, it requires minimal expansion to provide primary care.

The matter of an industrial health program concerned with nonoccupational health hazards is, however, a subject of considerable debate. Some employers believe that nonoccupational health services result in better work attendance, improved job performance, reduced insurance costs, improved workforce stability, and a higher level of employee morale, whereas others see no benefits at all in such efforts, and are skeptical of the merits. Still other employers feel that to enter into the area of nonoccupational health hazards would be to infringe on the employees' freedom of choice in the selection of a physician and on their rights of privacy. Another group is concerned over the effects of such an endeavor on employee relations, pointing out the distrust that is often felt toward an employer-established program.

One aspect of an industrial health program that can be important to the troubled employee is that of periodic physical examinations. Through this means, the possibility of a diagnostic evaluation of mental, emotional, or personality disorders exists, whether the causative factor is occupational or nonoccupational in nature. Since the earlier the onset of a mental disorder is detected the greater the likelihood of cure (or, if not cure, substantial amelioration of the symptoms), the industrial physician can play a substantial role not only in detecting the condition, but in counseling the employee and suggesting referral for treatment where such is indicated.

The compatibility of employees with their particular job is an important factor to be borne in mind in such examinations. The findings of the 1974 Conference Board survey are significant in this respect. They showed that only 57 percent of the employers of more than 500 employees provided periodic health examinations in an attempt to determine the compatibility of the employees with their job, or to determine any harmful effects that might be inherent in the working environment.

Some employers, such as Du Pont, combine a statistical analysis of absenteeism with the findings of physical examinations to obtain further clues to the presence of potential hazards or abnormal reactions to the working environment. Of interest also is the program at the American Cyanamid Company, where the top 60 people in the corporate structure are required to have an annual physical examination, including an emotional evaluation. Should any mental abnormality be evidenced, the employee is required to seek appropriate help. Another program that should be noted is one set up by General Electric, which is aimed at the identification of mental health problems and the recommendation of appropriate care.

Dr. David B. Robbins, a psychiatric consultant to IBM, has expressed the opinion that the occupational physician is in a unique position to study emotional problems in the world of work, that such a program has contributed significantly to the tertiary and secondary prevention of emotional illness, and that industry should now focus its efforts on the primary prevention of such illnesses, as Robbins calls it: "a difficult, vexing, even risky shift of emphasis."

John Mullins of Johnson and Johnson has said of its industrial health program that if it never treated a practical illness it would have paid for itself many times over because of the way its personnel have been able to calm frustrations and help troubled employees with their problems.

Dr. Alan A. McLean of IBM is another who feels that an industrial health program can do much in the areas of preventive psychiatry and the stimulation of mental health by forestalling the occurrence of serious mental disorders. Noting that it is estimated that anywhere from 15 to 85 percent of employees are maladjusted and that one-third could benefit from treatment for mental, emotional, or personality disorders, McLean believes that the positive worth of such effort could not be measured in dollars.

While such findings indicate a considerable interest by, and availability of, industrial health professionals in places of employment, they also make it clear that the advancement of industrial health has a long way to go. This is particularly so in smaller places of employment and in certain types of businesses, particularly in wholesale and retail trade and in agriculture. A few years ago, for example, John A. Stoudenmire, an experienced student of the subject, stated that mental health consultation and education has been given relatively little attention by industry.

Despite the divergence of opinion concerning how much an industrial health program can do for the troubled employee, it must be observed that today a growing number of employers are engaging psychiatrists on a full-time or on a consulting basis. By 1960, the American Psychiatric Association reported that 183 of its members were employed by private business on a full-time or part-time basis. In 1977 Marilyn M. Machlowitz wrote in *The New York Times* that in 1960 the latest figures available indicated that 200 psychiatrists and 150 clinical psychologists were working for places of employment. Today, she comments, these proportions are much greater, with many employers using such professionals on a consultation basis, while others rely on the services of community mental health centers or HMOs, and still others employ psychiatric nurses or social workers. And more recently, Dr. Alan A. McLean said that fewer than 500 psychiatrists are employed by private business, although their number doubled between 1967 and 1971 alone.

Another aspect of an industrial health program that can benefit the troubled employee is that of health education. A health education campaign can include the distribution of literature, the display of posters, the showing of films, and the inclusion of articles on the subject in the corporate journal. More direct, however, are group or seminar discussions and individual counseling. The Conference Board survey in 1974 found that one-third of the companies surveyed engaged in health education activities. More than half of these provided health counseling in connection with periodic health examinations and held film showings, while 85 percent distributed printed matter in various forms.

Health education techniques used today are often subject to criticism, particularly in terms of the lack of employee interest observed. Dr. Jerry Cassuto of the Western Electric Company has commented that most health education programs in places of employment are traditional stereotypes (posters, pamphlets, films), many of which are quite excellent, but that in terms of actually reaching employees and their families they are "often sadly lacking." Dr. Cassuto notes that the Industrial Medical Association conducted a survey in 1967 of 400 directors of industrial medical programs (of whom only 200 replied), and found that two-thirds had a specific health education program. Of these, 89 percent utilized individual counseling supported by the more customary means of health education, but only one company employed a health educator specialist.

Dr. Cassuto notes the value of individual or group counseling but comments that "the percentage of employees currently being reached is relatively small." He laments the "few attempts to inaugurate new concepts," "the apparent reluctance to utilize the professional health educator in industry," the fact that "outside agencies are also largely ignored," and that "little attempt is being made to objectively analyze the efficacy of existing programs." He cites as imaginative approaches to health education those taken by the New York Telephone Company and the Illinois Bell Telephone Company. IBM, too, has a program, one part of which is specifically devoted to the prevention of mental illness.

That there are positive results from such industrial health efforts is evident from the positive approaches being taken today by more than 600 employers toward the early identification and treatment of alcoholic employees. Where well-conceived alcoholism control programs have been instituted, the recovery rates being reported range from 60 to 80 percent of the alcoholic employees. Considering that these employees tend to be skilled and experienced people, and on average employed by the same employer for 12 years, the cost effectiveness of these efforts is apparent from any viewpoint. Today such control programs are being effectively enlarged to include the troubled employee who has mental or emotional disturbances. One such program is that in effect at the Illinois Bell Telephone Company.

Relationship to Insurance and Employee Benefit Programs

Another aspect of the role of the employer is the determination of the relationship of insurance and employee benefit programs to the problems of the troubled employee, where these are not dictated by collective bargaining agreements. The importance of such financial sources to the troubled employee was shown in the preceding chapter. To be discussed here is the extent to which health insurance coverages provide for the treatment of mental disorders.

Louis S. Reed of the American Psychiatric Association reported in 1975 that among 148 employee benefit plans, almost all had some insurance coverage for the treatment of mental disorders. In 68 percent of the plans coverage was equal to the health insurance benefits for hospital care for other conditions, and the same was the case for outpatient care in 42 percent of the cases. A year earlier, a Conference Board survey showed that more than 94 percent of the companies surveyed had hospital insurance for the treatment of mental disorders, but with special limits on the number of days covered. For outpatient care, there were such special limitations as 50 percent coinsurance and a limit to the episodes of treatment covered, usually 20 a year.

In 1976 the U.S. Department of Health, Education, and Welfare (HEW) recommended that a comprehensive insurance system, whether public or private, should include diagnostic and treatment services on either an inpatient or ambulatory basis, including such specialized services as nursing care and day care, and such supportive services as vocational counseling. In 1972 the National Association for Mental Health said that hospital care benefits should be the same for mental illness as for other illnesses, that short-term intensive therapy should be encouraged, that prescribed drugs should be covered, and that insurance should not favor a particular profession.

The decision with respect to insurance coverages, as was shown in the preceding chapter, rests with the purchaser: the employer or the union through collective bargaining. In either instance, insurance for the treatment of mental disorders can be a matter of secondary importance. Employees tend to be uninterested because they are certain that they will never become mentally ill. Despite the fact that mental disorders can devastate their finances, they clearly show a distinct preference for insurance protection against the costs of dental care or vision care, neither of which can be bankrupting, but both of which are used continually by most employees, thus having distinct visibility as a benefit.

A digest of 134 selected health and insurance plans prepared by the U.S. Department of Labor shows how the purchaser of insurance determines the extent, or even the exclusion, of coverage for the treatment of mental disorders. For hospital care, one program covered 365 days, one covered 300 days, one 180 days, two covered 120 days, one 90 days, several covered 70 days, and a great many were limited to 30 days. One was limited to 21 days. The variations in hospitalization coverage, then, ranged from 365 days down to 21 days.

For outpatient care, coinsurance (or patient cost sharing) was general, but the proportion of costs to be borne by the employees ranged from 20 percent to 40 percent, but was most generally 50 percent. At the Detroit Edison Company, the cost sharing was reported as 20 percent of the first $1,000 for ambulatory care, 30 percent for the second $1,000, 40 percent for the third $1,000, and thereafter 50 percent. Time limits were also placed on coverage for outpatient care, the range being from 40 visits a year to 100 visits, with many plans having a 50-visit limit per year. In all instances the amount paid per outpatient visit was limited to a specified dollar amount, usually $20.

A great many of the plans provided for a maximum dollar limit for benefits payable for the treatment of mental disorders. In a few cases, the maximum was on a lifetime basis, ranging from $5,000 to $25,000. For the large majority of cases, the maximum dollar amount was on an annual basis, but encompassed a wide range in amounts from $1,500, to $1,200, to $1,000. Many were limited to $625, $500, $400, or $300, with one being limited to $214.50.

The variations of benefit patterns under multiemployer collectively bargained plans are of equal interest. These are discussed in the following chapter.

The benefits for the treatment of mental disorders under the Federal Employees Benefit Plan, instituted in 1960, is of interest since this is the largest employee group in the nation, the plan providing health insurance protection for 7.6 million federal civilian employees and their dependents. The plan is administered by Blue Cross/Blue Shield, insurance companies and, as was indicated in the preceding chapter, by several of the prepaid group practice plans or HMOs, with the choice resting with the employee. There are two basic benefit options under the plan: a high option and a low option. The premium cost is shared by the federal government and the employees, although if an employee elects the high-option benefit, he or she must pay the difference in the premium cost over the low-option benefit. Most people elect the high-option benefit.

Under this plan, Blue Cross/Blue Shield provides for 365 days of hospitalization for mental disorders under the high option, and for 30 days of hospitalization under the low option. For ambulatory care, 80 percent of the costs are paid subject to a $100 deductible (75 percent and $150, respectively, under the low-option benefit). The insurance companies pay up to $1,000 of hospital care at full cost and 80 percent of such costs thereafter. For ambulatory care, 80 percent of the costs are paid, and more recently the benefit was limited to 20 visits a year to a psychiatrist's office or to 40 visits a year to a community mental health center. Dr. William Guillette of Aetna Life and Casualty reported in 1976 that the average claim payments per case were totaling $5,601 for care by a psychiatrist, $8,125 for care by an analyst, and $5,248 for care by a psychologist. The average claim duration regardless of the type of professional exceeded two years.

Malcolm McIntyre of Aetna Life and Casualty has said that in 1973 claims for the treatment of mental disorders under the plan were 12.4 percent of all claims. Most of these claims were for outpatient care, and one-half were for the treatment of neuroses. It was this experience that led to the limitations on ambulatory care noted earlier. The result was that mental illness claims dropped to 7.3 percent of all health insurance claims. The insurance companies are now experimenting with coverage for partial hospitalization in an endeavor to further reduce costs. This form of care, to be covered, must be licensed, accredited by the Joint Commission on the Accreditation of Hospitals, and approved by the insurer. It must be adequately staffed and equipped, have a written treatment plan, maintain complete records, and have an agreement for transfer to a hospital if necessary.

The diversity of benefit patterns for the treatment of mental disorders would seem to defy reason. Certainly in some instances troubled employees are provided minimal protection, after which they must either have recourse to their own resources or to public programs, or must cease treatment.

The Problem of Small Employers

In many ways, coping with the health and disability of employees is admittedly more difficult for the smaller employer than it is for the larger employer. To begin with, there is no established in-house medical department to rely on. Furthermore, the small business does not have the advantage of being able to spread costs over large numbers, and in some instances the professional resources are not readily available.

Be that as it may, small employers encounter the same health problems among their employees as do larger employers. Some say that this is a greater problem among small employers, while others claim that the small employer is better off in some ways. First, smaller employers tend to develop an awareness of the direct role they play, especially in an owner-managed business, where the day-to-day habits of every employee are no secret to the owner-manager. Second, the atmosphere of a smaller workplace can make for an intimacy between employer and employee that makes personal relationships more meaningful. Thus, the employer can observe the onset of health problems, including mental disorders, and suggest corrective measures. Unfortunately, there is no conclusive evidence that compares the onset of mental disorders among employees to the size of the place of employment.

The importance of smaller places of employment in the entire spectrum of employment is evident from the Statistical Abstract of the United States, which shows that half the workforce (excluding the self-employed, government, and railroads) is employed in places that employ fewer than 100 people. Furthermore, a quarter of the workforce is employed in places that employ fewer than 20 employees, and about 3 million people work in places that employ one to three employees. The relationship of small employers to the health of workers is, therefore, a matter of very considerable significance.

Yet, as the U.S. Department of Health, Education, and Welfare noted in 1970,

> With relatively few exceptions workers in small industries do not have the benefit of occupational health services . . . Small businessmen . . . may

recognize the value of occupational health services but find that individual programs are expensive and that other employers are hesitant to engage in cooperative projects. . . . The smaller the work group, the more difficult it is to arrange for health services. . . . These industries . . . could use to advantage part-time nursing in conjunction with periodic visits to the plant by a physician. When services available through voluntary and public health agencies in the community are also used, small industries can provide health benefits that compare favorably with those of larger establishments.

The record shows that industrial health services in smaller places of employment are less complete than those made available by larger employers. A study made by the Brookings Institution for the National Association of Manufacturers in 1952, for example, showed that for places employing 1 to 250 employees, only 33.9 percent provided any in-plant medical services for employees, and that only 21 percent made any attempt at introducing a health education program. On the other hand, 84 percent did make some provision for out-of-plant medical services. Six years later, HEW found that in manufacturing plants with fewer than 100 employees, 23.5 percent arranged for pre-employment physical examinations, but periodic examinations were only provided in 8 percent of those plants, medical advice was available in only 7.2 percent, plant health inspections were made in only 3.9 percent of the plants, and only 2.8 percent made any attempt at health education. Only 0.5 percent of the plants provided for adequate physician services, and only 1 percent had adequate nursing services.

Still, the problems of smaller places of employment are not insurmountable. The most usual approach taken is the employment of a part-time physician or nurse. Dr. Robert O'Connor of U.S. Steel has expressed the opinion that for 150 to 200 employees, a part-time nurse working 4 hours a day, 4 or 5 days a week, would be sufficient, functioning in conjunction with a part-time physician working 1 hour a day, 4 or 5 days a week, and with provision made for first-aid treatment when no professional services are available. An alternative to this approach could be the cooperative use of an industrial nurse by several separate businesses. In either instance, periodic health examinations could be provided through the use of community resources.

Dr. O'Connor recognizes that the establishment of an industrial health program is extraordinarily difficult for places with 50, 25, or fewer employees, but remains firmly convinced that certain aspects of an industrial health program can be accomplished. A local physician, for instance, can be used for the conduct of pre-employment examinations and for the treatment of occupational injuries. An industrial health physician can be used on a monthly or semi-monthly basis to counsel management in the handling of personnel and job placement problems and in the development of safety measures.

Other approaches taken by smaller employers can involve some type of cooperative endeavor, as was mentioned earlier. This might involve the joint use of existing services or facilities available in the community. It might require the establishment of services and facilities on a cooperative basis. In either instance, the catalyst can be the smaller employers in the community, the trade organizations to which employers belong (which are frequently used to enable small employers to purchase group insurance coverages), a group of independent physicians providing services on either a contract basis or on a fee-for-service basis, or a local hospital or health maintenance organization (HMO).

A similar approach that can be taken is the formation of a consortium of smaller employers in a community, using a centralized form of industrial health service. The advantages are essentially the same: the avoidance of the need for each employer to make his own arrangements, and the spreading of costs over larger numbers. While more experimentation, experience, and information in such an approach are sorely needed, it is worthy of note that today consortia in various parts of the country are proving valuable for employers in coping with the problem of alcoholism among their employees.

Yet another approach can have possibilities for smaller employers where union employees are involved. That would be the establishment of an industrial health program under the aegis of the union, or of several unions in a community acting cooperatively. Such centers, working cooperatively with small employers, could form the basis for an industrial health program that would be economically feasible, since the services would be spread over larger numbers. Requisite, of course, would be a cooperative attitude between employers and the union, which admittedly does not always exist.

Examples of different types of cooperative approaches developed for the benefit of employees working in smaller places of employment are the Hartford Plan, jointly sponsored by the Manufacturers Association of Connecticut and the Connecticut State Medical Society; the Industrial Health Council program in Birmingham, Alabama; and the Philadelphia Medical Society–Chamber of Commerce Small Plant Program. The needs of small employers are also met by clinics or hospitals in various parts of the country. By 1966 more than 20 private clinics were serving 9,100 places of employment. One such clinic is the Industrial Clinic in Minneapolis. Others include the Portland, Oregon, Industrial Clinic; the Petrie Clinic in Atlanta; and the Manufacturers Health Clinic at Winder, Georgia. Some of the larger employers have generously made their industrial health services available to smaller employers in the community. The Cummings Engine Company in Columbus, Indiana, and the Gates Rubber Company in Denver are among those that have taken such action.

It should also be noted that today small business can receive federal loans for the development of industrial health programs through the Occupational Safety and Health Administration (OSHA).

Although the extent to which such efforts on the part of smaller places of employment can benefit the troubled employee can only be speculated upon, at the very least, where a troubled employee is observed by a nurse or a physician, or has available the consultation of a physician, the possibility of referral for psychiatric diagnosis and treatment is present.

Employment of the Troubled Employee

A final aspect of the role of the employer with respect to the troubled employee is the matter of employing a person who has been treated for mental disorders, of reemploying a former employee who has undergone such treatment, and of employing mentally retarded persons.

Employing a person who has been treated for mental disorders. The stigma against mental illness noted earlier pervades the concepts of many employers. Others, however, quite willingly give fair and reasonable consideration to the application of an individual with a history of mental disorders. Dr. Alan A. McLean of IBM has aptly commented that in such cases the interview with the applicant should not be conducted with a view toward excluding the applicant from employment. Rather, he says, what should be determined is the possibility that the applicant will find the work sufficiently distressing to produce a subsequent disability, or whether the applicant is handicapped to the point that unsuccessful job performance might be anticipated.

In recent years the efforts of the President's Committee on Employment of the Handicapped and subsequent legislative enactments have provided a very considerable impetus to the employment of persons with various types of handicaps. Du Pont, for example, is reported to have employed 1,452 handicapped people among its 100,000 employees since 1947, and has found that most of those employees achieve average or better than average job performance, safety records, and attendance records, and that their rate of turn-over is low. The scope of the subject is indicated in a 1970 report of the U.S. Bureau of Census that among the handicaps of workforce age Americans, 250,000 were listed as "mentally restored."

A test frequently applied for the employment of any handi-capped person is a determination of whether the handicap is nonpro-gressive, will not interfere with the work performance, and will not present a safety hazard to other employees. This determination is generally made by the medical department of the place of employ-ment or its medical or psychiatric consultant. In most instances the health evaluation is made in a pre-employment health screening ex-amination and/or a health questionnaire. Such examinations also as-sist in the placement of employees in the jobs for which they are best suited and provide protection against future workmen's compensa-tion claims based on preexisting conditions.

Where persons with a previous history of mental disorders are concerned, the factors to be determined are (1) the type and length of the treatment received, (2) the psychiatric diagnosis that was made, (3) the psychiatric prognosis, and (4) the type and demands of the job under consideration.

Here the legal aspects of the role of employers regarding mental and emotional problems among employees are of interest. In 1977 the New York City Department of Social Services was involved in a case in which, after erratic behavior on the part of an employee, the department head arranged for an examination by the agency psy-chiatrist. Upon refusal by the employee, discharge was ordered. The employee sued on the grounds that such an order was libelous by implying that the individual was psychotic and that it violated the right of the worker to privacy. Both the lower courts and the U.S. Court of Appeals upheld the employer, contending that an employer may order a psychiatric examination to determine job fitness and that such an order did not violate any rights of the employee. Similar positions have been taken by the courts in cases where the employer insisted that an alcoholic employee either receive outside help or be dismissed.

Finally, a word should be said concerning the employment of

drug addicts who have undergone treatment, particularly since this is becoming a problem of growing proportions in the workplace. The approach to employment would be similar for drug addicts to that for applicants with mental disorders, except that a urinalysis is used to detect the presence of drugs, and a history of the case is obtained from the treatment agency. Some employers require that the applicant must have had treatment for at least one year; and some will not employ methadone patients. Of interest is a survey by the Drug Abuse Council in 1973, which found that employers hiring former addicts noted little if any effect on the rate of accidents, labor turnover, insurance costs, employee morale, or thefts.

Reemployment following an episode of treatment for mental disorders. Employers have a more direct responsibility to the troubled employee who would like to be rehired, or put back to work after a leave of absence due to mental disorders. Reemployment is a very important part of the rehabilitation of released mental patients. It helps individuals reestablish contact with reality, by increasing their control over their own behavior, and it reestablishes their self-esteem.

Today a great many employers give considerable attention to the rehabilitation and reemployment of disabled employees. In part, the interest of employers is spurred by the costs of workmen's compensation and disability insurance, since otherwise the troubled employee might continue to be disabled. The effort should be to provide every encouragement to foster the complete rehabilitation of the employee, including changing the job assignment or helping bring about any necessary changes in the work environment. The process is helped all the more when there is a definite formulation of management policy to provide guidance. Employers differ widely in the degree of their willingness to be helpful in such cases, but many do make every effort to rehabilitate the troubled employee.

Employment of the mentally retarded. Of the 6 to 7 million mentally retarded persons in the United States, some 5 million are considered to have a mild degree of retardation (IQ 50–70), and some 3 million of these are age 20 or older. These persons are identified as having slow development, but as being educable to a functional level. With training, they are able to work in competitive employment and to live independent lives. Of these adult mild retardates, 87 percent of the men are reported to be gainfully employed (for women, the proportion is 33 percent). Their earnings are reported to be more than 85 percent of the average wages for comparable employment. Obviously the type of employment depends on the intelligence level and training of the individual. The forms of employment frequently available to the retarded include work in the service industries, farm or garden work, domestic services, delivery and messenger services, office work, janitorial work, and various types of unskilled or semiskilled laboring or factory work. Many are also employed by government.

The mildly mentally retarded, then, present a sizeable labor pool. Employers consider them reliable, dedicated employees capable of performing a variety of tasks. Their work records demonstrate a much lower rate of absenteeism and job separation in comparison with other workers of similar work grades, and an above-average ability to get along with fellow workers.

BIBLIOGRAPHY

Asher, Janet, and Jules Asher. *Psychological Consequences of On-the-Job Injury.* Washington, D.C.: American Psychiatric Association, undated.

Bachman, George W. Washington, D.C.: Brookings Institution, 1952.

Carone, Pasquale A., et al. *The Emotionally Troubled Employee.* Albany: State University of New York Press, 1976.

Cassuto, Jerry. "New Health Education Programs." *Journal of Occupational Medicine,* December 1967.

Collings, G. H., Jr. Presented before the American College of Preventive Medicine, November 13, 1972.

Collison, N. H. "Management and an Occupational Health Program." *Archives of Environmental Health,* February 1961.

The Conference Board. *Industry Roles in Health Care.* New York: 1974.

———. *Profile of Employee Benefits.* New York: 1974.

———. *Top Executives View Health Care Issues.* New York: 1972.

Conklin, Clifford A. *An Enlightened Business Investment.* Presented before the Pennsylvania Mental Health, Inc., Pittsburgh: January 26, 1968.

Fischer, Gloria J. "Socio-economic Factors and Outcome of Released Mental Patients: Influence of Type of Placement, Occupational Adjustment, Compensation and Type of Hospital." *Journal of Health and Human Behavior,* Winter 1964.

Follmann, J. F., Jr. *Alcoholics and Business.* New York: AMACOM, 1976.

———. *The Economics of Industrial Health.* New York: AMACOM, 1978.

———. *Insurance Coverage for Mental Illness.* New York: AMACOM, 1976.

———. *The Mentally Retarded and Insurance Protection.* New York: Health Insurance Association of America, 1973.

Guillette, William. Presented before the National Association of Private Psychiatric Hospitals, November 1976.

Halpern, Susan. *Drug Abuse and Your Company.* New York: AMACOM, 1972.

Hilker, Robert J. *Behavioral Problems in Industry.* Chicago: Illiniois Bell Telephone Company, 1976.

Hoskin, W. D. *The Practice of Occupational Health.* Chicago: American Medical Association, 1976.

Institute of Management and Labor Relations. *A Community Venture in Mental Health.* State University of New Jersey, June 10, 1970.

Jend, William. "Where Do We Want to Be in Occupational Medicine?" *Journal of Occupational Medicine,* July 1973.

Kinkle and Plummer. "Life Stress and Industrial Absenteeism." *Industrial Medicine and Surgery,* August 1952.

Klipstein, Kenneth H. *Your Health and Industry.* National Health Council, New York: 1960.

Levinson, Harry. *Emotional Health: In the World of Work.* New York: Harper & Row, 1964.

Machlowitz, Marilyn M. "An Age of Industrial Psychiatry." *The New York Times,* April 3, 1977.

McIntyre, Malcolm. Presented before the National Association of Private Psychiatric Hospitals, November 1976.

McLean, Alan A. "Job Stress and the Psychosocial Pressures of Change." Presented at the Hawthorne Studies 50th Anniversary Symposium, undated.

————."Mental Health Programs in Industry." Chapter 53 of *American Handbook of Psychiatry.* New York: Basic Books, 1974.

————. *Mental Health and Work Organizations.* New York: Rand McNally, 1970.

————."Occupational (Industrial) Psychiatry." Chapter 45 of *Comprehensive Textbook on Psychiatry.* Baltimore: William and Wilkins, 1975.

————."The Problem of Change and Adaptation." Presented before the Worshipful Society of Apothecaries. London: March 25, 1977.

————(ed.). *To Work Is Human.* New York: The Macmillan Company, 1967.

————."Who Pays the Bill?" *Journal of Occupational Medicine,* May 1967.

————,et al. *Mental Health in Industry.* New York: McGraw-Hill, 1958.

Melchiode and Jacobson. "Psychiatric Treatment Barriers to Employment Programs." *Journal of Occupational Medicine,* February 1976.

National Association for Mental Health. *Does Your Health Insurance Cover Mental Illness?* Arlington, Va.: 1972.

National Health Council. *The Health of People Who Work.* New York: 1960.

O'Connor, Robert B. "The Role of Industry in the Health of the Nation." *Journal of Occupational Medicine,* October 1968.

Reed, Louis S. *Coverage and Utilization of Care for Mental Conditions Under Health Insurance.* Washington, D.C.: American Psychiatric Association, 1975.

Riedel, Donald C., et. al. *Federal Employees Health Benefits Program.* Washington, D.C.: HEW Publication No. (HRA) 75-3125, 1975.

Robbins, David B., et al. "The Psychiatric Patient at Work." *American Journal of Public Health,* July 1976.

————."Occupational Mental Health." *Journal of Occupational Medicine,* November 1974.

Schacter, Festinger, Willerman, and Hyman. "Emotional Disruption and Industrial Productivity." *Journal of Applied Psychology,* August 1961.

Stessin, Lawrence. *The New York Times,* April 3, 1977.

Stoudenmire, John A. "Mental Health Education of Supervisors." *Mental Hygiene,* Spring 1972.

U.S. Bureau of the Census, 1970.

U.S. Department of Health, Education, and Welfare. *Community Health Nursing for Working People.* Washington, D.C.: 1970.

————. *Small Plant Health and Medical Programs.* Washington, D.C.: 1958.

————. *The Financing, Utilization and Quality of Mental Health Care in the United States.* Washington, D.C.: April 1976.

U.S. Department of Labor. *Digest of Health and Insurance Plans, 1974,* Supplement. Washington, D.C.: 1975.

Ward, Hugh. *Employment and Addiction: Overview of Issues.* The Drug Abuse Council, Inc. New York: June 1973.

13

THE ROLE OF UNIONS

ORGANIZED labor can play a significant role in seeing that the troubled employee receives proper attention. Mental health is just another aspect of the overall concern for the welfare of workers.

For many years organized labor has worked to eliminate adverse working conditions, to improve working hours and working conditions, to increase wage levels, and to improve employee benefits through social security and pension programs, workmen's compensation insurance, and unemployment compensation. More recently, unions have bargained for paid vacations and for health insurance programs.

Unions have also fought for improvements in areas outside the work scene, but which affect the general well-being of workers, both on and off the job. They have backed public education, improvements in housing conditions, and government funding for the provision of mental health services. Not only have the strivings of unions brought about a better standard of living for workers, they have contributed immeasurably to their general well-being and mental health.

Organized labor has also developed a direct interest in the mental health of workers, as exemplified in a 1961 AFL-CIO publication, *The*

Worker's Stake in Mental Health. This pamphlet took the position that local unions should provide mental health education to their members in as many ways as possible, including the conduct of conferences and the provision of counseling to troubled employees and their families, and referral for diagnosis and treatment. Once a member is receiving treatment, it is the responsibility of the union, according to the AFL-CIO, to follow up the patient, provide any necessary assistance to the family, be warmly supportive, and provide assistance to get the recovered patient back on the job.

In 1963, furthermore, the National Institute of Labor Education stressed the need for increased availability of facilities for the treatment of mental disorders in a great many communities, and particularly for workers and persons in the lower economic levels of society who could benefit from outpatient treatment. The same group urged that public funds be used to support such outpatient services as well as an extension of health insurance coverages to include the treatment of mental disorders. Educational programs were advocated to acquaint blue collar workers and their families with the nature of the various types of mental disorders and with the forms of treatment available to them.

Naive though it is to expect such concepts to have become fully operative among labor circles, it must be said that they serve, at least, as the guiding principles for the efforts of organized labor.

Union Attitudes

That many leaders in organized labor have at best only a mild or passing interest in the troubled employee is perhaps not an unfair statement. The stigmas and public attitudes which pervade the subject of mental, emotional, and personality disorders have their effect on blue collar workers, perhaps more so than in other strata of society. Such attitudes tend to demotivate union members from coming to grips with the problem of mental disorders. This general apathy cannot help but cross over into the actions of the union leaders who represent their concerns and demands. Thus, as with all politicians in a democratic society, union leaders often tend to avoid issues not raised by their constituency, passing over the problems of mental illness in favor of more popular programs or employee benefits.

Fortunately, such attitudes are changing. More and more, union leaders are showing active concern for the problem. Some of the changes they have brought about in recent years include the treatment of mental disorders in some of the union health centers and the extension of coverage for the treatment of mental disorders in a number of collectively bargained health insurance programs. The developments in these areas are discussed later in this chapter.

The attitudes of three important figures in union circles as respects mental health are indicative of the change taking place. In 1965 Walter P. Reuther, then president of the United Automobile Workers, noticed that modern technology was forcing more and more employees to view their work as a means of earning a living rather than as a source of satisfaction. Reuther held that this resulted in increasing problems of tension and stress among the workers. He pointed to the fact that in the preceding year his union had gone on strike for "more rational and humane treatment on the job, for relief from the incessant pounding of the assembly line, for improved protection against abusive and arbitrary decisions by the foreman, and for the right to resist invasions of their privacy." It was an attempt, he said, "to produce more wholesome environments . . . , environments which will not continue to diminish the stature of the human being."

Leo Perlis, director of community service activities of the AFL-CIO, is another labor spokesman who has several times voiced his opinion on the mental health of workers. Noting such fears among working people as loss of the job, their health, youth, and even purpose, as well as concerns for their family, Perlis takes the position that employers have a direct responsibility for their employees and that they cannot separate problems that originate away from the workplace from those that are work-related. Urging a cooperative approach to such problems on the part of management and labor, Perlis argues that one answer lies in industrial health programs supplemented by counseling by the union. Commenting that it takes more "than music in the air, pastels on the walls, and the smile of the supervisor to banish the boredom of the job," he acknowledges that many employees are reluctant to undergo psychiatric treatment for fear that the employer's reaction will jeopardize their job security. What is needed, Perlis feels, is a program that promotes mental health in industry under joint union–management sponsorship outside the controversial area of collective bargaining.

Melvin A. Glasser, director of the social security department of the UAW, has said: "The organized labor movement of today is concerned with far more than wages and hours. . . . [It] has as a major goal the achievement of comprehensive medical care for its workers."

Speaking of the experiences of the UAW, Glasser comments: "Our own observations bear out . . . that working class people are by and large antagonistic to the aims of psychotherapy. They do not understand it and hence they fear and ridicule it. . . . They resist the slim possibility of outpatient psychiatric help as it is now offered to them." In making these remarks, Glasser made it clear that he does not speak for all of organized labor.

Clearly, then, there are union leaders who have a distinct and active interest in, and concern for, the mental health of workers.

Provision of Care

An important role played by some unions with respect to the well-being of their members is through the direct provision of health care at the union health center. In the case of large unions, this can be very complete care, and might include the diagnosis and treatment of mental, emotional, and personality disorders. In other instances, particularly programs established by local unions, the health care provided might be of a quite limited nature, or specialize in only certain aspects of care, such as dental or vision care. Or the local union might make arrangements with a clinic in the community to provide specified types of care or physical examinations. Similar arrangements might also be made with a prepaid group practice program or with a health maintenance organization (HMO).

Twenty-five years ago, the American Medical Association (AMA) expressed its concern about the development of union health centers. At that time the American Labor Health Association (ALHA) said, "A major deterrent to the growth and development of the health center movement has been the opposition of segments of organized medicine." It noted that it was not too uncommon, then, for physicians in group practice to be barred from local medical society membership and from hospital staffs. The ALHA noted, however, that "to the extent that this represents the desire for careful safeguarding of hard won medical standards, it is understandable." One of the concerns of the AMA at the time was that a health center would restrict the patient's freedom of choice of a physician.

In 1958, the AMA made a study of 50 labor union health centers. Eighteen of these were set up by the ILGWU located in various cities throughout the country, and four were operated by the Amalgamated Clothing Workers of America in Chicago, Mobile, New York, and Philadelphia. Other programs were operated in the New York City area by the laundry workers, the lithographers, the bakery workers, the butchers, the food handlers, the hotel and restaurant employees, the building service employees, the bartenders, the seafarers, the Hotel Trades Council, and the Wire, Metal, and Machine Trust Fund; and by the meat cutters, truck drivers, culinary workers, bartenders, and automobile workers in various parts of the country. Multi-union clinics were operating in Baltimore, Chicago, New York, Philadelphia, St. Louis, and Washington, D.C. The oldest plan was the ILGWU plan in New York, organized in 1913. The extensive health care program of the United Mine Workers was not included in the study.

Most of the 50 plans were financed in part by contributions made by employers, as stipulated in collective bargaining agreements. Total membership in 28 of the plans studied at that time was 766,178. For 19 of those plans 5,259 employers were involved, indicating a considerable service on behalf of workers engaged by small employers. Ten of the plans provided only diagnostic services. Most engaged in health education activities, including counseling, but only one, the Union Health Center in Philadelphia, included mental health education. At that time, only one of the plans studied, the Union Health Service, Inc., in Chicago, provided for the treatment of mental illness, having one part-time psychiatrist on the staff. Ironically, several of the plans provided dental care, vision care, and prescribed drugs.

During the same period, the AMA promulgated guides for the evaluation of management and union health centers. These guides covered a wide range, from ethical principles to the physical facility, the medical and auxiliary staff, and the maintenance of medical records, on to promotional publicity, community relations, and professional relations. Psychiatric staffing or treatment was not mentioned.

The activities of specific union health programs today where the diagnosis and treatment of mental disorders are included in the benefits are discussed in Chapter 15.

Mental Illness in Collective Bargaining

Particularly since the rulings of the federal government during the wage-price freeze of World War II, the process of collective bargaining has been an important factor in extending health insurance coverage for union members. Collective bargaining has also served as a catalyst (1) in extending insurance protection to the vast majority of employed people, (2) in gradually broadening those insurance coverages, and (3) as has been shown, in increasing the portion of the costs of such insurances borne by the employer. Collective bargaining has also been a factor in bringing about the continuation of health insurance coverage for workers who are laid off. In fact, in 1976 the U.S. Department of Health, Education, and Welfare found that almost one-half the health insurance plans at places of employment continued health insurance coverage during periods of layoff, half of these in turn continuing the coverage for at least three months, and half being completely financed by the employer.

Collective bargaining has, in some instances, served to extend health insurance plans to include the costs of the treatment of mental disorders, within certain limits. This inclusion is an innovation of the past decade.

The UAW negotiated the first nationwide collective bargaining agreement to cover mental health care on an outpatient basis. The coverage became effective in 1966 for 2.5 million workers and their dependents, including retired workers and their families, in 77 communities in 34 states. The objectives were to make readily available to the covered population short-term therapy for nervous and mental disorders, and to remove any economic deterrent to their early diagnosis.

The coverages under the program for the treatment of mental disorders include 45 days of hospital care for each episode of treatment (with a waiting period of 90 days between episodes) and inhospital treatment by a physician with no cost to the patient. The cost of prescribed drugs and electroshock therapy is covered whether in or out of hospital. Outpatient care benefits are limited to $400 a year. Within this limit, the patient does not bear any of the cost for hospital outpatient care, or that provided by day-care programs or child guidance centers. For group psychotherapy, the patient bears 15 percent of the cost. For treatment in a psychiatrist's office, family counseling, or psychological testing, the patient pays nothing toward the cost of the first five visits. After that, the patient pays 15 percent of the cost for the next five visits, 30 percent toward the next five visits, and 45 percent thereafter. The program is insured by several Blue Cross/Blue Shield plans, insurance companies, and prepaid group practice plans, of which the Kaiser Foundation Health Plan is the largest.

Certain aspects of the experience of this program are of interest. The utilization rate among workers and their dependents is about 30 per 1,000 covered persons, with practically no utilization by retired workers. The cost has been running about $1 to $1.25 per covered family per month. Of those seeking treatment under the program, more than half suffered from neuroses, more than a third had character disorders, and 18.9 percent had psychoses. By type of treatment, three-quarters of the patients saw a private psychiatrist, while only 6 percent participated in group therapy. Some 5 percent had undergone psychological testing, and only 3 percent had had electroshock therapy. Others used hospital outpatient services or community mental health centers. The plan is considered economically viable.

The program of the United Steelworkers of America, which covers 50,000 workers and their dependents, includes several different plans arrived at through negotiations. Under these plans, hospital care for mental disorders ranges in duration from 30 to 120 days, depending on the plan. Ambulatory care for such disorders is not covered. The International Association of Machinists program also differs among the negotiated plans, some of which do not cover ambulatory care. In other union-negotiated plans that include major medical expense benefits, 80 percent of the costs of hospital care for mental disorders are covered, and 50 percent of the costs of ambulatory care are covered after a $50 deductible, with a limit of 50 visits a year.

Other negotiated multiemployer insurance plans for mental disorders today include the Amalgamated Clothing Workers, the retail food industry, the dress industry, the retail drug industry, the personal services industry, the upholstering industry, the fur manufacturing and retailing industry, the furniture industry, the warehouse industry, the Pullman Company, the Jewelry Manufacturers Association, the Massachusetts Leather Manufacturing Association, and the Metropolitan (New York) Taxicab Board of Trade. There are broad variations in the coverages of these negotiated multiemployer health insurance programs for mental disorders, as reported by the U.S. Department of Labor. Hospital care ranges from 21 days (the retail drug industry) to 70 days (the retail food industry), with several plans providing 30, 45, or 60 days of care. Ambulatory care most generally is restricted to 50 visits a year and to $20 a visit. The maximum benefits in a year range from $300 for the Massachusetts Leather Manufacturers Association to $1,500 for the retail food industry.

Interestingly, of the health insurance plans reported by the U.S. Department of Labor, those of the maritime industry, the teamsters, the brewers, the doll manufacturers, and in New York City the hotel association, the restaurant industry, and the building services employees specifically excluded nervous and mental disorders from their health insurance plans.

Participation in Industrial Health Programs

Unions can also play a role of importance in the conduct and operation of an industrial health program. Through cooperative endeavor with the employer, maximum effectiveness of such a program can be achieved, and the frequent employer mistrust of such a program can be dispelled. This is of particular importance for the troubled employee. Unions should certainly encourage workers to take advantage of the services of an industrial health program, of a union health center if such exists, or of available services within the community in the interest of the early detection of the onset of a mental disorder. Shop stewards should be trained in the detection of the early signs of mental disorders and should be informed of the sources of help to which a troubled employee might turn. They should cease the long-standing practice of covering up for the troubled employee. Such a practice will only harm the troubled employee in the long run, and can be dangerous to fellow employees as well.

Unions can also play an important role in developing meaningful health education programs and can help dispel the stigma that marks people with mental illness. Union leaders tend to be more credible to employees than are employers, so it is natural that troubled employees would be better guided by the people they trust.

Beyond this, the union should actively work toward the elimination of hazards in the workplace and in the community that can threaten the health and safety of employees and their families. Practically all such hazards can produce an influence on the mental health of everyone involved. Employees should be aware that their rights and responsibilities in this respect are now delineated and strengthened by the provisions of the Occupational Safety and Health Act (OSHA). Yet, as the Conference Board survey in 1974 reported, OSHA "appears to have stimulated a long-simmering controversy of the relationship of labor and management to both the occupational and nonoccupational health functions."

Not everyone would agree with what is said here. Not infrequently, skepticism or downright antagonism colors relations between organized labor and management. This can be a matter of long standing, and where it occurs is probably the result of mutual fault. Not infrequently, friction or suspicion develops among employees concerning the functioning of industrial health programs. Employees become concerned that a violation of confidentiality may jeopardize their chances for advancement, promotion, pay increases, and even the job itself and future employability. The position of the union can thus stand in the way of the effectiveness of an industrial health program.

Recently, Melvin Glasser of the UAW said:

> An alternative must be found to the present company doctor system. The workplace should be used more extensively as a focal point for providing health services, not only for job-related diseases, but for preventive health services, health education, and indeed all health problems.

A few years earlier, Sheldon W. Samuels of the AFL-CIO interpreted the views of union officials toward industrial health programs as follows:

1. Company doctors are no less a part of management than are other company officials.
2. Company medical programs must justify their existence by dollar benefits.
3. The company doctor often cannot protect the confidentiality of patients' records.
4. In-plant medical care is poor in quality.
5. There is growing difficulty in accepting plant programs as resources unrelatable to, and separate from, the total medical care delivery system.

In 1959 Dr. William Sawyer, then with the International Association of Machinists, reported to the National Health Council that:

> Generally organized labor does not consider its role in occupational health to be particularly significant. Since occupational health programs are the outgrowth of Workmen's Compensation law requirements, and must be provided by the employer, union labor has had little part in them . . . labor regards itself as the recipient rather than the participant. . . . [However,] with labor unions' concern about the inadequacies of in-plant occupational health programs . . . there is gradually emerging a belief that the over-all health of workers should not be arbitrarily and

inefficiently divided as it is now. . . . As a result, more than seven million trade union members have collective bargaining agreements which contain safety and health clauses. . . . Such programs today are concerned with the total health of the workers.

Such statements by important spokesmen for organized labor cannot pass unheeded. They reflect a deep and long-standing concern with industrial health programs on the part of the unions.

For management's part, there are many who feel that an industrial health program neither belongs on the bargaining table nor constitutes an appropriate subject for collective bargaining. One such is N. H. Collison of the Olin Corporation, who, while taking cognizance of the fact that a "union can be, and very often is, an important contributor to the success of an industrial program," nevertheless says that

[Such a program] has no place in collective bargaining discussions. . . . [To do so] invades the personal and confidential area of relationship between worker and management . . . [which is] an individual relationship . . . foreign to the whole collective bargaining concept.

However, the problem is not insurmountable. When a joint employer–employee effort is made with guaranteed confidentiality, the inhibition can be overcome. Experience has shown, for example, that when an alcoholism control program is approached as a joint employer–union effort at the outset, with full and equal participation by the union, a workable program emerges with considerable enthusiasm. But when these conditions do not exist, the program tends to fail.

The importance and necessity of a cooperative approach by labor and management in the field of industrial health was recognized by David R. Lavalette of General Dynamics Corporation, who recently made the point that of "all the issues of mutual concern to employees, unions, physicians, and management . . . [which should] be devoid of controversy" the matter of industrial health is most important. He went on to say that unfortunately "this commonality of interests is not universally recognized." That labor and management can work cooperatively is evident from a recent contract negotiation by the United Rubber Workers with the Goodyear, Firestone, Uniroyal, and General Rubber companies which led to a study of the health hazards of 18,846 workers in the rubber industry. The research project is jointly financed by the management and the union.

The general concern among workers over occupational hazards

was made evident in a 1969 survey by the U.S. Department of Labor, in which it was reported that 71 percent of workers considered occupational safety and health a more important issue than wages. Among the unions that have been in the vanguard of active interest in job safety and health are the United Steel Workers of America; the United Automobile Workers; the United Paperworkers International Union; the International Association of Machinists; the United Rubber Workers; the Boilermakers Union; the United Mine Workers; and the Oil, Chemical, and Atomic Workers International Union.

Through collective bargaining, the Oil, Chemical, and Atomic Workers International Union requires that a survey of plant health and safety conditions be made by independent consultants at the expense of the employer. The employer is also required to pay for medical checkups and to furnish the union with annual statistics on the incidence of disease and death among the workers.

Another subject of union concern is the control of excessive noise in the workplace. The UAW introduced this issue into its contract negotiations in July 1976. The union had found that 20 percent of a random sample of workers had suffered severe hearing loss and that 60 percent had a measurable hearing impairment. It was further suspected that noise could be a co-causative factor in diseases associated with toxic materials, that it reduced visual acuity, and that it was responsible for accidents as well as shoddy workmanship. The United Steel Workers of America, the United Rubber Workers, and the Boilermakers Union have also expressed concern over the hazards of occupational noise.

Unions are also getting involved in other job-related health hazards. Examples are the concerns of the International Association of Machinists over the control of dermatitis, and the actions of the unions in the roofing, paint, textiles, printing press, typography, oil, chemicals, paper, steel, automobile, and atomic energy fields in setting up scientific studies and surveillance systems to detect cancers and other diseases attributed to occupational hazards. Contract negotiations have also been developed by the United Paperworkers International union to make the company medical records available to the union in order to determine the extent of the problem of asbestos. For instance, the high incidence of lung cancer among asbestos workers has been attributed to the fibers in the materials to which they are exposed.

Going beyond the workplace to environmental hazards in the community at large, the stance of the unions might be described as "hands off." Not infrequently, where steps are contemplated the purposes of which are to eradicate actual or suspected health hazards from the environment, workers display concern over job layoffs, plant shutdowns, or complete job loss, and frequently stand along with management in opposition to proposed corrective measures.

In a study made for the Ford Foundation, Nicholas Ashfort, at the Massachusetts Institute of Technology, recognized the concern of workers over the loss of jobs that can ensue when their companies try to comply with environmental protection demands. Many workers fear that environmental controls will force their companies to lay them off, to shut down the plant while corrective steps are being taken, or to relocate the plant to another area. Here, Dr. Ashfort takes the position that workers are operating under a false assumption and that, in fact, more jobs may be created. He points to the fact that when it was discovered that polyvinyl chloride caused liver cancer it was contended that banning the use of the chemical would cost 500,000 jobs. Ashfort says:

> In fact, Goodrich designed a whole new technólogy . . . and throughout the country less than a hundred people lost their jobs. And the price of polyvinyl chloride rose by just 3 percent. . . . Environmental compliance is not the kind of financial ogre that it is alleged to be.

The same unfounded fear on the part of workers of job loss through plant shutdowns as a direct result of the ecology movement or of environmental health and safety improvements was noted by Stellman and Daum in their book. But these authors write that "those plants which were shutting down were marginal (unproductive) operations" and that "according to the latest federal data, unemployment due to pollution control numbered fewer than 1,500 people in all."

The fact is, however, that the health and welfare of people is too basic and important a matter to be endangered by partisan disputes. What is called for is statesmanship on the part of both sides out of a recognition that this is quite clearly to the mutual interest of labor and management. It might also be recognized that an industrial health program presents a rather clear avenue through which antagonisms can be put aside and through which a cooperative approach can be developed. It simply must be willed.

In summary, it is perhaps fair to say that the labor unions, while vastly interested in occupational health and safety, and while they have supported many types of legislation which have benefited their members as well as other workers, could do much more to improve the occupational health and safety of workers as well as the nonoccupational aspects of such health and safety. Whether or not the approach should be through collective bargaining is perhaps a question, unless no other avenues are open. Most certainly an industrial health program which is cooperatively conceived by management and labor can be the most productive form of such programs. The result could be of very considerable help to the troubled employee.

Relationship to Small Employers

The problems of small employers in relation to the health of their employees—both troubled and untroubled—were discussed in the preceding chapter. Where unions are involved, they can play a considerable role in relieving this problem both through the provision of insurance coverages for the treatment of mental disorders and through the actual provision of care for the troubled employee. Many of the multiemployer programs discussed earlier are the domain of the smaller employer. It is probably safe to say, however, that with relatively few exceptions, the unions do not do all that they could to relieve this problem.

A good example of what can be done within labor union circles has been described by Gerald R. Waters, Sr., of the New York City Central Labor Council. The Council is composed of some 600 local unions in the New York area, with a combined membership of 1,475,000 workers who, with their families, comprise a group of some 4 million people. In 1963 the Council, initially with a grant of federal funds, formed the Central Labor Rehabilitation Council of New York with a staff made up of a psychiatric social worker, a public health nurse, a vocational guidance counselor, and a job developer, as well as medical and psychiatric consultants.

The purpose of the staff was to interview workers and their families who had problems, to counsel them and, where necessary, to refer them for treatment. No charges were made for the services. By 1968, 3,261 referrals had been made, 21 percent of which involved alcoholism, drug abuse, and crime or delinquency. One-third of all referrals were spouses, children, or retirees. Today the program is supported by annual contributions from 365 local unions and three community agencies and the case load approaches 10,000 persons.

The Council is an attempt to create a greater awareness of the

problem of the troubled employee among unions, to help union
counselors identify the signs of the troubled employee, to reduce
many of the problems and grievances which exacerbate a situation, to
bring about the early detection of the troubled employee, and to
strengthen labor–management relationships to their mutual advantage. The program recognizes a present weakness in not adequately
following up the troubled individual after counseling and treatment
have taken place.

BIBLIOGRAPHY

AFL-CIO. *The Worker's Stake in Mental Health.* Publication No. 69, April 1961.
American Labor Health Association. *The Physician and Labor Health Plans.* New York:
    undated.
American Medical Association. *A Survey of Union Health Centers.* Chicago: 1958.
————. *Guides for Evaluation of Management and Union Health Centers.* Chicago: 1958.
Ashfort, Nicholas A. *Crisis in the Workplace: Occupational Disease and Injury.* Cambridge,
    Mass.: M.I.T. Press, 1976.
Carone, Pasquale A. (ed.). *The Emotionally Troubled Employee.* Albany: State University
    of New York Press, 1976.
Collison, N. H. "Management and an Occupational Health Program." *Archives of
    Environmental Health,* February, 1961.
The Conference Board. *Industry Roles in Health Care.* New York: 1974.
Follmann, J. F., Jr. *Alcoholics and Business.* New York: AMACOM, 1976.
————. *The Economics of Industrial Health.* New York: AMACOM, 1978.
Glasser, Melvin A., et al. "Prepaid Psychiatric Care Experience with UAW Members."
    American Journal of Psychiatry, November 1969.
————. "Worker's Health." *American Journal of Public Health,* June 1976.
Kerr, Lorin E. "An American Labor Health Program." *Gyldendal Norsk Forlag,* 1962.
————. "A Labor Health Program." *Physical Therapy Review,* November 1960.
Lavalette, David A. "Medical Relationships with Unions and Management." Presented
    before the American Medical Association, September 21, 1976.
McLean, Alan A. (ed.). *To Work Is Human.* New York: The Macmillan Company, 1967.
Michigan Blue Shield. *Research Report.* Detroit: January 1971.
Munts, Raymond. *Bargaining for Health.* Madison: University of Wisconsin Press, 1967.
National Health Council. *The Health of People Who Work.* New York: 1960.
National Institute of Labor Education. *Issues in the New National Mental Health Program
    Relating to Labor and Low Income Groups.* Washington, D.C.: June 1963.
————. *New Approaches to Mental Health Treatment for Labor and Low Income Groups.*
    Washington, D.C.: February 1964.
National Institutes of Rehabilitation and Health Services. *Till We Have Built Jerusalem.*
    Washington, D.C.: 1965.
Perlis, Leo. "The Human Contract in the Workplace." *United Rubber Worker,* April
    1976.
————. *Labor Approach to Mental Health in Industry.* Washington, D.C.: AFL-CIO, March
    25, 1961.
————. *Leisure-Opportunity for Public Service.* Washington, D.C.: AFL-CIO, March 24,
    1961.
————. *Workers Have Emotions.* Washington, D.C.: AFL-CIO, May 3, 1955.

Pollack, Jerome. "The Union Health Movement as Voluntarism." *New York Academy of Medicine,* April 27, 1961.

Reuther, Walter P. "The Worker and His Mental Health." Washington, D.C.: American Psychiatric Association, February 20, 1965.

Samuels, Sheldon W. Presented before the New York Academy of Medicine, May 31, 1972.

Sawyer, William A. *Role of Organized Labor in Occupational Health.* New York: National Health Council, 1960.

Shain, Max. *Survey of the Union Health Center and Hospital Benefit Program.* Ann Arbor: School of Public Health, University of Michigan, December 1967.

Sidney Hillman Health Center of New York. *Helping Blue-Collar Workers in Trouble.* New York: September 1967.

Simons, John H. *The Union Approach to Health and Welfare.* Institute of Industrial Relations, University of California, Reprint No. 259. Berkeley: 1965.

Stellman, Jeanne M., and Susan M. Daum. *Work Is Dangerous to Your Health.* New York: Vintage Press, 1976.

UMWA Welfare and Retirement Fund. *Annual Reports.* Washington, D.C.

U.S. Department of Health, Education, and Welfare. "Health Benefits for Laid-off Workers." *Social Security Bulletin,* 1976.

―――. *Management and Union Health and Medical Programs,* 1953.

U.S. Department of Labor. *Administration of Negotiated Pension, Health and Insurance Plans.* Bulletin 1425-12. May 1970.

Weiner, Hyman J., et al. *Mental Health Care in the World of Work.* New York: Association Press, 1973.

14

THE INDUSTRIAL
HEALTH PROGRAM

WHAT can the place of employment—the office, factory, school—do to help its troubled employees? In Chapter 16 you will find a discussion of the role of the individual, the family, the personal physician, and the clergy in helping others find the various sources of help and guidance currently available. This chapter covers the very important role that can be played by employers and labor unions, preferably functioning cooperatively, to help the psychiatrically or emotionally disturbed employee.

Why Set Up a Program?

Today an increasing number of employers are establishing programs for troubled employees which are turning out to be of considerable value to employees and their families, as well as to employers. In some instances, these special units have grown out of programs established to help alcoholic employees. The possibilities for programs set up for troubled employees can be almost limitless if they are properly executed and fully exploited. Experience has proved that it is not enough for the place of employment to attempt to avoid the onset of some mental disorders through such means as thoughtful job placement and adequate job training, preparation of the employee for job adjustments and transfer, and the elimination of any working conditions that are stressful to employees. In addition, employers should take the responsibility for the early identification of mental, emotional, or personality disorders.

A successful program not only saves employees from considerable anguish and suffering, unemployment, and bankruptcy, but can pay dividends to the workplace through reduced absenteeism and labor turnover, improved morale and efficiency, savings on insurance and employee benefit costs, and increased production.

In coming to grips with the problem, and setting up a special program to handle it, management and the designers of the program must become informed about mental disorders, their types, their various probable causes, and their signs and symptoms. They must become aware that employees have many types of problems and that some people have great difficulty in surmounting them. Problems range from family or financial difficulties, to many types of job-related grievances, to a general sense of insecurity. Left unresolved, the consequences can be anxiety, nervousness, dissatisfaction with the job, overzealousness about the job, deteriorating job performance, accident proneness, and physical ailments. In setting up a program to help these employees, it must be recognized that people are different, have differing emotional makeups, and display different degrees of adaptability to situations. Because people, like machines, can break down, there must be a basic appreciation of, and sympathy for, the problems besetting the troubled employee.

It also must be recognized that today's workers are at a much higher educational level and are more affluent than was true of prior generations. As employees, they expect to derive satisfaction from their work and an opportunity to develop skills and abilities. They resist monotonous routine more frequently than was the case at one time. They are more mobile, restless, and changeable. Their sense of what they are entitled to assumes a broadening horizon. Today's employees have a changed attitude toward authority and increasingly insist in having a voice in matters that concern them. They evidence a decline of confidence, or even mistrust, in many established institutions, including big business. A consequence of this is that today there are new concepts developing within the workforce in all industrialized nations. Some of the recent demands of organized labor in the United

States, discussed in the preceding chapter, exemplify these broad-ened concepts.

More and more, employees are demanding that they be included in the planning phase of their production systems, in the organization of the work processes, in experimentation with variations in work hours, in the elimination of unsafe and stressful working conditions, and in the organization of the chain of authority. In essence, what we are experiencing is a demand for increased democracy in the deci-sion-making process. Overall, the aim is to humanize the work process.

Before discussing this role of the industrial health program fur-ther, let us take a brief look at the development and at the general concepts of industrial health programs in this country.

Changing Concepts

As was shown in Chapter 12, the basic and original concept of industrial medicine was essentially limited to coping with occupational accidents and diseases, coinciding somewhat with the enactment of workmen's compensation laws. An expanded concept of such pro-grams has been developing in more recent years. However, there is increasing concern over nonoccupational hazards that affect the health and well-being of employed people. Recognizing that it is diffi-cult, if not impossible, to dissociate the effects of occupational hazards from nonoccupational ones on such matters as absenteeism, disability, and insurance costs, employers are increasingly broadening the scope of their medical programs to examine possible nonoccupational caus-ative factors.

This newer, exceedingly broader concept of industrial health programs is reflected in the fact that places of employment, both private and public, are increasingly being called upon to employ the socially, economically, and educationally disadvantaged, as well as the physically handicapped. This development, given impetus by the Equal Employment Opportunity Act, places new, and at times diffi-cult, demands on employers. It means that more and more, organiza-tions and businesses of all types will be employing people who have a relatively low level of health care awareness. It means that there will be increasing numbers of employees who have a backlog of unmet medical needs. The new industrial health program must make an effort to become familiar with different ethnic cultures and subcul-tures, and must take a different approach to on-the-job education and training and to the development of an awareness of the value of good health.

This broadened concept of an industrial health program has already been recognized by management in some places of employment. Dr. John Foulger of E. I. Du Pont de Nemours has said: "Management must be concerned with the total health—there is no such thing as occupational and nonoccupational health—industrial medicine has the greatest potential for supervising total health."

Dr. G. H. Collings, Jr., of the New York Telephone Company, recently stated:

> We, in occupational or industrial medicine, are involved with and to some degree responsible for the health of large semi-captive populations. In addition, our companies pay hundreds of millions of dollars annually to protect the worker against adverse health effects on the job and to purchase medical care for employees and their families. We are, therefore, likely to visualize health care in its broadest connotations as it affects such populations.

He then notes such in-house supplements to primary health care as the health education of employees, early diagnosis in the form of periodic health inventories or multiphasic screening programs, and general health counseling to employees.

Unquestionably there is no unanimity in these broader concepts of industrial health programs, yet they continue to receive more general acceptance. In any instance, it is increasingly recognized today that industrial health programs are primarily engaged in preventive medicine. This is made evident by a 1960 definition of occupational and industrial health by the American Medical Association:

> A program that embraces the principles of preventive medical care as provided by management to deal constructively with the health and safety of employees in accordance with their work environment and job description.

Industrial health programs have two distinct and unique aspects that can be brought into play: (1) They are concerned with gainfully employed adults in their productive years, and (2) they function in a controlled setting, one that permits observation on a continuing basis and that can influence individuals or groups in ways that are usually not possible in less structured settings. Recognizing this, Dr. George James has said: "American industrial plants represent a natural point of first contact with the health care system for the employed population. A health center at the workplace would have a very high potential for being used as the multipurpose primary care center for emphasizing health promotion and preventive medicine." Similarly, Dr. William Jend, Jr., of the Michigan Bell Telephone Company, has said:

> The only concerted, planned, large-scale, personal, adult health mainte-
> nance programs in this country today are in the occupational health
> programs of American industry. The workplace is probably the ideal
> locale to practice real preventive medicine on a wide and effective scale.

The Contribution of the Health Team

The responsibilities of the physician in an industrial health program generally include the diagnosis and treatment of occupational injuries and illnesses in addition to the treatment of minor nonoccupational illnesses and injuries. The employee who needs more extensive treatment is counseled and referred to a personal physician or to a community health agency. Where preemployment, periodic, or special-purpose health examinations are involved, these are conducted by the physician or by the staff under his or her direction. The physician can provide counsel to management, personnel directors, and supervisors, with respect to job placement, job transfer, the employment of handicapped persons, and early retirement based on the health status of the individual employee. In instances where certain health- or safety-related responsibilities cross multidepartmental lines, the physician often works cooperatively with the personnel department, supervisors, the safety program, and the industrial hygiene department.

The physician should also be responsible for the general health education and counseling of employees as respects both occupational and nonoccupational health hazards. Not only can such efforts have a positive effect on the health of employees and their families, but they make clear to employees that management is concerned with, and interested in, their health and safety. Many health education programs emphasize lifestyles for healthful living, and help employees become actively aware of the importance of such matters as weight control and diet, exercise and rest, and the avoidance of excessive smoking or the abuse of alcoholic beverages.

The medical director should participate in plant inspection tours in an effort to identify hazards to the health and safety of the employees. The industrial physician should also be responsible for maintaining and studying the health records of individual employees. Such records not only document the onset of physical or emotional disorders, but can serve to pinpoint occupational health hazards not otherwise identified.

Today such recordkeeping is required by OSHA, and government inspectors have access to the files on demand. Under OSHA, employee representatives have the right to review the health records at any time. Therefore, adequate health records are now a requirement of business operations. But a sound system of health records should not be confined to OSHA requirements alone, since they can furnish valuable information about many nonoccupational health hazards.

The physician in the industrial health field is supported by a nurse who has special education and training in industrial health. He or she should have a general knowledge of occupational health hazards, of workmen's compensation laws and OSHA, of health resources available in the community, of health education techniques, and of all aspects of preventive medicine.

Industrial health nurses work under the orders of the physician. They can administer first aid and certain forms of treatment, and can assist in conducting health examinations. They can contribute to the preparation of health and safety reports and the maintenance of health records. Industrial health nurses can be of considerable help in providing health educational information and health counseling, assisting handicapped workers, and visiting disabled employees in their homes. Nurses should be alert at all times to the signs and symptoms that identify mentally ill or emotionally disturbed employees. They should also have working relationships with all other departments of the place of employment, particularly those concerned with personnel and safety, and should participate in all periodic inspection tours organized to detect health hazards in the plant.

Because there are increasing numbers of industrial health programs, many are branching out into areas that are specifically useful to the subject of our study—the troubled employee. Many programs now include psychiatrists, psychologists, psychiatric nurses, and social workers, either as full-time staff, or on a consulting basis. Where such a program does not exist, those responsible for personnel can tap other resources, by establishing contact with psychiatrists in private practice, local hospitals, community mental health centers, or other available psychiatric clinics or centers.

Dr. Alan A. McLean of IBM and Harry Levinson of the Menninger Foundation are among those who have written extensively on the role of psychiatric professionals involved in industrial health programs in the workplace. Recognizing the need for early recognition of the onset of symptoms, many writers on the subject feel that the company dispensary or the community source of outpatient care can be beneficial for most troubled employees after just a brief period of therapy. On the other hand, it is felt that prolonged treatment is not feasible in an occupational setting. Here it is recognized that a substantial number of troubled employees have well-established patterns of personality disorders, but that relatively few have major incapacitating disorders.

Recognition and treatment of mental disorders. The onset of mental disorders may be detected by any of several sources. It may become apparent to the occupational physician or nurse in the course of an employee's visits to the dispensary or as a result of certain findings in a physical examination. Similarly, telltale changes in behavior may be detected by the manager, the personnel department, or the supervisor or shop steward at the place of employment, by the person's family, or even by troubled employees themselves.

It is the job of the psychiatrist to train the supervisors and shop stewards at the place of employment as to what signs and symptoms point to the onset of mental disorders. Alert to such signs as undue absenteeism, deterioration in the level of work, performance, job dissatisfaction, low morale, unusual anxiety and nervousness, carelessness and unnecessary risk-taking, memory loss, faulty decision making, unusual emotional reactions, changes in behavior patterns, suspiciousness and friction with other employees, or unexplainable physical ailments, the trained supervisor or shop steward can sit down with the troubled employee and present him or her with the facts as observed, but with warmth, friendliness, compassion, and patient listening.

In cases where it is warranted, the troubled employee may be referred to a psychiatrist for counseling, diagnosis of the problem and, if necessary, referral for treatment. The supervisor or shop steward should also be trained in working constructively with the troubled employee after treatment has been completed. (See the section on Making the Program Work for more about what the first-line supervisor can do.)

It is also the responsibility of the psychiatrist to provide emotional first aid for troubled employees and, where warranted, to refer them to an appropriate source of treatment in the community. Not infrequently, the troubled employee evades or resists the suggestion of treatment. The psychiatrist must then firmly present the employee with the alternatives—treatment or job jeopardy. Once treatment has taken place, the psychiatrist is called into play in the rehabilitative process, perhaps to recommend a restructuring of the job or a change to another type of job or work situation for the employee.

The role in prevention. Industrial health psychiatrists can also do much to prevent the onset of mental disorders. They can counsel employees in such matters as their personal problems, job changes or transfers, career changes and job advancements, the effects of aging, and shifts in management responsibilities, and can even counsel the family where transfer is anticipated to a foreign country. Another area in which the psychiatrist can participate is in the review of both the prospective employees to determine the applicant's qualities in relation to the demands of the prospective job, and in a review of any history of mental disorders in order to determine the person's fitness for the job.

A further responsibility of the psychiatrist should be that of providing mental health education to management, personnel departments, employees, and supervisors on the one hand, and to the employees on the other. The purpose should be to increase the awareness of mental disorders and to overcome popularly held misimpressions and stigmas surrounding mental illness.

Another important preventive concern of the psychiatrist in the industrial health field should be to identify hazards in the workplace that could trigger or exacerbate mental problems, including both physical factors and stressful situations. Here a study of employee health records can be most informative. In addition, the psychiatrist might counsel management on ways to create a more mentally healthy climate in the workplace, including such matters as incentives, greater job satisfaction, and the encouragement of initiative, as well as such matters as rest periods and vacations.

Making the Program Work

As in any industrial health program, a program geared toward the needs of the troubled employee must have the full and active support of top management. Management must be convinced of the importance of the program out of both humane and economic considerations. It is up to management to give the program a sense of vision and vitality. It is management's responsibility to appoint personnel to administer the program and to provide the necessary staff and facilities. The entire operation should be guided by a written statement of policy so that there will be no doubt in anyone's mind about what is being done and why it is being done. It also attests to management's interest in the health and well-being of its employees. Where union labor is involved, management should make every effort to gain the full cooperation of the union through joint planning, drawing up of a policy statement, and administration of the program.

Leo Perlis of the AFL-CIO aptly stated recently:

> Both labor and management now realize that personal problems can and often do result in absenteeism, turnover, low labor morale, reduced productivity, and curtailed production. But not all are aware that they must address themselves to the human causes. . . . A cooperative and positive approach to the alleviation of personal and family problems . . . can be spelled out in a supplementary agreement.

Beyond these considerations, the program should be applicable to all employees, at whatever level, on a nondiscriminatory basis. Except where otherwise prescribed by law, the health records of all employees should be confidential to the medical director as a professional matter. Employees should be assured of this; otherwise, employees with mental or emotional problems will have no confidence in the intent of the program, fearing that their job status or even their employability will be jeopardized.

To be workable, such a program must provide for the adequate training of supervisors and shop stewards in the early identification of the signs of impending mental, emotional, or personality disorders. Obviously, they are not expected, or equipped, to make a diagnosis, but through daily observation they can become aware of impaired work functioning, undue absenteeism, accident proneness, tenseness, changed or unusual behavioral patterns, or friction with other employees. To be observed are the work performance and the functional effectiveness of the worker, his or her competence, sense of well-being, and job satisfaction. It is also important to develop an awareness of such highly personal matters as marital or family troubles or the accumulation of debts.

Once the supervisor or shop steward suspects that a mental problem exists, referral should be made to the medical staff for consultation and diagnosis. The employee should then be informed of the professional opinion and, to the degree warranted, referred for care. Subsequent progress evaluation and follow-up should then be made, and should continue after the employee has returned to work. Every effort should be made to help the employee in the rehabilitation process, including the possibility of limited duty or responsibility for a time, or even a change of job assignment.

Is It Cost Effective?

Management has a perfect right to ask about the cost effectiveness of industrial health efforts. Unfortunately there is no ready answer. Extant studies are quite scattered and fragmentary. Economists fail to agree on which factors should be included in any such computations. Furthermore, as was shown in Chapter 8, certain costs of illness and injury, including the development of mental disorders, are not measurable on the basis of presently known techniques.

While economic approaches to the value of health have been apparent since the work of Sir William Petty in the late seventeenth century, of Adam Smith a century later, and of Edwin Chadwick in 1842 and Gary Calkins in the 1880s, not very much is known of the cost effectiveness of today's industrial health programs. Practically nothing is known with respect to programs designed to help the troubled employee, with the exception of those set up to help people suffering from alcoholism.

Handicaps to Collecting the Data

Among the many problems in collecting data on the cost effectiveness of industrial health programs are the methodological difficulties of evaluation, deciding which factors should be included and which excluded, placing values on each factor, and retrieving the data prior to the inception of the program, for comparative purposes. Statistical gathering is a costly endeavor, and choices must be made as to the relative value of data gathered in relation to such costs.

A further problem concerns the collection of comparative data once a statistical process has been established, since many factors are subject to change with time: the industrial processes; materials and equipment used; plant design and layout; the makeup of the workforce by such factors as age, sex, and education level; the amount of overtime work; and the details of union contracts. Finally, it is difficult to make a meaningful comparison of the findings in one plant with those of a similar type of plant. No two places of employment at present maintain comparable statistics, using the same parameters—if they have any at all.

It should also be noted that an industrial health program involves many elements of cost other than those incurred by the medical department. The data must include the cost of time spent by executives, personnel staff, and supervisors; fees charged by outside engineers, chemists, architects, and specialized consultants; new safety devices and equipment, restructured plant layout, provision for adequate ventilation and lighting, and of substituted processes, equipment, or materials; training workers; health education; health and disability insurance and salary continuance programs; and workers' time off for medical department consultation.

In 1972 the Conference Board solicited the views of business executives on the subject. Several executives spoke of the cost benefits of a strong preventive medical and health maintenance program. They expressed the view that in-plant health facilities can minimize the work time lost for minor medical attention, can provide prompt attention in the case of health problems of a serious nature, and can retain maximum control over such problems as malingering, unnecessary treatment, absenteeism, and the level of medical fees. The general view was that an expansion of in-house medical services in many situations is a more effective and less costly solution than relying primarily on outside services.

Despite these comments, a study made by the Conference Board two years later indicated that industry had made little effort to validate the cost-benefit assumptions behind in-house employee health care programs, or even to test them against the traditional standards of accountability used by management. The study showed that three out of four employers had made no attempt to evaluate the effectiveness of their nonoccupational care programs. Of those who had made such an effort, a few mentioned attempts at cost-benefit analysis. Some employers reported statistical analyses that had verified definite benefits, but without any relation to the costs. Several employers reported that their workforce was unquestionably healthier since the inception of their industrial health programs. They cited a marked reduction in loss of time and in absenteeism, as well as increased productivity as positive signs. Other employers reported that evaluations were either planned or pending. The inadequacy of cost-benefit evaluation was laid to such matters as (1) the difficulty in conducting the research, particularly on a comparative basis with conditions before the program was established; (2) the problem of determining short-term gains in comparison with long-term gains, and relating these to changing health conditions unrelated to the industrial health program; (3) some ambiguity concerning the aims of the program; and (4) the reaction that an industrial health program includes compassionate goals as well as profitability.

Yet a survey conducted by the National Association of Manufacturers found that of 1,625 industrial health programs, all but five considered their programs "paying propositions." More than 90 percent of the employers included in the survey reported a reduction in accident frequency, in the incidence of occupational diseases, in absenteeism, and in insurance premiums. Labor turnover, on the average, dropped 27.3 percent; absenteeism declined 29.7 percent; and workmen's compensation premiums dropped 28.8 percent.

What the Records Show

Experiences Among Larger Companies. Following are a few examples of the cost effectiveness of specific industrial health programs at some of the larger places of employment. The details of these statistics are discussed in greater depth in a recently published book, *The Economics of Industrial Health.*

Socony–Vacuum Oil Company, East River plant: In 1949 it was reported that as a result of its in-plant medical department, established in 1946, there had been a substantial decrease in working days lost among its 1,500 employees and in the amount of sickness benefits paid. Disability payments decreased from $115,726 in 1946 to $66,-565 in 1949. Work days lost as a result of nonoccupational illness decreased from 10,466 in 1947 to 5,435 in 1949.

Denver Federal Center: In 1960 a health service for the 3,425 federal employees at the Center cost $38,000 a year. During its first year of operation, sick leaves declined by more than 20,000 hours, producing a saving of $32,800 in that one area alone. By contrast, for federal employees not covered by the program, sick leave at that same time increased 13 percent.

Olin Corporation: In 1961, a program that was described by Norman Collison reduced workmen's compensation costs alone by $28,000 a year. It also reduced labor turnover, absenteeism, and time lost due to accidents. At the company's North Carolina plant, with 2,400 employees, an industrial health program was established in 1950. By 1959, workmen's compensation claims were half the rate for all other places of employment in North Carolina, health insurance claims were reduced 30 percent, absenteeism was reduced 10 percent, and the rate of labor turnover was half the national average. In addition, lost-time accident cases declined from 60 per year to 9 (1 in

1954), days lost from accidents declined from 7,000 a year to 4,800; accident frequency dropped from 18 to 3; and the accident severity rate dropped from 2,000 to 1,400 (none in 1954). (The reason for the especially good record in 1954 was not explained.)

Mountain States Telephone Company: With 27,000 employees in 1967, the following results took place concerning the cost effectiveness of the program, which had been instituted at the end of 1963. Over the five years preceding the program's inception, sickness disability benefits paid by the company for nonoccupational illnesses and injuries averaged $20.73 per $1,000 of payroll. In the four years following the establishment of the program average payments dropped to $17.79. Total days of absence due to sickness per employee per year dropped from 10.03 to 5.92, representing more than a 40 percent decrease. The dollar saving for 1967 for nonoccupational disability benefits was $894,999. For job-related injuries, for which the company pays disability benefits usually higher than those required by workmen's compensation, as well as complete medical care, the cost per year dropped from 86¢ per $1,000 of payroll to 61¢, a decrease of 25 percent, producing an estimated saving of $169,839 from the period 1964–1967. Savings in sickness-absence payments for the years 1964–1967 were estimated at $2,329,811. The cost effectiveness of the fitness examinations for employees whose work performance reflected a health condition, such as mental disorders or alcoholism, was not evaluated. It was recognized that other factors, such as improved job design, increased attention by supervisors, and an improved safety program, could have a bearing on the results shown.

The Norton Company, Worcester, Mass.: According to Dr. Karl T. Benedict, the company found that its industrial health program, introduced in 1911 but considerably expanded since that time, has reduced its disability rate to the point where it is only 40 percent of the national average. The services provided for its 4,500 employees include, beyond the usual physical examination, special surveys to determine the levels of dust, chemicals, and radiation.

Supreme Aluminum Industries, Ltd., Scarborough, Canada: Safety committees of workers and management were established in 1975. In one year the number of lost-time accidents and the number of working days lost as a result of accidents decreased more than two-thirds, according to the *Atlas World Press Review.* The company estimated that it saved more than $200,000 in indirect costs. When the 5-day 40-hour work week was reduced to a 4-day 36-hour week in 1972, production at the company increased by 12 percent.

Experiences Among Smaller Companies. Here are some of the cost benefits found among small places of employment.

One small firm provided part-time nursing services to its employees at a yearly cost of $1,000. The first year, workmen's compensation losses were reduced by $4,700.

A company with 300 employees established an industrial health program. The result was a 61 percent decrease in workmen's compensation costs.

A heavy foundry with 200 employees, which had had a yearly accident frequency rate of considerable severity, established an industrial health program in 1947. By 1950 the accident rate at the plant was zero.

A plant with 115 employees installed a dispensary and thereby reduced labor turnover by 25 percent.

In a plant with 160 employees, workmen's compensation claims were reduced by $4,500 during the first year of operation of an industrial health program. The cost of the medical department was $1,200.

In 1946 the *Allen Manufacturing Company* joined the Hartford Small Plant Medical Service, a cooperative effort for making industrial health services available. During the next six years, labor turnover at the plant was reduced 87 percent, workmen's compensation premiums were reduced 24 percent, and the incidence of occupational accidents dropped to zero.

At a plant with 115 employees, direct savings from absenteeism alone were more than double the cost of its industrial health program.

A plant with 175 employees employed a nurse. In one year there was a 52 percent reduction in lost-time accident frequency and an 82 percent reduction in lost-time accident severity.

Although many of the gains reported, such as reductions in labor turnover and absenteeism, improved employee morale, and increased efficiency and production, are not equated in dollars, their economic value to the workplace is readily apparent.

Unfortunately, there is practically no information on the cost-effectiveness of programs set up to help the troubled employee. One reason for this is that such information becomes a part of any data on the cost-effectiveness of the industrial health program as a whole. Another reason is that attempts to help the troubled employee are for the most part relatively recent, not permitting sufficient time for the accumulation and study of specific data on this aspect of an industrial health program. There is, however, some information available with respect to one aspect of attempts to help the troubled employee: the cost-effectiveness of alcoholism control programs. One reason for this is the encouragement and assistance provided by organizations such as the National Council on Alcoholism and the National Institute on Alcohol Abuse and Alcoholism. The following is a brief condensation of some of the findings at various types of places of employment, the details of which are contained in the book *Alcoholics and Business.*

Scovill Manufacturing Company, which had 27,000 employees in 1973, reports a 78 percent recovery rate. This translates into an estimated savings of $186,550 annually, after an average cost of $1,100 per alcoholic employee for treatment and rehabilitation has been deducted.

Illinois Bell Telephone Company, with 45,000 employees, has experienced a recovery rate of 72 percent of the identified alcoholic cases. While the savings that resulted from reduced overtime pay, employee turnover, premature deaths, and insured medical costs, as well as increased production, were not rigorously evaluated, it was found that sickness disability cases lasting more than 7 days dropped from 662 in the 5 years before the program was started to 356 in the following 5 years. This produced a saving of $459,000. In the same time period, off-the-job accidents declined 66 percent, and job accidents decreased 80 percent.

At the Pontiac Division of *General Motors,* the alcoholism control program saved $9,878 on disability insurance benefits and 10,850 hours lost from work each year on 25 alcoholic employees alone. At the Oldsmobile Division, the program experienced a 49 percent decrease in lost man-hours, a 29 percent decrease in disability insurance benefits, and a 56 percent decrease in leaves of absence among 117 workers.

Allis-Chalmers Corporation has experienced, as a result of its alcoholism control program, an estimated saving of $80,000 a year.

McDonnell Douglas Corporation saved $3 million over a 4-year period in lost productivity alone, thanks to its alcoholism control program.

The New York Transit Authority saves $2 million a year. Cost of the program: $130,000 a year.

The *Federal Civilian Employees* program has projected a saving of $1.25 billion over a 5-year period; or a saving of $17 for every $1 spent on the alcoholism control program.

The *U.S. Postal Service,* experiencing a 75 percent recovery rate through its program, estimates a potential net saving of $1,864,000 over and above the costs of the alcoholism control program.

An unidentified manufacturing company reports an annual saving of $100,650 against a cost of $11,400 for its alcoholism control program.

These examples of the cost-effectiveness of industrial health programs unfortunately are not comparable to one another, nor are they complete evaluations of either the costs of the programs or of their economic effectiveness. They leave one wanting to know considerably more than is shown. Nonetheless, they do make it reasonably clear that industrial health programs are cost-effective from a solely economic point of view.

BIBLIOGRAPHY

American Labor Health Association. *National Conference on Labor Health Services.* New York: 1958.

American Medical Association. "Scope, Objectives, and Functions of Occupational Health Programs." Chicago: December 1971.

American Psychiatric Association. "Troubled People on the Job." Washington, D.C.: 1959.

Ashfort, Nicholas A. *Crisis in the Work Place: Occupational Disease and Injury.* Cambridge, Mass.: M.I.T. Press, 1976.

Atlas World Press Review. *Humanizing Work.* June 1977.

Benedict, Karl T. "Industrial Health Protection." *National Safety News,* June 1975.

Cohen, Steven R. "Another Look at the In-Plant Occupational Health Program." *Journal of Occupational Medicine,* November 1953.

Collings, G. H. "What Is Primary Care—An Occupational Health Perspective." Presented before the New York Academy of Medicine, April 22, 1976.

Collison, Norman. "Management and an Occupational Health Program." *Environmental Health,* February 1961.

Colwell, Miles O. "The Balance Sheet in Employee Health Conservation." Presented before the Industrial Health Foundation, October 13, 1970.

The Conference Board. *Industry Roles in Health Care.* New York: 1974.

———. *Top Executives View Health Care Issues,* 1972.

Felton, Jean Spencer. "Organization and Operation of an Occupational Health Program." *Journal of Occupational Health,* June 25, 1965.

Follmann, J. F., Jr. *Alcoholics and Business.* New York: AMACOM, 1976.

———. *The Economics of Industrial Health.* New York: AMACOM, 1978.

Goldstein, David H. "The Changing Scope of Occupational Medicine and Environmental Health." *American Journal of Public Health,* April 1970.

Hoover, A. Walter. "The Future of Occupational Health Programs." *Journal of Occupational Medicine,* June 1973.

James, George. "The Teaching of Preventive Medicine and Paramedical Education." *Inquiry,* 8:1, 1970.

Jend, William, Jr. "Where Do We Want to Be in Occupational Medicine?" *Journal of Occupational Medicine,* July 1973.

Joselow, Morris M. "Occupational Health in the U.S.—The Next Decades." *American Journal of Public Health,* November 1973.

Klem, Margaret, et al. *Small Plant Health and Medical Programs.* Public Health Service Publication No. 215, 1952.

Levinson, Harry. "The Abrasive Personality at the Office." *Psychology Today,* May 1978.

———. *Emotional Health: In the World of Work.* New York: Harper & Row, 1964.

Manufacturing Chemists Association. *Air Pollution.* 1974.

McLean, Alan A. "Mental Health Programs in Industry," Chapter 53 of *American Handbook of Psychiatry.* New York: Basic Books, 1974.

———. "Occupational (Industrial) Psychiatry," Chapter 45 of *Comprehensive Textbook of Psychiatry.* Baltimore: Williams and Wilkins, 1975.

———. "Who Pays the Bill?" *Journal of Occupational Medicine,* May 1967.

Metropolitan Life Insurance Company. *Your Employee Health Program.* New York: undated.

———. *Health Education in Industry.* New York, undated.

National Health Council. *The Health of People Who Work.* New York: 1960.

Perlis, Leo. "De-Ciphering Workers." *The New York Times,* July 14, 1977.

———. "The Nature of Meaningful Work." Presented at the Conference on Ethics and Economics, University of Delaware, Newark, Delaware, November 10, 1977.

President's Report on Occupational Safety and Health. GPO Document No. 4000-00288, December 1973.

Renwick, Patricia A., et al. "What You Really Want from Your Job." *Psychology Today,* May 1978.

Robbins, David B., et al. "The Psychiatric Patient at Work." *American Journal of Public Health,* July 1976.

15

HOW MANAGEMENT AND UNIONS ARE HELPING

MORE and more employers are making provision for the diagnosis and treatment of mental, emotional, and personality disorders among employed people through their industrial health programs or arrangements for outside consultation. Labor unions are also increasingly making arrangements through their health centers. These programs have been set up in direct response to recognition of the fact that troubled employees are costly to their operations in a great many ways, and that there is much they can do about the problem in an organized effort. Industrial health programs, where such are in operation, have expanded their concerns to nonoccupational illnesses and accidents and to environmental hazards, are now developing concern for the troubled employee.

A 1958 survey by the U.S. Department of Health, Education, and Welfare, of 333 industrial establishments in the United States and Canada, showed that only nine of those establishments had a full-time psychiatrist or psychologist on their staff, that only eight had such professionals employed on a part-time basis, and that only 23 had such professionals on-call. Today, as has been shown, some 500 psychiatrists are employees of, or consultants to, industrial health programs.

What Employers Are Doing

The number of places of employment having established industrial health programs is not categorically known. Therefore, the number of places of employment having developed programs for the troubled employee is not known. That the concept, scope, and services provided by industrial health programs varies quite extensively goes without saying. Some are quite complete, others are relatively rudimentary. Some are limited to occupational hazards only.

The book *The Economics of Industrial Health* gives a partial listing of industrial health programs in places of employment that were operative in 1977 in 239 manufacturing plants of various types, 21 transportation companies, 33 utilities, 7 retailing establishments, 8 financial institutions, 19 insurance companies, and 9 communications sources. Since industrial health programs provide the initial point of contact with the troubled employee, this listing—although partial—is important.

Furthermore, as is shown in the book *Alcoholics and Business,* more than 600 places of employment have established alcoholism control programs, including those specifically listed in the book. These include 60 manufacturing plants, 14 transportation companies, 19 utilities, 4 financial institutions, 13 insurance companies, 15 governmental agencies, 2 universities, and 6 employers in communications, services, and retailing. The alcoholism control programs are important because they are obviously concerned with at least one aspect of the troubled employee.

The following is a listing of a number of organizations and institutions that have active programs set up to help the troubled employee, at least to some extent. Although the listing is by no means all-inclusive, it serves to illustrate the variety of employers involved.

AT&T
Allied Chemical Corp.
Allis-Chalmers Corp.
Aluminum Co. of America
American Can Co.
American Cyanamid Co.

American Fore Insurance Company
American Motors Corp.
Armco Steel Corp.
Armstead Industries, Inc.
Armstrong Cork Co.
Bell Telephone Laboratories, Inc.

Carnegie Corporation
Caterpillar Tractor Co.
Chase Manhattan Bank
Chrysler Corp.
Colgate-Palmolive Co.
Combustion Engineering Inc.
Corn Products
Crown-Zellerbach Corp.
Detroit Edison Co.
Diamond Crystal Salt Co.
Dow Chemical Co.
Eastman Kodak Co.
E. I. du Pont de Nemours and
  Company
Electric Storage Battery Co.
Eltra Corp.
Equitable Life Assurance Society of
  the United States
Ex-Cell-O Corp.
Federal Civilian Employees
Federal Electric Corp.
Federal-Mogul
First National City Bank
Fluor Corp.
Ford Motor Co.
General Dynamics Corp.
General Electric Co.
General Motors Corp.
General Telephone & Electronics
  Corporation
Goodyear Tire & Rubber Co.
Gulf & Western Industries, Inc.
Hercules Incorporated
IBM
Illinois Bell Telephone Co.
Insurance Co. of North America
Ionac Chemical Co.
IT&T
Johns-Manville Product Corp.
Johnson & Johnson
Johnson-Carper Furniture Company
  Inc.
Jones & Laughlin Steel Corp.
Kennecott Copper Corp.
Lane Bryant, Inc.
Lever Brothers Co.
Magee Carpet Co.
Marine Midland Grace Trust
  Company of New York

McDonnell Douglas Corp.
McGraw-Hill Book Co., Inc.
Metropolitan Life Insurance Co.
Minnesota Mining & Mfg. Co.
Morgan Guaranty Trust Co. of New
  York
Mountain States Telephone &
  Telegraph Co.
New Holland Machine Co., Ltd.
The New York Telephone Co.
The New York Times Company
The New York Transit Authority
Northern Electric Co., Ltd.
Olin Corp.
Pacific Telephone & Telegraph Co.
Pan American World Airways, Inc.
Paramount Pictures Corp.
Parker Pen Co.
Phillips Petroleum Co.
Polaroid Corp.
Procter and Gamble Co.
St. Joseph Lead Co.
Scovill Mfg. Co.
Shell Oil Company
Sinclair Oil Corporation
Smith, Kline & French
Socony Mobile Oil Co., Inc.
Southern California Edison Co.
Sperry Rand Corp.
E. R. Squibb & Sons, Inc.
Standard Oil Co. of California
Standard Oil Co. of New Jersey
Supreme Aluminum Industries, Ltd.
Tennessee Valley Authority
Time Inc.
TWA
Union Carbide Corp.
Union Oil Co. of California
United Air Lines, Inc.
United Artists Corp.
United Shoe Machinery Co.
U.S. Navy
U.S. Postal Service
United States Steel Corp.
Western Electric Co., Inc.
Western Gear Corp.
Westinghouse Electric Corp.
Wohlert Corp.
Xerox Corp.

A brief description of a few of these programs will indicate how concern for the troubled employee has been integrated with concern for the total health of employees under an industrial health program. Those selected for illustrative purposes are representative of various approaches by different types of employers, or are indicative of unique attempts to help the troubled employee.

The Western Electric Co. is engaged in manufacturing, installation, distribution, purchasing, and defense activities for the Bell System. It is a subsidiary of AT&T, and its subsidiaries include Teletype Corporation, Sandia Corporation, and Nassau Smelting and Refining Company. It maintains 14 major plants, 39 distributing houses, and mobile crews of trained technicians. It has more than 150,000 employees located in 29 states. Its manufacturing locations range in size from 1,500 to more than 20,000 employees.

According to information made available by W. B. Cowen, medical administrator of the company, the medical program employs 37 full-time physicians, including a psychiatrist, 99 part-time physicians, 178 nurses, and 28 technicians at the various company locations. At distributing centers, whose staffs range from 120 to 1,200, employees who constitute the mobile force of the company receive care from the Bell Systems medical departments or from local private practicing physicians.

The medical program at Western Electric has as its written objective "the conservation and improvement of [the] employee's physical and emotional health . . . under a concept of preserving the dignity of the individual." Emphasis is placed on preventive medicine.

All otherwise acceptable applicants for employment are given a pre-employment physical examination to help management come to a decision as to the degree of employment risk. Applicants having certain impairments, either correctible or permanent, are given consideration provided their disabilities neither interfere with the job requirements nor threaten the safety and welfare of other employees. In either case, those employed are given work assignments compatible with their physical and emotional health capabilities.

Once employed, workers are given periodic health examinations if they are exposed to occupational health hazards. For these types of high-risk jobs, examinations are provided to employees prior to placement, at subsequent designated intervals, and when the employee leaves. Examinations are also provided for those assigned to work outside the United States, and prior to personal leaves of absence, to transfer within the company, and to retirement.

Periodic health examinations are also given annually on a voluntary basis to department chiefs, buyers, research leaders, and to those in higher supervisory positions. Examinations are available every two years to section chiefs, professional administrative employees, secretaries, information systems employees, and wage practices associates, as well as to such professional employees as engineers, physicians, nurses, and lawyers for those between ages 30 through 49, and annually thereafter. The results of such examinations and the health records of all employees are held in strict confidence by the physicians and are only released, except where otherwise required by law, at the request of the employee. For statistical compilation and study purposes, a coding system is used for such records.

In addition, fitness-for-work examinations are provided on the recommendation of a supervisor in cases involving occupational injury or disease, disability absences, undue absence from work, decreased job performance, disruptive behavior, or pregnancy (pregnant women are not assigned to jobs that involve either excessive lifting or straining or exposure to toxic materials or radiation). In these cases, health counseling must be provided at the employee's request.

The medical care provided to employees includes first aid treatment in emergency situations and care for all job-connected injuries and diseases. Care is also provided for minor nonoccupational conditions, followed by referral to a personal physician, if necessary.

The Western Electric employee is encouraged to have an interest in health maintenance and safety awareness, both on and off the job. To this end, health and safety instruction is provided through company publications, periodic bulletins, demonstrations, lectures, and conferences on a continuing basis. The company considers the verbal link between its supervisors and its employees paramount in its efforts on behalf of the health and safety of the employees. Therefore, the supervisor is responsible for noting the early development of illnesses, as well as careless safety practices. Furthermore, all employees may consult the medical program physician for counsel and advice concerning any matters affecting their health, and they are encouraged to do so.

Western Electric also maintains an alcoholism control program. Moreover, as part of its basic research efforts, it studies the effect on the employee's health of such personal habits as excessive smoking and inadequate diet, as well as the effects of personality factors on health and safety.

Finally, the medical director, the design engineer, the factory engineer, the safety supervisor, the industrial hygienist, the machine and tool designer, the industrial engineer, and the functional supervisor are responsible for reviewing potential occupational hazards on a continuing basis. The purpose is to reduce or eliminate such hazards as excessive noise levels, air or water pollution, and toxic chemicals or radiation. Such a comprehensive program cannot fail to be of considerable help to the troubled employee.

An interesting program designed to help the troubled employee is the Insight program developed by the Utah Copper Division of the Kennecott Copper Corp. in July 1970 for its 8,000 employees and their dependents. Headed by a psychiatric social worker, the program was organized to penetrate the problems of employees before they get out of hand. The Insight program grew out of an established alcoholism control program.

According to the April 15, 1972, issue of *Business Week,* the program has the enthusiastic support of the 19 unions involved. It is also supported by a company policy statement developed in 1969, with implementation responsibility vested in the company's director of industrial relations.

The program is voluntary, although disciplinary action with warning and probation is the alternative presented to those who refuse to seek help. Confidentiality through guaranteed anonymity is assured. The program provides counseling on a 24-hour-a-day, 7-day-a-week basis. Where warranted, the employee is referred to the appropriate social agency. There are 220 social agencies, both private and public, available in the Salt Lake City area alone. One-third of the cases require only a single session of counseling. Insight also follows up the treatment process and, through various media, provides educational materials about the program.

By 1977, a total of 7,971 troubled employees and their dependents had sought the help of the Insight program, averaging 102 new referrals each month. Most referrals came from the individual involved, followed by referrals from the employee relations department, the family of the employee, supervisors, and the union in that order. The problems involved were principally familial or marital, alcoholism and drug addiction, and psychological-emotional disturbances, in that order. Other problems were financial debts, personal distress, suicidal tendencies, and psychotic or psychophysical disorders. Most of those seeking help were dependents of employees.

The results of the program are impressive. Those who sought

help showed a marked decrease in absenteeism (by one-half), a decrease in weekly indemnity payments (by almost two-thirds), and a decrease in health insurance benefits paid (of almost one-half). After 7 years, of the 7,971 persons seeking help, 193 had walked off the job or quit, 114 had been discharged, 43 were pensioned, and 38 were deceased.

The Pacific Telephone and Telegraph Company in San Francisco inaugurated its own Insight program for its 21,000 employees in 1972. Similar programs were then set up for the 120,000 civil service employees in the San Francisco Bay Area and for public employees in Hawaii.

At the Illinois Bell Telephone Co., a program for troubled employees has been developed as part of its industrial health program. As described by Dr. Robert R. J. Hilker, medical director of the company, the purpose of the effort is to give employees a source of professional help and support not otherwise generally available.

The troubled employee is usually identified by the immediate superior's observation of job deficiencies, but it also occurs when professionals in the medical department observe certain patterns in the employee. But nine out of ten referrals for help start with the supervisors. The tenth referral will come as a result of the medical department's observations or because the individual concerned recognizes the need. Next, the medical department personnel make a diagnosis and, where deemed necessary, recommend referral to an outside consulting psychiatrist at company expense. The medical department then maintains a follow-up progress report on the treatment and, after the employee has returned to work, assists in whatever means are dictated by the individual case in the processes of rehabilitation. The program includes the early identification of, and referral for, treatment of cases of alcoholism and drug abuse.

The program's effectiveness is evidenced by the fact that the number of disability cases (disability lasting more than 7 days) has been halved, with annual savings in this area alone ranging from $291,000 to $500,000.

The Insurance Co. of North America in Philadelphia published a guide on emotional and mental illness for department heads and managers. Stating that it is company policy "to provide competent professional assistance to employees who need it because their work performance is being adversely affected by an emotional or mental health problem," the guide states that "it is in the best interests of both the employee and INA that these illnesses be identified early and appropriate treatment recommended as soon as possible." The employee is free to undertake the recommended treatment or to reject it, and all such situations are handled in strictest confidence within the medical department. An attempt is made to dispel all stigma against mental disorders, and it is recognized that the troubled employee is either unable or unwilling to accept the fact that he or she is mentally or emotionally ill. The attempt is "to head off potential trouble and to retain a valuable employee." The possible signs and symptoms of mental disorders, discussed earlier, are identified in the guide.

The department head or manager is considered the keystone of the program. This is where the responsibility rests for early detection of the troubled employee, since these managers are in a position to observe deterioration in work performance, personality problems, friction with other employees, confusion, the commission of errors, an inability to concentrate, alterations in temperament, and restlessness. Where such behaviors are observed, the facts are discussed with the employee and referral is made to the medical department. If the need for treatment is identified after diagnosis, the employee is referred to the appropriate source of treatment. Treatment is not provided by the medical department itself, but through the employee insurance program, which covers the expenses for necessary care.

If a treatment program is prescribed, the employee's career is not affected. But if the employee rejects treatment, the consequences are the same as in any other case of unsatisfactory work.

At IBM a complete industrial health program has been operative for some time for its employees at its 35 locations in the United States and Canada. In 1968 the company instituted a health screening and medical data system for all its employees. As described by Dr. F. W. Holcomb, Jr., the objective of the voluntary program, which keeps all results confidential, is to detect disease early on and to accumulate health data. Some three-quarters of the employees have participated in the program. Among the conditions shown to exist by the screening program are diseases of the nervous system and physical illnesses that might well originate in psychiatric conditions.

Dr. David B. Robbins has described the efforts of IBM at its New York headquarters to bring about the early detection of mental, emotional, and personality disorders at all levels of employment. Consulting psychiatrists are available to help the troubled employee on his or her own referral, on the referral of the employee's family, or of management, the personnel department, or the medical department. Seldom does the psychiatrist provide treatment, except for an acute psychiatric episode or where the disorder is job related. In other instances, referral is suggested to an appropriate treatment agency or to a private psychiatrist, although the consulting psychiatrist follows up the treatment process. Company policy precludes release of an employee on the basis of a psychiatric diagnosis per se.

A large majority of cases of the identified troubled employees at IBM involve neuroses, anxiety, tension, transient situational disturbances, or personality disorders. Ten percent of the cases involve alcoholism, another 10 percent involve psychoses (including depression), and 15 percent of the cases show no evidence of psychiatric disease. One out of ten troubled employees has family problems. Others have suicidal tendencies or sexual problems, or suffer from drug abuse. One-quarter of the cases exhibit such job-related symptoms as excessive absenteeism or lateness, friction with fellow employees, or a lack of initiative.

Every effort is made to retain the troubled employee, including selective job placement or transfer. A study of the experiences of the program shows that 61.7 percent of the identified troubled employees were still employed by the company three years after identification and appropriate treatment. Of these, one-half were reported to be giving outstanding job performances or to be exceeding the job requirements; one-third were satisfactorily meeting their job requirements; and the remaining one-sixth were reported to be coming short of the job requirements. Another 38.3 percent of the identified troubled employees were no longer with the company three years after their problems had been identified. Most of these terminations were voluntary on the part of the employee or by mutual agreement. In the remainder of the cases some were fired, some had retired, one was totally disabled, one was deceased, and one was in jail.

At the Olin Corporation plant in North Carolina, which is located in open country 30 miles from the nearest large city, an industrial health program was established in 1950 with well-defined objectives. The company recognized that this type of program is doomed to failure unless it has the support of all levels of management, as well as the confidence and acceptance of employees and the cooperation of the local medical profession. A medical center with adequate facilities was established under a medical director. The program includes complete physical examinations for all employees, including those with physical abnormalities. The medical records are strictly confidential. The program is closely correlated with the plant safety program. According to N. H. Collison, special services provided by the program emphasize the early detection and prevention of such chronic conditions as hypertension, diabetes, cancer, arthritis, and emotional disorders.

What Unions Are Doing

As was shown in Chapter 13, certain labor unions have developed an active interest in the treatment of mental, emotional, and personality disorders. In several instances, this has taken the form of collective bargaining for the inclusion of certain costs for the treatment of mental disorders in the health insurance benefits. Elsewhere the treatment of mental disorders has been included in the services of the union health center. Some of the latter services are discussed here.

In 1948, the United Mine Workers health services joined forces with the Russellton, Medical Group at New Kensington, Pa., and the Centerville Clinic at Centerville, Pa., to provide for the diagnosis of, and short-term therapy for, mental disorders among its more than one-half million members and their dependents. Child guidance, drugs, and vocational rehabilitation were also provided. For more intensive care, referral was made to a hospital.

Two years earlier, the St. Louis Labor Health Institute, serving some 39,000 union workers, made provision for psychiatric consultation and short-term treatment where needed and for 90 days of hospitalization for more intensive care. Five psychiatrists serve on the staff of the Institute. The Institute has found that 9.2 percent of all hours of care it provides are for psychiatric treatment. Psychiatric cases also account for 2.5 percent of hospital admissions and for 5.7 percent of all days of hospital utilization. The vast majority of cases treated are for neurosis (41.3 percent) and for behavior or character disorders (21.2 percent). Psychosis accounts for 4.8 percent of the cases, and organic brain syndrome for 3.7 percent. The remainder of the cases are characterized as "other" diagnoses.

In 1975 the Carpenters Family Service Plan was commenced in Philadelphia to provide diagnosis, individual and group counseling, marital counseling, and child guidance. It also provides treatment for alcoholism, physical complaints, and compulsive gambling. Vocational guidance and rehabilitation services are part of the service, as well as speech therapy and psychological testing.

Other union health centers that provide some degree of diagnosis and treatment for mental disorders include the following:

The Amalgamated Clothing Workers of America in Philadelphia provides short-term individual psychotherapy, drugs (subject to charges), and referral for cases requiring more intensive therapy for its 35,000 members and their dependents.

The Union Family Medical Fund of the Hotel Industry of New York City provides ambulatory mental health care at its seven centers (two providing unlimited treatment and five being limited to consultation and short-term therapy) and 10 days of hospitalization for electroshock therapy.

The AFL-CIO Medical Service Plan, a multi-union service in Philadelphia, provides psychiatric diagnosis and treatment, and hospitalization.

The Eleanor Roosevelt Union Health Guidance Center is a Chicago-based multi-union service.

The New York City Central Labor Council is described in Chapter 13.

However, some established union health center programs for the diagnosis and treatment of mental disorders subsequently terminated such services. Perhaps the most notable, because it was reputedly the most extensive of such programs, was that of the Retail Clerks Union Local 770 in Los Angeles. The program was a joint management–union arrangement between the Food Employers Council and the union. Through its Mental Health Development Center, as well as an arrangement with the Kaiser Foundation Health Plan, the program in 1961 made psychiatric services available to 50,000 union members and their dependents. At its own center, employing 8 psychiatrists, 3 clinical psychologists, and 12 psychiatric social workers, the clinic provided unlimited individual and group therapy. Provision was also made for family, marital, and premarital counseling; parent–child guidance; psychological testing; and occupational therapy. Mental health education was made available to the union membership and their families, and provision was made for up to 111 days of hospitalization for the treatment of mental disorders. At the clinic, the patient paid $2 per service up to a maximum of $20 a month.

In mid-1970, after nine years, the center was closed because of the cost of the program, which was running 2¢ an hour per employee and totaling some $600,000 a year. There were also reportedly disagreements between management and the union over certain aspects of the therapy provided.

Another attempt that was terminated was that of the New York Joint Board, Amalgamated Clothing Workers of America, in New

York City. Established in 1964, and combining the resources of the union and the New York Clothing Manufacturers Association, the purpose of the program was to provide treatment for members and their families aimed at getting employees back to work. It was a crisis-oriented program providing short-term therapy concerned with those symptoms that interfered with work production. The treatment consisted of an initial interview, group therapy, medication (in 40 percent of the cases), and hospitalization (involving 12 percent of the cases) up to 90 days covered by the insurance program. Ambulatory treatment was provided at the union's Sidney Hillman Health Center.

The program involved 20,000 workers: more than half female, 72 percent born outside the United States, and most with at least a grade school education. Most of the workers ranged in age between 45 and 54 years, and four out of five had worked in the industry for five or more years, mostly with the same employer. The size of the shops where they worked varied from 10 to 100 or more employees. The work performed was on a piecework basis.

Over the three-year period of the program, 718 persons were identified as in need of help, one-quarter of these being family members of workers. Of those needing help, 61.6 percent received treatment, the remainder choosing not to do so. In 43 percent of the treated cases, relatives of the worker were involved in the treatment process. Referrals for treatment came from the employee or his/her family, from the union, from the employer, or from the insurance company. Most of those who received treatment (62.8 percent) had neurotic disorders, personality disorders, transient situational disturbances, psychophysiological disorders, or no specific diagnosis. The remainder had psychotic disorders (35.2 percent) or organic brain syndrome (2 percent).

Four out of five of those treated under the program had undergone one to twelve treatment sessions, with more than half having made less than five visits. At the other extreme, 12.7 percent had made more than 21 visits for treatment. The period of treatment to completion was less than one month in 11.4 percent of the cases, one to two months in 18.3 percent of the cases, and two to three months in 13.7 percent of the cases. Treatment ran over a period of three to six months in 28.9 percent of the cases, and for six to twelve months in 18.3 percent of the cases. One year or more of treatment was required in 9.4 percent of the cases.

The earnings (based on piecework) of workers suffering from mental disorders were found to be not significantly different from the wages of other workers. Neurotic patients, in fact, tended to earn more than other workers. Those with organic brain disorders, psychotic disorders, and psychosomatic disorders earned less than other workers.

The program was terminated in 1968, after funding by the National Institute of Mental Health expired.

BIBLIOGRAPHY

Akabas, Whelley. "Mental Health: A Report on Labor, Management, and Carrier Co-operation." *Pension and Welfare News*, June 1967.

Bond, Buckwalter, and Perkins. "An Occupational Health Program." *Archives of Environmental Health*, September 1968.

Business Week. "He Cures Kennecott's People Problems." April 15, 1972.

Collison, N. H. "Management and an Occupational Health Program." *Archives of Environmental Health*, February 1961.

The Conference Board. *Industry Roles in Health Care*. New York: 1974.

Follmann, J. F., Jr. *Alcoholics and Business*. New York: AMACOM, 1976.

————. *The Economics of Industrial Health*. New York: AMACOM, 1978.

————. *Insurance Coverage for Mental Illness*. New York: AMACOM, 1970.

Hilker, Robert R. J. *Behavioral Problems in Industry-Proposed Solutions*. Chicago: Illinois Bell Telephone Company, 1976.

Holcomb, F. W., Jr. "IBM's Health Screening Program and Medical Data System." *Journal of Occupational Medicine*, November 1973.

Howe, H. F. "Distribution of Occupational Physicians Among American Industries." *Journal of Occupational Medicine*, 11:191, 1969.

Insurance Company of North America. "A Guide for Department Heads and Managers on Emotional Illness." Philadelphia: undated.

Kennecott Copper Corporation. *Insight: A Program for Troubled People*. 1977.

National Health Council. *The Health of People Who Work*. New York: 1960.

Reed, Louis S., et al. "Health Insurance and Psychiatric Care." *American Psychiatric Association*, 1972.

Retail Clerks Local 770. "Employee Benefit Plan Review." April 1970.

Robbins, David B., et al. "The Psychiatric Patient at Work." *American Journal of Public Health*, July 1976.

Sidney Hillman Health Center of New York. *Helping Blue-Collar Workers in Trouble*. New York: September 1967.

————. *Mental Health Rehabilitation in a Union Population*. June 1, 1965.

Simons, John H. *The Union Approach to Health and Welfare*. Berkeley: Institute of Industrial Relations, University of California, 1965.

Stoudenmire, John A. "Mental Health Education for Supervisors." *Mental Hygiene*, Spring 1972.

U.S. Department of Health, Education, and Welfare. *Small Plant Health and Medical Programs*. Washington, D.C.: 1958.

Weiner, Hyman J., et al. *Mental Health Care in the World of Work*. New York: Association Press, 1973.

Yarvote, Patricia M., et al. *Journal of Occupational Medicine*, September 1974.

16

WHERE TO RECEIVE HELP AND GUIDANCE

A great many sources of help, guidance, and information are available to those concerned with mental, emotional, and personality disorders, whether the concern is at the personal or family level, or at the workplace itself. These many sources of help are at the national, state, and community levels.

The assistance available at the many sources of help and information is invaluable to those concerned with the problem of mental disorders, if only they will be taken advantage of. Unfortunately, those who do become concerned, whether for personal or job-related reasons, have difficulty knowing where to turn for guidance. This is because most people do not think they will ever have to be concerned with mental conditions and therefore tend to remain uninformed on the subject. The stigma, the misunderstandings, and the prejudices that pervade the subject all tend to lessen a sound concept of mental disorders, what they are, what exacerbates them, and what to do about them. The not-infrequent lack of confidence in the available services and the forms of care, at times not totally lacking in justification, undoubtedly acts as a further deterrent to sound understanding.

The result, in too many instances, is that what needs doing remains undone until more damage has occurred than need be the case.

Coping with many of the types of mental disorders is not an insurmountable matter if the signs of the condition are detected early and if diagnosis and appropriate treatment are brought about. The opposite can be dangerous. This is why it is so important to have an awareness of the subject and at least a general knowledge of where to seek help and guidance.

Sources of help, information, and guidance are discussed here first as they pertain to the troubled employee or to the members of his or her family, and then as they relate to concerned employers or labor unions.

Sources for the Individual

Troubled employees, or the members of their families, have available to them many sources of information on the subject of mental, emotional, or personality disorders. These can be helpful in overcoming the prevalent stigmas about such disorders and can aid in an understanding of the subject. In many communities there are also many sources for help and guidance, as well as diagnosis and treatment, should the symptoms of such disorders become apparent.

Individuals must recognize that they have just as much responsibility for keeping themselves in reasonably good mental health as they have with respect to their physical health. Beyond that, they have a responsibility to bring about the early identification, and any necessary treatment, of apparent mental, emotional, or personality disorders or, failing this, to heed the suggestions for help from knowledgeable people.

Mentally healthy individuals are the fortunate product of a unique and complex personality in reaction to the total life situation. Such individuals, according to the Menninger Foundation, are those who have a wide variety of interests and sources of gratification. These people are not tied up within themselves, are flexible in situations that would otherwise produce stress, are aware of the alternatives to problems that arise, and have a realistic understanding of both their assets and their liabilities. Mentally healthy people recognize that there are systems of value other than the ones they adhere to, and they do not overtly attempt to inflict their values on others. They have realistic life goals and, within their competence, are active and productive. While this may or may not be the ideal personality, it most certainly constitutes healthy behavior.

There are a great many things that people can do to maintain a healthy sense of mental balance. To begin with, they must recognize that every other living mortal is constantly beset by all kinds of problems from unhappy childhood experiences, rejections, and frustrations, to marital problems or problems with their children, to a failure to achieve to the fullest, to economic setbacks, financial worries, and even unemployment. We all have to function under considerable stress and tension at times. Many have to face stark and overwhelming tragedies. Yet most people, while suffering under such problems, remain functional, survive, and eventually overcome those problems.

In the process, individuals should be given to self-observation, just as they do with their physical health. It is in their own self-interest to do so. Self-observation calls for an awareness of the importance of maintaining reasonably good physical health through proper nutrition, sleep, rest, relaxation, and exercise. It calls for making every effort to establish and maintain a stable and close family life, as well as an interest in other people, in one's work, in learning and improving one's capabilities, in cultural pursuits, and in sports and hobbies. Such extensions of effort are important safety valves for avoiding inactivity and immobility and for enhancing self-esteem and the pride of accomplishment. They increase the ability of the individual to be realistic, flexible, and adaptable in the face of the situations which life inevitably presents. Life is not a TV commercial, a soap opera, or a Hollywood movie with a guaranteed happy ending. It is a real process, at times overbearing and grim, at times repetitive and dull, and sometimes fulfilling and joyous.

It is also important to be alert to the following symptomatic reactions, any of which can become serious. In a great many cases, these symptoms can be controlled and overcome:

Physical symptoms, such as sleeplessness, restlessness, or digestive upsets.

The development of overindulgence in work.

Overdependence on others.

Excessive ambition.

The presence over any extended period of time of such patterns of behavior as impatience, anger, hostility, anxiety, or fears.

Self-destructive characteristics, such as unnecessary risk-taking, dependence on alcohol or drugs, compulsive gambling, extramarital relationships, or the contemplation of suicide.

Above all, it must be recognized that the greatest waste of human energy and the most contorted use of the human mind is that of engaging in such nonproductive practices as:

Unfounded guilt for things that have happened or for things undone.

Envy of others.

Odious self-comparisons with others.

Concern with blame for what happens to oneself or to others.

Greed or avariciousness.

Submission to, or control by, fads, whether thought patterns, concepts, one's own health, or even the clothes one wears.

At the very least, such uses of the mind are childish, yet unfortunately they consume far too many people. They are destructive and a wasteful and unproductive use of one's energies.

Long since the great religious leaders have given us some very sage counsel on how we might avoid mental disorders. Moses, in the Ten Commandments, told us we should not covet our neighbor's house, his wife, his servants, his oxen, or anything that is his. He further cautioned against bearing false witness, stealing, and committing adultery, and proposed one day a week for rest, relaxation, and contemplation after laboring the other six days.

Then came the teachings of Jesus, advising temperance in all things and, in the Beatitudes, cautioning us to beware of covetousness, for a man's life consists not in the abundance of the things which he possesses; not to lay up treasures, for where your treasure is there will your heart be also; and reminding us that we are the salt and the light of the earth; that we should be pure of heart and merciful; that we should love our enemies as well as our neighbors; that we should hunger after righteousness; and that we should take heed that the light which is in us be not darkness.

Later came the teachings of Mohammed. The Koran teaches of the falaciousness of a poor diet, of wine drinking, and of gambling and usury, and that by their intentions should men's works be judged. Buddha set an example with his sage concept of the value of meditation. And then came the caution of St. Gregory the Great against the seven deadly sins: gluttony, sloth, lust, pride, covetousness, envy, and anger, any and all of which can contribute to the onset of mental disorders.

Our religious leaders gave us sound advice in the interest of mental health. Certainly, if followed, these tenets could serve to avoid many occurrences of neuroses and emotional and personality disorders. Yet despite an avowal of faith in such doctrines, many people too often ignore such teachings, while those who tend to disregard or disdain religious beliefs simply lose the benefit of wise counsel. Hear ye!

This is not to say that everyone should expect to be completely docile all the time, to be without desires or ambitions, and to be eternally free of cares, concerns, and worries. Such influences can, within bounds, bring out the best in people, spur them to greater effort and achievement, and benefit not only themselves, but society as a whole, through increased productivity and initiative and creative contributions, as in the case of the Beethovens and Dostoevskys. It is when the process of functioning becomes impaired that the destructive aspects of such characteristics become apparent—and should be heeded.

Such positive acts on behalf of mental health failing, people should observe any developing symptoms within themselves of mental, emotional, or personality disorders. These symptoms, experienced by people who need help, were discussed in Chapter 6. Recognition of such symptoms means, however, that people have a responsibility to themselves to have at least a passing familiarity with the major types of mental disorders and with the signs of their onset. Most people develop an awareness of many types of physical ailments. The same could be true with respect to mental conditions. People owe it to themselves and to their families. In perhaps too many instances people fail to recognize the signs of impending trouble or insist on trying to work their way through it alone, with considerable damage being done while they try to muddle through.

Eventually the anguish becomes unbearable, behaviors become flagrantly abnormal, and anxiety reaches the point of distraction and inability to work or function. Depression can result in complete withdrawal. Finally, after all this damage has been done, the individual recognizes that he or she is in need of help.

Where does the troubled person turn? There are many sources of help, depending on the services available in his or her community. As was shown in Chapter 9, the family physician can be a valuable source of guidance, but here the attitudes of some physicians toward mental disorders and toward psychiatry, noted earlier, must be borne in mind. The clergy, too, can be a source of guidance, and it should be noted that the Academy of Religion and Mental Health at 16 E. 34th Street, New York, N.Y. 10016, has 24 branches in various parts of the country. More specifically, there is the private practicing psychiatrist, the clinical psychologist, or the psychiatric social worker, who can offer guidance for the obtainment of diagnosis and needed treatment. Each of these professions has a national organization (see the Appendix) as well as state and local organizations, which can recommend individual practitioners in the community.

Many communities have mental health clinics or centers of various types that can furnish valuable guidance to the individual needing help. Some furnish child guidance, others provide family or marriage counseling, and still others provide general mental health services. Information on such sources of help can be obtained from such organizations as the Family Service Association of America at 445 E. 23rd Street, New York, N.Y. 10010; the American Association of Marriage Counselors at 270 Park Avenue, New York, N.Y. 10017; the American Association of Psychiatric Services for Children, at 1701 18th Street, Washington, D.C. 20009; or the National Society for Autistic Children, 169 Tampa Avenue, Albany, N.Y. 12208.

Still other sources of help are the community mental health centers which, over the past decade, have cropped up in communities throughout the United States. These centers have been described in Chapter 9. Information about them can be obtained from the National Council on Community Mental Health Centers, 2233 Wisconsin Avenue, N.W., Washington, D.C. 20037. An illustration of the services provided is found in the Peninsular Hospital Community Mental Health Center at Burlingame, Calif., which provides family-focused community service programs for families, parents, and teenagers, including crisis intervention for emergencies, diagnosis, and treatment.

Another example is the Maimonides Community Health Center in Brooklyn, N.Y., which, among other services, provides programs for senior citizens, rehabilitation services, and tutor therapy. Other notable examples are the Hall-Mercer Community Mental Health Center at the Pennsylvania Hospital in Philadelphia, the Hennepin County Community Mental Health Service at Minneapolis, the Community Mental Health Center Plan of New Haven connected with the Yale–New Haven Medical Center, and the Sound View–Throgs Neck Community Mental Health Center connected with the Albert Einstein College of Medicine in New York.

Another valuable source of services that has become increasingly available is that of the outpatient mental health services of many general hospitals. Two examples of these services—of which there are many—are the Downriver Adult Out-Patient Services at Lincoln Park, Mich., which provides consultation, education, and short-term treatment for blue collar and salaried employees; and the Mental Health Clinic of South Nassau Communities Hospital at Rockville Center, N.Y. If the individual is a subscriber to a prepaid group practice plan or HMO that provides mental health services, that too is a valuable source of help and guidance. Veterans can make use of the services of the VA hospitals, which can be a valuable source of help.

Unquestionably troubled employees should take full advantage of whatever counseling or treatment is available through an industrial health program at their place of employment, or at their union health center, provided these facilities exist. With respect to the place of employment, the distrust that can arise in the mind of the employee has been noted previously, including the concern of the effect mental disorders can have on continued employment. Whether such concerns are warranted can only be appraised by the employees themselves based on their own observations. In any event, the employee would do well to pay attention to any health education information made available at the place of employment or by the union. In this way, people can develop some basic information on the subject of mental disorders.

There are also many sources of help, including self-help, for special types of problems. People with suicidal tendencies can turn to many local sources of help, such as the Los Angeles Suicide Prevention Center; Rescue, Inc., in Boston; Friends in Miami; and the San Francisco Suicide Prevention Center. Information concerning such sources is available through the National Save-A-Life League, at 505 Fifth Avenue, New York, N.Y. 10017. For those with alcohol problems, there are the many local organizations, throughout the United States, of Alcoholics Anonymous, Al-Anon, and Alateen. Those under stress can try the StressControl Center at 210 East 49th Street, New York, N.Y. 10017, or other facilities listed in the Appendix. There are also such locally established organizations as Neurotics Anonymous and Schizophrenics Anonymous.

There is no simple or easy way in which to advise the troubled individual where to seek help and guidance. In the final analysis, people must make the decision, based in part on what is available in their own communities. The fact is that there are a great many potential sources of help and guidance. Unfortunately, opinions of the services provided by many of the sources of help vary, and at times are quite critical. But this may be partly explained by the varying concepts of treatment discussed earlier. Again, the troubled person must have recourse to sound sources of information.

Employers and Unions

Employers and labor unions have a responsibility to assist the troubled employee to the greatest extent possible. It is in their own self-interest, as well as in the best interest of employees and their families. Once the employer or the union accepts this responsibility, they will find many sources to turn to for information, guidance, and help.

At the outset, the employer or the union should become informed on the subject of mental, emotional, and personality disorders. Several universities conduct courses to this end. One of these is the Harvard University Health Services at the Harvard Business School in Boston. The employer or the union should also actively pursue a program of mental health education for its employees or members to ensure that they are better informed on the subject. Many sources of literature, films, and other educational materials, certain of which are listed in the Appendix to this book, are readily available.

Where an industrial health program is functioning, at whatever level, much can be done to help the troubled employee. Counseling can be made available to the worker with mental, emotional, or personality problems, and the supervisor or shop steward can play an important role in the early detection of impending trouble. Where treatment might be indicated, referrals for diagnosis can be recommended. In the fulfillment of this difficult responsibility, employers and unions can receive help and guidance from a great many sources. Included here are other employers who have become experienced in the subject (see Chapter 15), insurance organizations, state mental health departments, community mental health centers, mental health clinics, and HMOs. Health professional societies can help. Furthermore, consultants are available to employers and unions. To this end, employers and unions should remain aware of the various sources of help in the community available to them. The 200 community services established by the AFL-CIO can provide valuable aid.

An example of industry involvement in community mental

health centers is exemplified by the following statement by Clifford A. Conklin of the St. Joseph Lead Company:

> We feel the new comprehensive community mental health centers offer real hope of assistance to industrial management. . . . Industry can play an important part by providing a share of the local construction money. In Beaver County [Pa.], for example, industry (including some of the nation's biggest corporations) gave almost $200,000 for the construction of a mental health center.

An example of the help that can be provided by an HMO is found in the instance of the Rhode Island Group Health Association at 210 High Service Avenue, at North Providence, R.I. The Association has available to places of employment or unions a fully developed Employee Assistance Program.

Other examples of services available to places of employment at the community level are the Nebraska Psychiatric Institute; Pennsylvania Mental Health, Inc.; the Nassau County (N.Y.) Mental Health Association; the Long Island Industries Association; and the Esalen Institute at Big Sur, Calif. Assistance in coping with stress can be provided by the Biofeedback Research Society (see Chapter 10) at the University of Colorado Medical Center, 4200 E. 9th Avenue, Denver, Colo. 80220. There are many others. Also available are organizations that can provide help and guidance in coping with a specific problem, such as alcoholism. One example is the National Council on Alcoholism, at 733 Third Avenue, New York, N.Y. 10017, and its local affiliates.

Another aspect in coping with mental disorders, as has been shown, is that of making certain that the place of employment does not present conditions that can exacerbate the onset of such disorders. Included here are such matters as excessive noise, vibration, noxious odors and fumes, inadequate lighting and ventilation, extreme temperatures, the presence of harmful chemicals or toxic substances, and the presence of potential accident hazards. Help and guidance are available from the many technical and professional societies of engineers, chemists, and industrial hygienists listed in the Appendix.

Safety standards brought about by such organizations as the American National Standards Institute can be of invaluable assistance, as can the efforts of the National Safety Council. Insurance companies have some 10,000 safety engineers available to their policyholders to provide consultation in such areas as environmental health, monitoring and inspection, loss control, and recordkeeping. Many have helpful manuals, literature, and films, and some give courses of instruction in safety.

There are, then, a great many sources to which employers and unions can turn for guidance in their concern over industrial health and related hazards. Which source is most valuable in a particular instance can be determined by such differentials as the number of employees involved, the type of operation and hazards presented, the geographic location, and the discerned needs and problems to be solved.

Many of these sources of help, information, and guidance available to places of employment and to labor unions are listed, along with their addresses, in the Appendix to this book. There you will find the names of health professional organizations, organizations concerned with occupational hazards, and those concerned with such matters as rehabilitation, alcoholism, and drug abuse. Sources of information, educational materials, and films are also listed, as are some of the consultants available to places of employment and unions. Additional sources of help are identified in two earlier books published by AMACOM: *The Economics of Industrial Health* and *Alcoholics and Business.* Some sources of help available to small employers were given in Chapter 12.

The prerequisite is an earnest desire to help the troubled employee.

BIBLIOGRAPHY

AFL-CIO. *The Worker's Stake in Mental Health.* Publication No. 69, April 1961.

Conklin, Clifford A. "An Enlightened Business Investment." Presented before Pennsylvania Mental Health, Inc., Pittsburgh: January 26, 1968.

Felton, Jean Spencer, et al. "Mental Health Outreach of an Occupational Service in a Government Setting." *American Journal of Public Health,* December 1973.

Follmann, J. F., Jr. *Alcoholics and Business.* New York: AMACOM, 1976.

——. *The Economics of Industrial Health.* New York: AMACOM, 1978.

Leavell, H. R., and E. G. Clark. *Preventive Medicine for the Doctor in His Community.* New York: McGraw-Hill, 1965.

Solley, C. M., and K. T. Munden. "Behavior of the Mentally Healthy." *Bulletin of the Menninger Clinic,* Vol. 26: 178, Topeka: 1962.

Stone, Judson I., et al. "Innovations in Programs and Funding of Mental Health Services for Blue Collar Families." *American Journal of Psychiatry,* May 1972.

Vaughan, W. T., Jr., et al. "The Private Practice of Community Psychiatry." *American Journal of Psychiatry,* Vol. 130, 1973.

17

SOME SPECIAL PROBLEMS

FINALLY, there are some special problems that should be discussed, since they may or may not have psychiatric implications. They most certainly can affect the general health and well-being of employed people and can take their toll in the workplace environment.

In this final chapter, I would like to discuss some of the special problems related to the troubled employee: stress, whether on or off-the-job induced; alcoholism and drug abuse, which are generally considered a manifestation of a psychiatric disorder; excessive use of tobacco, which can have a psychiatric base; destructive gambling, which in many instances is compulsive to the individual; and suicide, which may result from the presence of mental disorders. Although aspects of these problems have been discussed elsewhere in this book, they are integrated here as a special topic.

Epilepsy is not included in the discussion because there is disagreement as to whether it can be considered a form of mental disorder. Most neurologists consider the affliction a disorder of the nervous system, some consider it a symptom of a diseased state, and some maintain that it is not a mental disease at all. While the causes of epilepsy are unknown, we do know that it is not a contagious condition. It can occur at any age, although it usually manifests itself in childhood. Characterized by sudden and recurring episodes of unconsciousness, the seizures are characterized as grand mal, petit mal, psychomotor, and focal, and can result in accidental death from a fall or from suffocation. Estimates of the number of epileptics in the United States range from $1/2$ to $1 1/2$ million persons. The goal of therapy is to render the patient as seizure-free as possible through the use of drugs and through the preservation of good health, temperance, and the avoidance of fatigue.

Similarly, a discussion of cerebral palsy is not included since, again, there appears to be no agreement on a definition of the condition. For example, some include all organic nervous system injuries incurred in the prenatal period, while others limit the definition to neuromuscular defects.

Persons suffering from either epilepsy or cerebral palsy can present particular problems at the workplace. Such persons might have to receive special considerations from the standpoint of job placement and training, in the interest of their own safety, as well as the safety of other employees. When employed in the right job and in the right environment, however, they have generally been found to be quite satisfactory workers with above-average attendance records.

Stress

While the subject of stress has been interwoven in the preceding discussion of mental, emotional, and personality disorders, the question remains whether stress is a symptom of mental disorder. Obviously, in some persons undergoing a period of stress it clearly is. In others, it may merely be a phase, although it has been known to trigger the onset of mental disorders. There is no satisfactory answer to the reason why one person under stress breaks down and becomes mentally ill and another does not. Clearly, what is stress to one person is stimulus to another. To many a certain amount of stress adds spice to life. Stress is a factor in everyone's life, with complete freedom from it occurring only in death. Hence the gravestone condolence: rest in peace.

What exactly is stress? As was shown in Chapter 4, the symptoms of stress can be found in many of the diagnoses of mental disorders developed by the American Psychiatric Association. Yet stress cannot simply be defined as the consequence of excessive demands, since different people respond in different ways to identical situations and have different breaking points. A stimulus that affects one person adversely will leave another unaffected, whether because of differing biochemical factors, genetic predispositions, early life experiences, cultural factors, or certain defense mechanisms. On the other hand, exposure to some stress produces distinctly beneficial results in the form of exhilaration, challenge, or excitement, and acts as a constructive force. Thus, everyone has a different level of toleration for stress, differing abilities to cope with it, and various ways of handling it.

Consequently, some define stress as intense exertion, the word itself deriving from the physical sciences. Others relegate stress to the realm of external conditions, as forces that occur in all kinds of endeavor that induce strain within the individual. Others limit their definition of stress to those conditions which produce bodily or biological responses in the individual, whether in the form of a nonspecific response of the body to a demand placed on it, or in the form of an extreme or noxious stimulus that generally produces physiological changes, behavioral change, or even a perceptual change. Hence, the word stress is used in different ways to mean different things and is, in fact, a general catchall term for a large number of problems. It would help if mental health professionals were to make the subject more specific.

The causes of stress within an individual can be personal in nature, they can be job-related, or they can be closely interrelated, as often happens. They can be related to such personality traits as rationalization or life expectations; the demands one places on oneself; an inability to relax and play; the degree of compulsiveness, anxieties and fears within a person; or those discussed earlier: guilts, shame, invidious comparisons, jealousy, envy, or greed.

Stress can result from any number of occurrences in the personal life of an individual. These can include the death of a spouse or a loved one, marital difficulties and divorce, the event of marriage itself, pregnancy, sexual problems, or the onset of injury or illness. It can be brought about by changes in living conditions; excessive worry; sleepless nights; emotional disturbances; sociological isolation; problems in keeping up with the Joneses; or debts, mortgages, or other financial problems.

On-the-job stress can come about in many ways and, as Winston Churchill once commented: "Those whose work and pleasures are one are fortune's favorite children." Job-related stress has been defined as a work-related factor that produces a maladaptive response.

It can result from such physical working conditions as excessive temperatures, the presence of noxious odors or fumes, excessive noises and vibrations, faulty lighting, fear of physical harm, or crowded working conditions resulting from poor plant layout.

Beyond such physical factors, many other aspects of the workplace can cause undue stress in some people. Included here are certainly the inadequate selection, placement, and training of the individual for the particular job, the necessary person-to-job fit. Such factors as overwork, difficulties with the supervisor, unfair criticism, job pressures, the degree of responsibility, frustrations, repetitiveness of tasks, job dissatisfaction, and job monotony can produce stress in some people.

Various factors having to do with insecurity can be stressful to many people. These include fear of layoffs, concerns over aging or impending retirement, fear of demotion, fear of a changed responsibility and of possible failure, a failure to adapt to new processes or circumstances, or concerns over new management or work location.

More subtle factors can be extremely stressful to some employees, including such things as a narrow range of permissible behaviors, the impossibility of exerting imagination or creative abilities, confusion in management decisions, frequent changes in demands, changes in the organizational structure, role ambiguity for the individual, and the lack of the fulfillment of ambitions. Promotion and increased responsibilities can produce stress in many people, as can being responsible for either production levels or the welfare of other people. Such stress-producing influences are extremely difficult to understand and fully assess.

Nor are executives free from stress. Executive stress can arise out of the impersonalization and isolation of their position, competition, or promotion neuroses, overwork, the conflict of personal values and business responsibilities, the demands accompanying authority and responsibility, the need at all times to provide leadership, and the unending problems of decision making. Here are some of the demands that can be stress-producing for persons in responsible positions:

Price and product competition.
Increased production.
Increasing sales and the development of new products.
Dealing with governmental agencies and new legislative enactments.

Competing for markets at home and abroad.

Meeting changing trends in markets.

Corporate social responsibility.

Being concerned with customer relations and public relations, diversification and mergers.

Coping with inflation, recession, and shutdowns.

A great many stress studies have been made of such diverse pursuits as aircraft control personnel, men under combat conditions, telephone operators, executives, invoice clerks, miners, sales office personnel, clergymen, physicians, university professors, supermarket cashiers, paper mill workers, engine drivers, piecework employees, and salaried employees. A 1978 study by the U.S. Department of Health, Education, and Welfare showed that a feeling of tension on the job was more prevalent among foremen, followed by managers and supervisors, and least among workers. On the other hand, tension in their daily lives was highest among supervisors, followed by managers, foremen, and workers. Another study, by Group Health Insurance in New York in 1962, found that 31 percent of male blue collar workers suffered from psychiatric problems resulting from stress, and that 11 percent suffered from stress occasioned at home or at work.

The effects of stress on the physical health of people have been difficult to evaluate, since not much correlation has been made between stress and health. It has been substantiated, however, that stress from whatever cause increases epinephrine (also known as adrenaline) and thyroid activity, stimulates the heart rate, causes palpitations, affects the turnover of carbohydrates, lipids, calcium, and magnesium, and has an effect on the cholesterol level. One consequence of stress is an increase in the incidence of coronary heart disease and myocardial infarctions. One study, for example, showed three times the incidence of coronary heart disease among persons working under stress.

Another study, covering an $8^{1}/_{2}$-year period, of 3,000 men employed in ten California companies showed that for men between the ages of 39 and 49, those who worked under stress had twice the incidence of heart attacks compared with those who were more relaxed. Other physiological consequences of functioning under stress have been found to be an increased incidence of hypertension and stroke, of gastrointestinal disturbances and peptic ulcers (which result in 150,000 surgical operations each year), of diabetes, and of such conditions as migraine headaches, insomnia, asthma, colitis, rheumatoid arthritis, muscular aches, skin diseases, fatigue, and blood cancers, such as leukemia and lymphoma.

Stress has also been found to aggravate disabilities and to impede the recovery from various illnesses. It can be a cause of accidental injuries. It can bring about excessive use of alcohol and tobacco (to be discussed subsequently), and can trigger the onset of mental, emotional, or personality disorders.

The consequence among employed people can be an increased incidence of illnesses, accidents, disabilities, and premature deaths, with greater costs to an insurance program. Absenteeism and labor turnover are thereby increased, and work performance suffers from decreased productivity, an increased incidence of shoddy workmanship, error, faulty decision making, disrupted perception, increased rigidity in behavior, and impaired customer relations.

Stress is therefore a subject of concern for management. While the subject is not fully understood and merits more research, it is certainly clear that the elimination of the physical causes of stress, as well as other work-related situations that result in stress for some employees, can do much to alleviate its harmful effects in the workplace. It requires a recognition of, and an awareness of, the problem. Increasingly, this is happening among such employers as Kimberly-Clark, Chase Manhattan Bank, Exxon, Time Inc., Equitable Life, McGraw-Hill, Mobil Oil, and Occidental Life which, among other things, have established physical fitness programs as well as relaxation programs to combat stress.

People suffering from stress can do much to reduce it as a factor in their lives. There is no simple, easy solution, since everyone reacts differently, but such balancing influences as rest and relaxation, exercise, vacations, combining work with play, and learning to loaf a little can help relieve tension. Stress can be mastered by learning to accept situations and adapt to them, by not being humiliated by failures, by avoiding defensive or self-destructive reactions, by conquering frustrations, and by finding enjoyable elements in the job. Some find relief through psychiatry, biofeedback, encounter groups, zen, yoga, sufism, and transcendental meditation.

Alcoholism

The American Medical Association recognized alcoholism as an illness in 1956. Soon afterward the American Hospital Association in

1957 and the AFL-CIO in 1959 followed suit. It is considered by many to be a manifestation of a psychiatric illness, although this concept lacks unanimity. Alcoholism is, however, included in the diagnoses of the American Psychiatric Association as was discussed in Chapter 4.

The use and abuse of alcohol is evident throughout recorded history, the oldest drunkard of record being Noah. Religious leaders and rulers of nations throughout the ages have taken cognizance of the harm that can result from the abuse of alcohol.

Today alcoholism is a problem in every nation, although to varying degrees. It appears in all strata of society. In the United States it is estimated that there are 9 million alcoholics, although 34 percent of Americans are reported to be total abstainers, the greatest proportion in any nation maintaining such records. Fifty percent of American women and about one-third of men are said to be abstainers or infrequent drinkers.

The toll of alcoholism is serious. The alcoholic person has a 12-year-shorter life span and is more illness-prone than the nonalcoholic. One-half of all motor vehicle fatalities, one-half of suicides, one-third of homicides, and the vast majority of drownings are said to be involved in one way or another with a drinking problem. Of all admissions to hospitals, 13 percent are reported to result from alcoholism, and 10 percent of the resident population of public mental hospitals are alcoholic. The abuse of alcohol is a major cause of cirrhosis of the liver.

The cost of alcoholism in the United States has been estimated by the Secretary of Health, Education, and Welfare to exceed $25 billion a year. Of this amount, more than $9 billion is reported to result from lost production, more than $8 billion from the costs of medical care (12 percent of all health expenditures), and more than $6 billion from motor vehicle accidents.

The cause of alcoholism is not clearly known. It is evident, however, that the incidence of alcoholism is greater among men, among persons with a family history of the disease, among persons with no religious affiliations, and among those who are divorced, separated, or single or who come from broken homes. Unquestionably, stress within the individual or various types of mental, emotional, and personality disorders can lead to alcoholism. Unfortunately, physicians for the most part are not trained at diagnosing alcoholism other than the pathological or organic complications that can result from alcohol abuse. These complications include a poor nutritional state, convulsions, diseases of the nervous and digestive systems, parasitic diseases, infections, and cirrhosis of the liver.

The signs of alcoholism, however, have been discussed variously by many knowledgeable and experienced professionals. Among the early signs of impending trouble are such habits as sporadic drinking for relief from troubles or worries, gulping drinks, disassociating oneself from nondrinkers, feeling alcohol to be a necessary part of social contact, occasional memory lapses, the compulsion to drink more than others, finding an urgency for the first drink, drinking alone, drinking to build confidence, sneaking drinks, becoming defensive about excessive drinking, and the gradual development of a tolerance for alcohol.

More serious signs are the development of a dependence on alcohol, feelings of guilt and remorse, loss of time from work, the neglect of a proper diet, a reduction in interests, an impaired ability to reason or function adequately, the need to drink in the morning, an inability to control drinking, the development of tremors, and physical debilitation. Finally, left uncontrolled, drinking becomes an obsession accompanied by frequent and extended periods of intoxication. Eventually, there is a loss of tolerance for alcohol and delusions and hallucinations occur.

There are many forms of treatment for the alcoholic person, depending on the progress the disease has made and whether or not there are physical complications. Included are hospital inpatient care and a variety of outpatient facilities, such as alcoholism treatment centers, detoxification centers, family therapy sessions, HMOs, and certainly the highly effective Alcoholics Anonymous. Just as there is no known cure for diabetes, alcoholism is also currently incurable, but the disease can be brought under control.

Half the alcoholics are employed people, ranging in places of employment from 3 to 10 percent of the workforce. Another 10 percent of employed people are said to be problem drinkers. In the main, these employees are in the 35 to 55 age bracket, have been with the same employer some 10 to 12 years, and are therefore skilled and experienced personnel. Alcoholism occurs at all levels of the workforce, from the night elevator operator to the chairman of the board. It is found among upper and middle management, salespeople, clerks, and skilled and unskilled workers. Scientists, university professors, physicians, lawyers, and members of Congress are not excluded.

The effects of alcoholism on places of employment include two-and-a-half times the degree of absenteeism as other employees, three-and-a-half times the number of work absences due to off-the-job accidents, twice the incidence of respiratory and cardiovascular diseases as other employees, and three times the incidence of digestive and musculoskeletal disorders. Alcoholic employees have twice the incidence of disabilities lasting 30 or more days as other employees, and six times the incidence of disabilities lasting 90 or more days a year. Other effects include lateness, deteriorated work performance, faulty decision making, employee friction, impaired customer relations, reduced efficiency, material wastage, and on-the-job accidents. Consequences can be undue labor turnover and cases of early retirement.

The costs of alcoholism to places of employment have been estimated by various sources to range from $8 billion to $12 billion a year. In addition, the cost in poor productivity of goods and services, personnel turnover, and faulty decision making has been estimated to range from $1 billion to $2 billion yearly. Some specific examples of estimated costs are of interest. North American Rockwell Corporation, with 100,000 employees, has placed the cost of alcoholism to its operations at $250 million a year, or $50,220 per alcoholic employee each year. Gulf Oil Canada, Ltd., with 11,000 employees, has estimated the annual cost to be $400,000. The United California Bank of Los Angeles, with 10,000 employees, estimates the cost at $1 million a year. The Illinois Bell Telephone Company places the cost of alcoholism in wage replacements alone at $418,500 a year. The U.S. Postal Service estimates an annual cost of $168 million, and the U.S. General Accounting Office places the cost of alcoholism among federal civilian employees at $550 million a year.

Despite such findings, many employers are unaware of the problem of alcoholism within their workforce, others are concerned about the effect on their public image should they admit the presence of alcoholics, and still others simply discharge the detected cases. On the positive side, an increasing number of employers are establishing alcoholism control programs to help the employee with a drinking problem. The National Institute on Alcohol Abuse and Alcoholism recently estimated that 1,200 such occupational programs were operative by the end of 1976, double the number found to exist a few years earlier. Certain of these programs are discussed in the book *Alcoholics and Business.* Other programs include those established by Anaconda American Brass Company, the Canadian National Railways, Canadian Pacific, Westinghouse Electric Company, Lockheed-California Company, Dow Chemical Company, Alcan Fiduciaries Ltd., and Rocketdyne.

The approach taken requires all the necessary elements of an industrial health program discussed earlier in this book, even though the alcoholism control program might function as a more or less separate entity, as happens in some instances. Although penetration is not easy (since the employee with a drinking problem will inevitably deny that this is the case), the results in identified cases of alcoholism are remarkably good. Recovery is brought about in 60 to 80 percent or higher of the alcoholic cases identified. As a result, productivity is increased, absenteeism is reduced, there is less turnover in the workforce, employee friction is reduced and morale improved, and experienced and valuable personnel are salvaged. The cost-effectiveness of many of these programs was shown in Chapter 14.

A necessary part of such programs is an adequate insurance program to cover the costs of treatment in various types of modalities and the income lost while treatment is under way. Such insurance protection is generally available today. Another necessary element is inclusion in any health education program of a discussion of alcoholism, so that employees can be aware of the nature and extent of the disease and so that public attitudes and the stigmas attached to alcoholism might be overcome.

Many sources of help are available to employers in the establishment and operation of an alcoholism control program. Certain of these are listed in the Appendix. Not to be overlooked are the local affiliates of the National Council on Alcoholism, the counselors made available to employers by Alcoholics Anonymous, the Alcoholism Committee at 222 Park Avenue South, New York, N.Y. 10003, state government agencies, insurers, several universities, specialized consultants, and certainly those employers with operational alcoholism control programs. In various localities there are also available such programs as the Employee Health Program at the Johns Hopkins University School of Hygiene and Public Health in Baltimore.

In addition to any operative program at the place of employment, there are many sources of help for the alcoholic employee, including Alcoholics Anonymous, the Red Cross, the Salvation Army, the family physician, locally established alcoholism treatment centers, and such places for treatment as the Strecker Hall Program for the Treatment of Alcoholism at the Institute of the Pennsylvania Hospital in Philadelphia. Sources for treatment can be found in the Alcoholism Treatment Programs Directory of Information Planning Associates, Inc., 656 Quince Orchard Road, Gaithersburg, Maryland 20766.

Drug Abuse

Drug abuse and addiction is considered by many to be a manifestation of psychiatric illness, since it is an indication of a disordered mental functioning. Others maintain that there is no conclusive data to show a relationship between drug abuse and pre-existing personality characteristics or other mental disorders.

The abuse of drugs may take any one of essentially three forms: (1) the abuse of drugs and medications commonly purchased, such as barbiturates or antihistamines; (2) the misuse of prescribed drugs by overuse; or (3) the illegal use of mind-altering drugs, such as heroin and marijuana. We are concerned with the latter form of abuse here.

The report to the President by the Strategy Council pursuant to the Drug Abuse Office and Treatment Act of 1972 recognized that much controversy is generated over definitions of drug abuse, some defining it in terms of the law, others in terms of what is normative for a given society. The report defined abuse as "the illegal use of a controlled substance or use of a drug in a manner or to a degree that leads to adverse personal or social consequences," such as "impaired mental health, physical health, maturation, or inability to work effectively" or "involvement in socially disruptive or illegal actions."

The Expert Committee on Drug Dependence of the World Health Organization draws a distinction between drug abuse and drug dependence. Drug abuse is defined as the "persistent or sporadic excessive drug use inconsistent or unrelated to acceptable medical practice." Drug dependence is defined as a "state, psychic and sometimes physical, . . . characterized by behavioral and other responses that always includes compulsion to take the drug on a continuous or periodic basis in order to experience its psychic effects. . . . ."

Drugs associated with drug abuse are the opiates and synthetic opiate derivatives, such as heroin, morphine, methadone, and meperidine. Also involved are the hallucinogens, such as LSD, mescaline, psilocybin and psilocin, DOM, and DMT. Derivatives from the hemp plant *Cannabis*—marijuana and hashish—are included, as are the major stimulants amphetamines, methamphetamine, cocaine, methylphenidate, and phenmetrazine, as well as such sedatives as barbiturates and the tranquilizers Miltown, Valium, and Librium. Other forms are aspirin and salicylates and such inhalants as glue, airplane gas, ether, plastic cement, cleaning fluid, and nail polish remover.

Most of these drugs have legitimate uses in coping with many physical and mental disorders so long as there is strict adherence to the regimen prescribed by the physician, although the prescribing habits of some physicians with respect to these drugs are currently being subjected to question and criticism. Most of these drugs can be habit-forming and dangerous. Dependency can result, the functioning of the mind can be affected, and mental disorders can result. Physiological consequences can also occur, including hepatitis, bacterial infections, and skin diseases.

Death can result from drug abuse as well. In 1968, 1,692 deaths resulted from drugs in New York City alone. Overdoses accounted for 70 percent of these fatalities; barbiturates were the cause of 544 of these deaths, aspirin and related drugs, 175; opiates, 229; tranquilizers and related drugs, 646; and other drugs, 376.

In the United States each year some 8 billion dosage units of amphetamines and 4 billion dosage units of barbiturates are reportedly produced. The number of persons who abuse the use of these drugs is not known, although they have vaguely been estimated to be in the millions. The number of drug addicts (mostly an addiction to heroin) is variously estimated to be 150,000, 200,000, 400,000, and 600,000. Of these addicts, 85 percent are said to be male, 60 to 70 percent black or Spanish-American, and most are unmarried, unemployed, and in the younger adult-age brackets. A 1967 survey reported that of persons over age 18, 25 percent used psychoactive drugs and 27 percent used tranquilizers. Thefts attributable to drug abuse (mostly among heroin users because heroin is expensive) are estimated to amount to $1 to $2 billion yearly.

The types of people who abuse drugs have been found to be those with a personal adjustment problem, those who are aimless and lack a goal in life, or those who suffer from lonesomeness. Other characteristics include a mistrust of others, a tendency to defy authority or to rebel, or self-destructive tendencies. Peer-group pressures can affect some younger people. On the other hand, those with a high degree of self-esteem and a concept of self-worth generally are not vulnerable to drug abuse.

Many forms of treatment are available for those who abuse drugs or who are addicted. There are various types of detoxification centers, abstinence programs, multimodal programs, treatment programs for the users of monopiates, and antagonist programs aimed at withdrawal through the use of counterdrugs. There are also the various forms of civil commitment. Considerable debate surrounds these various treatment approaches, and their effectiveness is by no means clear. One approach that has attracted considerable attention in recent years is that of methadone maintenance. Methadone is a pure narcotic, and is used as a means of withdrawing from other drugs in a controlled situation. Included in the approach is detoxification, chemotherapy, group work, psychotherapy, medical treatment, and education and counseling. Opinions vary, at times strongly, over this approach since it is difficult for the patient, in turn, to withdraw from the methadone. Another approach, for which there are arguments both ways, is that of heroin maintenance.

The effectiveness of these various approaches is questioned by many. In certain instances it has been found that more than half the patients drop out of the program and that more than one-third make only one visit. Some 5 percent were abstaining one or more months after treatment, and a small percentage had decreased the use of drugs.

A study of the economics of heroin treatment by Maidlow and Berman in 1972 is of interest. The study notes that treatment for heroin addiction costs from $2,000 per addict per year for an outpatient substitution program to $30,000 per addict per year for an extensive inpatient withdrawal and rehabilitation program. It also notes that the two federal hospitals for drug addiction at Lexington, Kentucky, and Fort Worth, Texas, have a combined expenditure of $50 million a year; and that New York City alone spends nearly $6 million a year for narcotics rehabilitation. The study then examines alternative approaches to treatment and attempts a cost-benefit analysis based on a determination of direct case history, the theoretical benefit history, and the calculated expected net benefit. The study concludes that "the benefit per addict under the methadone maintenance modality is more than $130,000 above the net benefit of the therapeutic community." In arriving at this conclusion, the study shows examples of 17 percent drop-outs after 90 days from the therapeutic community and an addictional relapse rate of 35 percent, compared to a failure rate of 13 percent for methadone maintenance programs. Under the theoretical benefits, the study estimates that the heroin addict steals an average of $30,000 a year to support his habit, and that this is saved by treatment. It further estimates that the cured addict is capable of earning $5,084 per year. This is hardly a cost effectiveness approach, being more a comparison of two approaches to treatment, but it does indicate some factors that can be related to a cost effectiveness approach.

Drug abuse has become an increasing problem in places of employment in relatively recent years. It is not a problem which approaches the scope of alcoholism, however, in part because only about one-third of drug abusers are employed people. Because the problem is a relatively recent one in our society, not too much is yet known of its effect on places of employment. We do know, however, that drug abuse increases the incidence of accidents and absenteeism, that job performance declines, that it increases labor turnover, and that it increases the number of thefts. Premature death can also result.

The drug abuser in places of employment, unlike the alcoholic, is usually in the 20- to 25-age bracket, in 75 percent of the cases has been with the employer for less than four years, and therefore is not likely to be an experienced or valued employee. One examination found that of the drug abusers, 44 percent were factory workers and 35 percent were clerical or maintenance workers or messengers. However, 8 percent were professionals, 5 percent were in a supervisory capacity, and 2 percent were at the management or executive level. Whereas most were in the young age group, 30 percent were between ages 26 and 35, and 6 percent were between ages 36 and 50. The most-used drugs were marijuana, followed by amphetamines, heroin, barbiturates, LSD, cocaine, morphine, and glue, in that order.

A study of more than 31,000 admissions to various types of facilities for the treatment of mental disorders in 1969 is also revealing. Drug dependence accounted for 1.9 percent of such admissions, about half of whom were under age 25. By status of employment, they were unskilled workers, skilled workers, professionals, managerial personnel, executives, housewives, students, retired persons, and unemployed people.

One thing stands out in both these studies: that drug abuse also occurs among professional people and people in supervisory, managerial, and executive positions:

Despite the problem not too many employers are doing anything constructive about it. A 1970 survey by the Conference Board of 222 employers showed that nearly two-thirds saw drug abuse as a major problem. Two-thirds, however, said that they did not have the problem. The discharge of drug abusers, the practice in one-fifth of the places of employment, was frequently dependent on the length of time the worker had been employed, as well as his or her value as a

worker. The survey found that only 18 of the 222 employers had
written formal policy statements on the subject. Another survey, by
Susan Halpern for the American Management Associations in 1972,
revealed that while only two of the employers surveyed had a problem
of drug abuse in 1960, 52 reported such a problem in 1970.

Where employers have attempted to take a constructive approach to the problem of drug abuse the approach is quite similar to
that taken in coping with alcoholism and need not be repeated here.
Once management has established policy and delegated responsibility
the supervisors are appropriately trained to observe unsatisfactory
job performance, and referral is then made to the medical department or consultant and, where appropriate, treatment is recommended. Refusal of treatment calls for disciplinary action. Health
education on the subject is also provided. Furthermore, many employers today will employ addicts if they have undergone treatment
and rehabilitation and if they are recommended for employment by a
responsible treatment agency. Apparently, there are no union health
programs to cope with drug abuse, and it is reported that in only a
few instances does the union assist in identifying the drug abuser.

A few examples of the approaches being taken by employers
today will suffice. The Weyerhaeuser Company is one company that
has a management policy that specifically deals with the abuse of
drugs. Identification of the addict is based on deteriorated job performance and the education of supervisors to this end is provided.
Treatment is then recommended, and there is follow-up on the rehabilitative process. The buying and selling of illicit drugs on company
premises is not condoned. Known addicts are not employed. In 1972
the company found that 59 percent of the employees used marijuana
to some extent, 29 percent used psychedelics, 15 percent used sedatives, and 28 percent used speed. The extent to which such usage
constituted abuse was not known.

The policy of an unidentified large public utility company pro-
hibits the illegal sale, purchase, transfer, use, or possession of drugs
on company premises or while on company business, and an employee so doing is subject to disciplinary action. Employees otherwise
engaging in such acts can be referred to the medical department, if it
has been noted that their job performance has deteriorated, where
appropriate evaluation, counseling, recommended treatment, and
follow-up is provided. If the employee is uncooperative, he or she is
subject to suspension or dismissal.

The policy of an unidentified manufacturing company provides for referral for treatment, leave of absence, and follow-up measures. Treatment failing, the employee is dismissed. Applicants discovered to be on drugs or narcotics through pre-employment examination and urinalysis are not considered for employment.

Another case of employers handling drug addiction is the program of the Insurance Company of North America. Company policy requires caution and discretion in order to prevent libel or charges of defamation of character. Suspicious cases are handled on the basis of an evaluation of job performance by the department head or manager. In an attempt at early identification, the employee is referred to the medical department, which in turn will recommend appropriate treatment. Strictest confidence is observed in all cases and the basic salary continuance plan is available to the employee during the period of rehabilitation. If treatment is refused, or if it is unsuccessful, the employee is handled as in any other instance of failure to perform satisfactorily on the job. The telltale signs of drug abuse are seen as drowsiness, confusion, severe panic or anxiety, bizarre behavior, excessive energy, poor judgment, shakes or convulsions, dilated pupils, speech difficulty, tracks on the forearms, chronic cough, body odor, and the use of a peculiar jargon.

AT&T has management policy concerned with drug abuse, the program being generally similar to its alcoholism control program. In addition, educational materials on the subject are made available to employees, and meetings are held on the subject. The illegal sale, purchase, transfer, use, or possession of illicit drugs by employees on company premises or while on company business is prohibited.

At the Illinois Bell Telephone Company a physician with a background in psychiatry administers a rehabilitation program for drug abusers. A full-time qualified drug counselor conducts individual counseling and group therapy sessions. In 1974–1975, 89 employees, 62 of whom were males and 27 females, were referred to the program. Referrals to the program came principally from supervisors (63 percent), the remainder coming from the medical department (24 percent), the individual (2 percent), and relatives (11 percent). Of those referred to the program, 71 percent consented to treatment. Most of the drug abusers are young and have been with the company a relatively short time. Of the drug abusers, 38 percent used heroin, 29 percent poly-drugs, 13 percent marijuana, and 20 percent used other drugs.

Excessive Use of Tobacco

In recent years, an active campaign has been aimed at the cessation of, or reduction in, cigarette smoking. The subject can be highly subjective, since cigarette smoking is a deep-seated habit for many people. It is also a controversial subject, frequently oversimplified and ignoring other directly related factors. Data from the National Clearing House for Smoking and Health and the National Center for Health Statistics nonetheless gives evidence that over the past two decades an impressive proportion of the American population has either ceased cigarette smoking or decreased the consumption of cigarettes. Heavy smoking is quite prevalent, however, some 26.4 percent of men and 17.6 percent of women smoking more than 25 cigarettes a day.

The psychological aspects of cigarette smoking, particularly of heavy smoking, are not yet clearly understood. Some smokers say they smoke because they enjoy it, others because it helps them relax. Some find that tobacco gives them energy, since it is a stimulant. Some smoke out of a long-established habit or because it is ritual with them. Some do it, however, as a result of stress, tension, emotional disturbance, or neuroses, and for these people cessation of the habit is the most difficult.

Excessive cigarette smoking today is quite generally recognized to present a health hazard. There are considerable differences of opinion, however, on both the nature and extent of the hazard involved and on the relationship of smoking habits to other factors that can be deleterious to health. In 1975 a report to the President by the Strategy Council pursuant to the Drug Abuse Office and Treatment Act of 1972 took the position that "there is no doubt that chronic cigarette smoking is a form of drug dependence."

Cigarette smoking is said to be the chief cause of lung cancer; to be a major factor in heart disease, emphysema, and chronic bronchitis; to have a strong relationship to cancer of the mouth, oral cavity, larynx, tongue, and lips; to be a contributory factor in cancer of the urinary organs, the pancreas, and the kidneys; and, used excessively over long periods of time, to produce considerable tissue damage. In 1964 a panel of advisors to the Surgeon General of the United States, in noting these health hazards, said, however, that "statistical methods cannot establish proof of a causal relationship in an association." Since that time, there has been considerably more statistical gathering and the following are some of the findings.

Cigarette smokers are reported to have more than five times the mortality from lung cancer as nonsmokers, although the evidence is not always consistent. A recent study showed that men who smoked two or more packs a day had 15 to 20 times the mortality from lung cancer as nonsmokers. These relationships appear to increase when excessive smoking is combined with air pollution, or among those whose work subjects them to such substances as asbestos or dust. Those who work indoors, or who take little exercise, also have an added risk. Studies have also found that the cessation of smoking lessens the risk of cancer, although not to the level of those who have never smoked. Some 20 percent of persons who acquire lung cancer, however, have never touched a cigarette.

Concerning the relationship of cigarette smoking to heart disease, it is maintained that smoking is a major risk factor in the development of coronary heart disease, and that for men under age 50 it is a greater risk factor than any other. The risk of dying from CHD among smokers is reported to be twice that of nonsmokers and Buerger's disease occurs almost exclusively among men who smoke. Cessation of smoking is said to reduce this level of mortality. The evidence from various studies is not always consistent, however, and the relationship of excessive smoking to such causative factors as functioning under stress and tension has not been adequately determined.

Significantly, the overall death rate of men who smoke cigarettes has been found to be 70 percent higher than the rate among those who have never smoked. For women, that rate is 77 percent higher. Among heavy smokers the difference is even greater.

There are many who do not accept such findings, however. These people feel that the methodology employed establishes an oversimplified relationship between smoking and the incidence of disease and mortality and fails to consider such factors as age, height, and weight. The extent of inhalation and the manner of smoking, as well as the use or non-use of filters and other factors, can bring about the onset of diseases attributed to smoking. Thus the Tobacco Institute has maintained that no one knows whether or not smoking causes illness or death, that the question is still open, that there are major defects in the statistical evidence to date, that much research fails to support the charges made against tobacco, that other characteristics of the smoker can affect the health outcome, and that more objective research is needed. The Tobacco Institute has pledged itself to support further research into the subject.

Regardless, the evidence to date would seem to provide a cautionary alert to those who are excessive cigarette smokers in relation to their physical status, family health history, and such lifestyles as overworking, functioning under stress, overeating, not getting sufficient exercise, and consuming excessive amounts of alcohol.

Excessive cigarette smoking is not unrelated to places of employment. It has been found, for example, that men who had never smoked averaged 4.6 work-loss days a year. For those who smoked less than 11 cigarettes a day the work-loss average was 4.8 days. For those who smoked 11 to 20 cigarettes a day the average was 6 days, for those who smoked 21 to 40 cigarettes a day the average was 6.7 days, and for those who smoked 41 or more cigarettes a day the work-loss average was 8.4 days. For female employees the number of work-loss days a year was somewhat higher among each category of smokers, those who consumed 41 or more cigarettes a day averaging 10.3 work-loss days a year. Thus, the work loss among heavy cigarette smokers was found to be twice that of the nonsmokers, for whatever reason.

It is of interest to employers, then, to include the subject of excessive smoking in any health education efforts for the benefit of employees and, where excessive smoking is observed, counseling might be in order. In particular, places of employment should be alert to the correlation of excessive smoking to certain occupational exposures which, in combination, can produce chronic bronchitis, emphysema, other respiratory and pulmonary functional diseases, and lung cancer. For example, it has been found that among insulation workers functioning in close proximity with asbestos, those who are heavy cigarette smokers have 90 times the incidence of lung cancer compared to heavy smokers not presented with such an industrial health hazard.

While too little is known about the relationship of excessive smoking to the many other related factors noted here, it is a subject of sufficient importance to merit intensive research efforts. Meanwhile, individuals have a role to play on their own behalf. Although it has been reported that 70 percent of smokers recognize that there are hazards involved, the decrease in the habit is not said to be that significant. What is called for, of course, is self-control in reducing the quantity of cigarettes smoked. That, of course, is easier said than done, particularly among troubled employees.

There are many types of programs set up to help the excessive smoker, including group therapy, aversion therapy, individual therapy, alpha-wave biofeedback, and transcendental meditation. Examples of specific programs are the chemotherapy approaches at the New York Hospital–Cornell Medical Center in New York, the Roswell Park Memorial Institute in Buffalo, and the Smoking Cessation Program at the American Health Foundation in New York, which is offered to employers and to unions. The organization Smokenders, located in many communities throughout the country and meeting with considerable success, is made available to many employee groups by such employers as Chase Manhattan Bank, Mobile Oil, and AT&T.

Destructive Gambling

Gambling is a practice that enters into a great many people's lives. Office pools, informal bets with friends and relatives, the weekly bridge or poker game, the golf match, Mah–Jongg, bingo, crap shooting, and certainly the numbers, the horses, slot machines, and lotteries of all types are common. Today such practices are not uncommon under the auspices of religious groups, chain stores, and state and local governments, and in an increasing number of instances operate under legal sanction. For a great many people gambling is an enjoyable and intriguing pastime.

Elements of gambling also enter into "playing" the stock market, business ventures of various types, and in some few instances the writing of insurance coverages.

Behind the process of gambling would appear to be the desire for quick, easy money, and for most people no apparent harm results. In instances where it is legalized, the rationale is that people do it anyway through illegal sources among the underworld, so why not use the practice as a source of public funds and give the taxpayer a break? The merit and the morals of this type of rationale are of course debatable and, in fact, are a continuing source of public discussion.

Most states, however, have laws that prohibit at least certain forms of gambling. Of interest is the position of the American Civil Liberties Union in opposition "to gambling laws which prohibit an individual from risking property in a game of chance." The ACLU considers such laws as "an unconstitutional intrusion by government into the sphere of personal privacy, morality and conscience." This position does not, however, contravene laws for licensing or regulating commercial gambling.

The unfortunate thing is that for some people gambling becomes a compulsion or an obsession, regardless of adverse consequences. As with alcoholism, many people arrive at a point where they can no longer resist the impulse even though the ruinous effects become readily apparent. Then it becomes an uncontrolled mental disorder. This, in turn, can be seated in underlying mental, emotional, or personality disorders of various types. It can also trigger the onset of such disorders.

Once the compulsiveness of gambling becomes apparent, it must be diagnosed and treated before too much damage is done.

The compulsive gambler appears in places of employment. The resultant problems would follow the pattern exemplified by other mental disorders. Any program to help the troubled employee should, therefore, include a concern for the compulsive gambler and should attempt to provide help and guidance in order to alleviate the problem.

Suicide

Suicide, its propriety, and its relationship to mental disorders is a subject that has been debated throughout the ages. Societal groups have frequently taken strong positions against suicide and have passed laws prohibiting the act and providing penalties for those making an attempt on their own lives. Religious tenets have also counseled against suicide and established penalties for those committing the act. Closely related is the debate surrounding euthanasia.

Plato at one time was opposed to suicide but later reversed himself in cases of extraordinary sorrow, an inevitable turn of fortune, or conditions of extreme distress or poverty. Epictetus, however, took the broad view, saying: "Live as long as is agreeable, if the game does not please you, go; if you stay do not complain." With the Christian era, St. Augustine in the fifth century said that suicide was forbidden by the Sixth Commandment and as a consequence suicides were denied the last rites. In the thirteenth century, St. Thomas Aquinas argued against suicide as being contrary to our natural inclinations and that we had no right to take our own life, life and death being matters for God to decide.

Secular laws followed, commencing in the tenth century, holding suicide to be a crime, providing for the confiscation of property and for the incarceration of those who made the attempt and failed. Oddly enough, a few hundred years ago, one statute provided that the penalty for attempted suicide was death.

Today in the United States the legal status of suicide and attempted suicide varies among the several states. In some states reliance is placed in common law for sustaining convictions for attempted suicide. In seven states there are statutes that explicitly make it a crime to attempt suicide. Increasingly, however, state laws are holding that suicide is not a crime if the individual is judged insane, and many states have no law against suicide. Concerns in such cases rest on harm done to others, including the abandonment of a child or the abdication of family responsibility. Here the position of the American Civil Liberties Union, adopted in 1975, is of interest:

> The ACLU recognizes that society may intervene to prevent an act of suicide and thus assure that the individual has had the opportunity rationally to consider whether to take the irreversible action. An attempt at suicide is not a criminal act, nor shall it be the sole basis for commitment.

Closely allied to suicide is the continuing dispute over euthanasia to which Pythagoras, incidentally, was unalterably opposed. Pope Pius XII, however, took the position that "the removal of pain and consciousness by means of drugs is permitted by religion and morality to both doctor and patient even if the use of drugs will shorten life." There are those, nonetheless, who regard euthanasia as suicide on the part of the patient and as murder on the part of others.

The means of suicide are many and are generally familiar. An overdose of sleeping pills is a common means. So, also, is the use of confined automobile fumes, gas, or jumping from buildings or in front of subways or trains. Other attempts include the use of firearms, hanging, drowning, or slashing the wrist or jugular vein.

In the United States at least 30,000 men and women each year commit suicide by official cognizance. Other suicides occur to which other causes of death are ascribed. Incidentally, the rate of suicide in the United States is exceeded in several other nations—Sweden has the highest rate. In some societies, such as the Japanese, suicide has long been considered an act of honor or duty under certain circumstances. There is no way of knowing the number of attempted suicides, although one estimate is that there are 200,000 each year in the United States. Beyond that are the many persons who, with suicidal tendencies, take various types of unnecessary risks that can result in their own death, as well as in the death of others. The terrorists, increasingly common today in many parts of the world, are unquestionably inviting suicide.

Suicide has been found to be more common among men than women, among whites than nonwhites, and among those with a higher standard of living than among the poor. It is more common in large cities than in smaller communities. It is more frequent among older people and among those who live alone as a result of being widowed, divorced, or unmarried. The types of people who attempt suicide vary from those who for whatever reason want to die, to those who with daring ignore the realities of death, to those who have suffered profound personal loss, to those having a family history of suicide, to the altruist who does it for the benefit of a social group, to those suffering from severe social isolation as a result of serious illness or disability, old age, a broken marriage, financial reverses, or unemployment. There are also those who want to attract attention to themselves and select an outstanding site such as the Empire State Building, or the Golden Gate Bridge.

Generally, however, the public reaction to suicide is that it is an indication of the presence of mental illness. Unquestionably, many suicides are based in mental disorders. Certainly a suicidal tendency is not uncommon among persons suffering from depression, with the risk apparently' being greatest following recovery and shortly after discharge from a hospital. Schizophrenics are also considered to be a high risk group, although one study found that only 0.2 percent of schizophrenics took their own lives. Also considered high-risk groups are neurotics, as well as alcoholics.

Most, perhaps 80 percent, of attempted suicides are preceded by warnings and the large majority of these have communicated their intent without receiving any effective response. Some 20 to 40 percent of successful suicides leave notes, which, incidentally, are frequently marked by a lack of emotion. In many instances, however, a suicide note is a cry for pity and help. Not infrequently the individual is not really sure he or she wants to die: What is wanted is relief. Often the urge is of short duration and where an unsuccessful case occurs it can act as shock treatment: to wit the concert pianist Artur Rubinstein and the literary critic and poet A. Alvarez.

The record is by no means consistent, however. Various studies have produced different findings: One source maintains that only 5 to 20 percent of suicides are truly mentally ill, and another source says that many of those who commit suicide do not have a clear-cut psychiatric diagnosis. Sigmund Freud, in his *Civilization and Its Discontents,* believed that we are driven by an instinct for destructiveness, and that the natural human instinct is toward aggression and self-destruction.

It is conceivable, then, that there are those who take their own lives without any apparent mental disorders. The successful movie star who simply said he was bored could serve as an example. Certainly those who are old or suffering from a deadly incurable disease could understandably take their own lives without being mentally deranged. It would, in fact, seem that the one privilege a person should have is that of disposing of himself. Many would, of course, dispute this; but it has a certain perverse logic in a world in which people are sent forth by their rulers to kill other people and even decorated if they succeed in doing a particularly good job of it.

Yet suicide continues to be considered a disgrace, marked with strong public stigma.

Suicide attempts are costly to places of employment. To the extent they occur, they are costly to the various types of insurance programs. The troubled employee harboring suicidal tendencies can also take unnecessary risks and thereby endanger not only himself or herself but other employees as well. Programs designed to help the troubled employee should therefore be alert to the presence of suicidal tendencies and should attempt to provide counseling and help. As was mentioned in the preceding chapter, many communities operate suicide prevention centers, which can be of great help to the person with suicidal tendencies.

BIBLIOGRAPHY

American Cancer Society. "Quit Cigarettes—Live Longer." New York: 1973.

American Health Foundation. "Smoking Cessation Program." New York: 1974.

American Public Health Association. "Smoking Survey." *American Journal of Public Health,* October 1973.

Avnet, Helen. *Psychiatric Insurance.* New York: Group Health Insurance, Inc., 1962.

Ayres, Stephen M. "Cigarette Smoking and Lung Diseases." *Respiratory Care,* July 1, 1976.

Bennetts, Leslie. "American Capitalism Sees the Profit in Physical Fitness." *The New York Times,* June 12, 1978.

Council for Tobacco Research. *1976 Report.* New York: 1976.

Culligan, M. J., and Keith Sedlacek. *How to Kill Stress.* New York: Grosset & Dunlap, 1976.

Drug Abuse Council, Inc. *Employment and Addiction.* New York: June 1973.

———. *Heroin Maintenance: The Issues.* New York: June 1973.

———. *Methadone Maintenance.* New York: May 1973.

Follmann, J. F., Jr. *Alcoholics and Business.* New York: AMACOM, 1976.

———. *The Economics of Industrial Health.* New York: AMACOM, 1978.

Ford Foundation. *Dealing with Drug Abuse.* New York: 1972.

Freese, Arthur S. "Understanding Stress." *Public Affairs Pamphlet* No. 538, New York: 1976.

Group for the Advancement of Psychiatry. *Drug Misuse: A Psychiatric View.* New York: 1971.

Gunderson, E. K. Eric, and Richard H. Rahe. *Life Stress and Illness.* Springfield, Ill.: Charles C Thomas, 1974.

Habbe, Stephen. "Controlling the Alcohol Problem: Not by Management Alone." *The Conference Board Record,* April 1973.

————."Management's Changing Views on Alcoholism." *The Conference Board Record,* October 1968.

Halpern, Susan. *Drug Abuse and Your Company.* New York: AMACOM, 1972.

Holmes, T., and M. Masuda. "Psychosomatic Syndrome." *Psychology Today,* April 1972.

Insurance Company of North America. "A Guide for Department Heads and Managers on Drug Abuse and Addiction." Philadelphia: undated.

Lipcomb, Wendell R. "An Epidemiology of Drug Use–Abuse." *American Journal of Public Health,* September 1971.

Maidlow, Spencer T., et al. "The Economics of Heroin Treatment." *American Journal of Public Health,* October 1972.

McLean, Alan A. *Mental Health and Work Organization.* Chicago: Rand McNally, 1970.

————(ed.). *Occupational Stress.* Springfield, Ill.: Charles C Thomas, 1974.

Metropolitan Life Insurance Company. "Drug Abuse in Industry." New York: October 6, 1970.

————. *Stress—And Your Health.* New York: undated.

National Center for Health Statistics. *Cigarette Smoking,* 21 (3), 1970.

National Safety Council. "Attitude, Anxiety, Tension Can Cause Accidents." *Safety Newsletter,* February 1977.

Norman, Michael. "Executives Learn to Manage Stress." *The New York Times,* March 26, 1978.

Peterson, Hal. "Suicide and the Law." New York: Columbia University, March 9, 1975.

Redfield, John T. "Drugs in the Workplace—Substituting Sense for Sensationalism." *American Journal of Public Health,* December 1973.

Renwick, Patricia A., et al. "What You Really Want From Your Job." *Psychology Today,* May 1978.

Rosenstock, Irwin M. "Psychological Forces, Motivation, and Nutrition Education." *American Journal of Public Health,* November 1969.

Rush, Harold M., et al. "The Drug Problem in Business." *The Conference Board Record,* March 1971.

Selzer, Melvin L., et al. "Fatal Accidents: The Role of Psychopathology, Social Stress, and Acute Disturbance." *American Journal of Psychiatry,* February 1968.

Snyder, Solomon H. *The Troubled Mind.* New York: McGraw-Hill, 1976.

Sterling, Theodore D. "A Critical Reassessment of the Evidence Bearing on Smoking as the Cause of Lung Cancer." *American Journal of Public Health,* September 1975.

Stress Control Center. "You Can Learn to Deal Successfully with Stress." New York: undated.

U.S. Department of Health, Education, and Welfare. *The Effect of the Man-Made Environment on Health and Behavior.* HEW Publication No. (CDC) 77-8318, 1977.

————.*Resource Book for Drug Abuse Education.* Washington, D.C.: National Institute of Mental Health, January 1971.

————.*Unless You Decide to Quit, Your Problem Isn't Going to Be Smoking: Your Problem's Going to Be Staying Alive.* HEW Publication No. (CDC) 74-8705, 1973.

West, Dee D., et al. "Five Year Follow-up of a Smoking Withdrawal Clinic Population." *American Journal of Public Health,* June 1977.

Wright, Mary. "Cigarettes Are Worse for Women." *Town & Country,* July 1974.

Zimmerman, David. "Are You a Workaholic?" *Mainliner,* November 1975.

APPENDIX

Selected Sources of Help, Information,

and Guidance

Academy of Religion and Mental
  Health
16 E. 34th Street
New York, N.Y. 10016

AFL-CIO
Community Services
815 16th Street, N.W.
Washington, D.C. 20006

Al-Anon Family Group
P.O. Box 182
Madison Square Station
New York, N.Y. 10010

Alcoholics Anonymous
P.O. Box 459
Grand Central Station
New York, N.Y. 10017

American Academy of
  Occupational Medicine
801 Old Lancaster Road
Bryn Mawr, Pa. 19010

American Association of
  Marriage Counselors
270 Park Avenue
New York, N.Y. 10017

American Association of
  Psychiatric Services for Children
1701 18th Street, N.W.
Washington, D.C. 20009

American Industrial Hygiene
  Association
66 Miller Road
Akron, Ohio 44313

American Medical Association
535 N. Dearborn Avenue
Chicago, Ill. 60610

American National Standards
  Institute
1430 Broadway
New York, N.Y. 10018

American Nurses Association
10 Columbus Circle
New York, N.Y. 10019

American Occupational Medical
 Association
150 N. Wacker Drive
Chicago, Ill. 60606

American Occupational Therapy
 Association
250 W. 57th Street
New York, N.Y. 10019

American Orthopsychiatric
 Association
1719 Broadway
New York, N.Y. 10019

American Psychiatric Association
1700 18th Street
Washington, D.C. 20009

American Psychoanalytic Association
1 E. 57th Street
New York, N.Y. 10022

American Psychological Association
1200 17th Street, N.W.
Washington, D.C. 20036

American Public Health
 Association
1015 18th Street, N.W.
Mental Health Section
Washington, D.C. 20036

American Social
 Health Association
1740 Broadway
New York, N.Y. 10009

American Society for
 Adolescent Psychiatry
24 Green Valley Road
Wallingford, Pa. 19084

American Society for
 Safety Engineers

850 Busse Highway
Park Ridge, Ill. 60068

American Society for
 Testing and Materials
1916 Race Street
Philadelphia, Pa. 19103

American Society of Heating
 and Ventilation Engineers
7218 Euclid Avenue
Cleveland, Ohio 44103

American Society of
 Mechanical Engineers, Inc.
345 E. 47th Street
New York, N.Y. 10007

Biofeedback Research Society
University of Colorado
Medical Center
4200 East 9th Avenue
Denver, Colo. 80220

Blue Cross Association
840 N. Lake Shore Drive
Chicago, Ill. 60611

Center for Applied Behavioral
 Sciences
 The Menninger Foundation
Box 829
Topeka, Kan. 66601

Center for Occupational
 Mental Health
New York Hospital–Cornell
 University Medical Center
White Plains, N. Y. 10605

Christopher D. Smithers
 Foundation
41 E. 57th Street
New York, N.Y. 10022

The Conference Board
435 Third Avenue
New York, N.Y. 10022

Cornell University New York State
  School of Industrial and
  Labor Relations
Ithaca, N.Y. 14853

The Drug Abuse Council, Inc.
1828 L Street, N.W.
Washington, D.C. 20036

EHE Stress Control Systems, Inc.
210 E. 49th Street
New York, N. Y. 10017

Employers with Established
  Troubled-Employee Programs
(see Chapters 15 and 16)

Family Service Association
445 E. 23rd Street
New York, N.Y. 10010

Forbes Associates
9 S. Downing Street
Denver, Col. 80280

Garden District Education Services
1528 Jackson Avenue
New Orleans, La. 70130

Group for the Advancement
  of Psychiatry
419 Park Avenue South
New York, N.Y. 10016

Harvard Business School
Cumnock Hall
Boston, Mass. 02163

Health Insurance
  Association of America
919 Third Avenue
New York, N.Y. 10022

Human Affairs, Inc.
Suite F
1401 E. 3900 South
Salt Lake City, Utah 84117

Human Service Group
5530 Wisconsin Avenue, N.W.
Washington, D.C. 20015

Illuminating Engineering Society
51 Madison Avenue
New York, N.Y. 10010

Industrial Health Foundation
5231 Centre Avenue
Pittsburgh, Pa. 15232

Industrial Hygiene Foundation
4400 Fifth Avenue
Pittsburgh, Pa. 15213

Institute of Social Research
University of Michigan
Ann Arbor, Mich.

The Levinson Institute, Inc.
Box 95
Cambridge, Mass. 02138

Life Extension Institute
1185 Avenue of the Americas
New York, N.Y. 10036

Manufacturing Chemists Association
1825 Connecticut Avenue, N.W.
Washington, D.C. 20009

Mental Health Materials Center
104 E. 25th Street
New York, N.Y. 10010

Metropolitan Life
  Insurance Company
1 Madison Avenue
New York, N.Y. 10003

National Association
  for Mental Health
1800 N. Kent Street
Rosslyn Station
Arlington, Va. 22209

National Association of
  Private Psychiatric Hospitals
1701 K Street, N.W.
Washington, D.C. 20006

National Association of
  Retarded Citizens
2709 Avenue E East
Arlington, Texas 76011

National Association of
  Social Workers
1425 H Street, N.W.
Washington, D.C. 20005

National Association of
  State Mental Health
  Program Directors
1001 Third Street, N.W.
Washington, D.C. 20004

National Clearinghouse for
  Mental Health Information
5454 Wisconsin Avenue
Chevy Chase, Md. 20203

National Committee
  Against Mental Illness
1101 17th Street, N.W.
Washington, D.C. 20036

National Council on Alcoholism
733 Third Avenue
New York, N.Y. 10017

National Council on
  Community Mental Health Centers
2233 Wisconsin Avenue, N.W.
Washington, D.C. 20037

National Council on
  Family Relations
1219 Woodcliff Drive
Madison, N.J. 07940

National Institute of
  Mental Health
5454 Wisconsin Avenue
Chevy Chase, Md. 20203

National Institute of
  Occupational Safety and Health
Room 532
U.S. Post Office
Cincinnati, Ohio 45202

National Institute on
  Alcohol Abuse and Alcoholism
5600 Fishers Lane
Rockville, Md. 20852

National Institutes on
  Rehabilitation and Health Services
1714 Massachusetts Avenue, N.W.
Washington, D.C. 20036

National Rehabilitation
  Association
1522 K Street, N.W.
Washington, D.C. 20005

National Safety Council
425 N. Michigan Avenue
Chicago, Ill. 60611

National Save-a-Life League
505 Fifth Avenue
New York, N.Y. 10017

National Society for
  Autistic Children
169 Tampa Avenue
Albany, N.Y. 12208

Neurotics Anonymous
1341 G Street, N.W.
Washington, D.C. 20005

Office of Vocational
  Rehabilitation
U.S. Department of Health,
  Education, and Welfare
Washington, D.C. 20201

Pennsylvania Mental Health, Inc.
1601 Walnut Street
Philadelphia, Pa.

Psychiatric Institute of America
1825 K Street, N.W.
Washington, D.C. 20006

Public Affairs Committee
381 Park Avenue South
New York, N.Y. 10016

Recovery Inc.
116 S. Michigan Avenue
Chicago, Ill. 60603

Rutgers University Institute of
Management and Labor Relations
New Brunswick, N.J. 08903

Schizophrenics Anonymous
56 W. 45th Street
New York, N.Y. 10036

State Departments of Labor

State Departments of
Mental Health

State Departments of
Vocational Rehabilitation

Strang Clinic
55 E. 34th Street
New York, N.Y. 10016

StressControl Center
210 E. 49th Street
New York, N.Y. 10017

Unions with established
mental health programs
(see Chapters 14 and 15)

United Automobile Workers
8000 E. Jefferson Street
Detroit, Michigan 48214

United Mine Workers of America
907 15th Street, N.W.
Washington, D.C. 20005

University of Cincinnati
Institute of Industrial Health
Cincinnati, Ohio 45204

Sources for Films Related to Industrial Health

Aetna Life and Casualty
Farmington Avenue
Hartford, Conn. 06115

Association Films, Inc.
347 Madison Avenue
New York, N.Y. 10017

Association Instructional
Materials
866 Third Avenue
New York, N.Y. 10022

Assn–Sterling Films
512 Burlington Avenue
La Grange, Ill. 60525

BNA Communications
9401 Recovery Hall Road
Rockville, Md. 20850

Center for Mass Communications
Columbia University Press
562 W. 113th Street
New York, N.Y. 10025

Encyclopaedia Britannica Films, Inc.
1150 Wilmette Avenue
Wilmette, Ill. 60091

Filmmakers Library, Inc.
290 West End Avenue
New York, N.Y. 10023

Films, Inc.
1144 Wilmette Avenue
Wilmette, Ill. 60091

Henry Strauss Productions, Inc.
31 W. 53rd Street
New York, N.Y. 10020

Human Relations for Industry
438 Delaware Avenue
Buffalo, N.Y.

International Film Bureau
332 S. Michigan Avenue
Chicago, Ill. 60604

McGraw-Hill Book Company
1221 Avenue of the Americas
New York, N.Y. 10021

Mental Health Materials Center
419 Park Avenue South
New York, N.Y. 10016

Metropolitan Life
  Insurance Company
1 Madison Avenue
New York, N.Y. 10003

National Safety Council
425 N. Michigan Avenue
Chicago, Ill. 60611

Peckham Productions, Inc.
9 E. 48th Street
New York, N.Y. 10017

Psychological Cinema Register
Pennsylvania State University
University Park, Pa. 16802

Pyramid Films, Inc.
Box 1048
Santa Monica, Calif. 90406

Smith, Kline and French
  Laboratories
1500 Spring Garden Street
Philadelphia, Pa. 19101

Consultants Available to Employers and Unions

American Health Foundation
1370 Avenue of the Americas
New York, N.Y. 10020

American Health Services
5530 Wisconsin Avenue, N.W.
Washington, D.C. 20015

Association of Labor-Management
Administrators and Consultants
  on Alcoholism
300 Wendell Court
Atlanta, Ga. 30336

Landis, Murray, Sutherland
420 E. 64th Street
New York, N.Y. 10021

Glen Slaughter
2001 Franklin Street
Oakland, Calif. 94612

Westinghouse Health Systems
Box 866
American City Building
Columbia, Md. 21044

INDEX